ABU

ALSO BY CHARLES LEERHSEN

Butch Cassidy: The True Story of an American Outlaw

Ty Cobb: A Terrible Beauty

Blood and Smoke: A True Tale of Mystery, Mayhem, and the Birth of the Indy 500

Crazy Good: The Story of Dan Patch, the Most Famous Horse in America

DOWN AND OUT IN PARADISE

THE LIFE OF
ANTHONY BOURDAIN

CHARLES LEERHSEN

Simon & Schuster

NEW YORK LONDON TORONTO
SYDNEY NEW DELHI

Simon & Schuster
1230 Avenue of the Americas
New York, NY 10020

First Simon & Schuster hardcover edition October 2022

The names and identifying characteristics of some individuals have been changed.

Interior design by Paul Dippolito

Manufactured in China

1 3 5 7 9 10 8 6 4 2

Library of Congress Cataloging-in-Publication Data is available.

ISBN 978-1-9821-4044-1
ISBN 978-1-9821-4046-5 (ebook)

For Frankie

AB: Is there anything I can do?

AA: Stop busting my balls.

AB: Okay.

—THE FINAL TEXT EXCHANGE BETWEEN
ANTHONY BOURDAIN AND ASIA ARGETO
ON THE NIGHT HE KILLED HIMSELF.

Contents

Prelude 3

Part One 17

Part Two 101

Part Three 181

Epilogue 275

Acknowledgments 279

Endnotes 281

Bibliography 293

Illustration Credits 297

Index 299

Prelude

He was the epitome of cool, a sad-smiling Jersey boy who combined supremely high standards with the underappreciated art of not giving a shit in ways that seemed to excite both sexes. You wanted either to be him or to do him, especially if you'd heard the gossip about his gargantuan member. He had the best job (if you could call it that) in the world, the best life in the world, applauded wherever he went. Cigarettes, booze, and time all looked good on him. So the question is, how did he get to the point where he wanted to kill himself? How does that scenario even begin to make the slightest bit of sense?

It all came down to the woman, or so the supposedly wise ones said. Darkly beautiful, you had to admit, and certainly no dummy, but trouble with a capital T, an old-fashioned femme fatale. Cocktail for cocktail, she could keep up with him all night long and then pull away like Man o' War in the rosy-fingered homestretch. He loved that about her, that she was tough and independent and always thirsty; he loved that fresh mouth. "I've never felt like this about anyone before," he told anyone within earshot. But her ballsiness also happened to be their biggest problem. Because for one thing it meant that she would screw anyone she pleased, sometimes, it was said, anyone within reach. Of course, he'd been around the block himself, and came from a world in which sex often didn't mean much, but since he was head over heels for her and had big plans for the two of them, and was such an incurable romantic at heart, such a goddamn Jersey boy, even the possibility of her sleeping with other people mattered to the point of making him physically sick. So many long, tortuous calls to Rome from which he would stagger back to the day's business pale and shaken, the people who'd been waiting around for him unable to look him in the eye. He could feel her slipping away. "Why don't you just get on with your fucking life!" she had screamed at him one night. As one of his friends said, "A billion fucking broads in the world and he's got to pick one who will take him or leave him!"

His fans hated her, refused to even say her name; he didn't care. His best pals were fed up with the teenage boy crap and at the same time nervous wrecks. Since leaving his first wife, Nancy, he had flirted with suicide several times. Would he take another shot at it—you know, once more with feeling? Yes, as a matter of fact, one especially drunken night he would.

Sirens, cops, reporters on the line. A complete fucking mess. When the sun came up, Frank Sinatra was still alive, but the whole world knew that he had tried to kill himself over Ava Gardner.

We actually can learn a lot from celebrities, who after all travel the furthest and the fastest in life and therefore accumulate the most edifying scrapes and bruises. A normal person's scars speak strictly of his or her probably prosaic personal history; the celebrity's, on the other hand, show what can and inevitably (and reassuringly) does go wrong even when one has money, beauty, and adulation in extravagant supply. Anthony Michael Bourdain—a chef, writer, and the host of a cable TV travel show who died by his own hand on June 8, 2018, at the age of sixty-one—was a crash test dummy extraordinaire. He didn't hide his scars and other imperfections as most celebrities do, and he told . . . well, not quite everything, as it turns out, but a good deal about his history of poor decision-making and worse luck and especially about what having "the best job in the world" meant when you were, like most of us, still caught up in the common comedy. From Tony we can learn not just practical tidbits like "why you probably shouldn't order fish on a Monday" (his single most famous piece of advice, related in *Kitchen Confidential: Adventures in the Culinary Underbelly*, the 2000 best-seller that first made him a star) and nuggets of wisdom like "travel isn't always pretty; you get scarred, marked, changed in the process; it even breaks your heart"—but also things about life that you didn't even know you didn't know. For example, if we really do wind up with the face we deserve—in Tony's case, a big, beautifully cragged-out Easter Island mask through which he somehow both eagerly and warily surveilled the world—the funeral we deserve is another matter entirely.

Consider: in the hours and days after Anthony Bourdain died, things did not proceed as they normally do in terms of arrangement making. No one called the Frank E. Campbell Funeral Chapel, the 120-year-old Upper East Side mortuary to the stars that three decades earlier had buried Tony's beloved father, Pierre (as well as Rudolph Valentino, Judy Garland, and Jackie O), to enlist its help in getting Tony into the ground or an urn or at least out of France, where he'd hanged himself on a bathroom doorknob. Nor, alternatively, did anyone from Tony's inner circle start pulling together a less formal but more colorful and celebratory ceremony inspired by one or more of the cultures he'd traded paint with in the course of his televised travels, an option that the deceased might well have found appropriate and—this was always important for him—amusing. After more than 250 episodes of, depending on how you count them, at least four cable shows, the possibilities were plentiful: New Orleans brass band festive, Japanese Zen, a traditional Maltese ceremony in which mourners sprinkle salt on the exposed stomach of the deceased, a Hindu pyre, one of those fantastic Taiwanese obsequies where the survivors hire strippers to ensure a strong turnout, a Kenyan wake where the eulogies are purposely strewn with lies—or even a Jewish service, for which Tony qualified as the son of the former Gladys Sacksman of the Bronx.

Yes, ethnically speaking, Tony identified as Jewish, and the traditional *levaya* with its ritual rending of the black ribbon, its Mourner's Kaddish and symbolic spadefuls of dirt, while it may not seem so exotic to people from the New York City area—where Tony grew up and maintained a home base—is both as spiritually riveted and heartbreakingly universal as anything he experienced in his seventeen-year career as a curator of far-flung ports. If in the end the Jewish option would not have flown—and it almost certainly would not have—that was only because of the fervor with which Tony detested his then-eighty-three-year-old mother. Although Gladys, like him, was nonobservant, any ceremony that seemed to acknowledge her influence on him, or even her existence, would have been rejected by Tony's true intimates as being insensitive to his presumed wishes. But we're getting tangled in hypotheticals here. In fact there was no one—neither intimates nor professionals—making any sort of arrangements for Tony. Nothing in the way of memorial planning was going on.

Instead, while the world gasped and grieved at the news of Tony's sudden death; and Google searches for "Bourdain suicide" spiked to more than one hundred million; and Donald Trump and Barack Obama proffered regrets and sympathies in uncharacteristically similar tweets; and thousands of mourners flocked spontaneously to the site of Les Halles, the already long-since shuttered steak frites place on Park Avenue South where Tony had once worked as head chef, to leave handwritten notes and bunches of flowers or affix greeting cards to the window with chewing gum and Band-Aids (*"We never met. . . . I've lost many people lately. Yours is a death I fear I won't get over"*)—in the midst of all the moaning and meshuggaas, the man of the hour lay largely ignored in the corner of a quiet, well-lit morgue in Colmar, France. The people who'd been traveling with him when he hanged himself at Le Chambard hotel in the nearby Hansel and Gretel village of Kaysersberg—that is, his TV crew and his good friend and occasional on-air sidekick, the renowned chef Eric Ripert—had headed back to the States as soon as the gendarmes gave them the go-ahead, some, it was said, slamming their hotel room doors in anger (at Tony) on the way out of Alsace. Having answered the predictable questions about his demeanor during his last few days, and having said, unsurprisingly, that his demeanor had been lousy indeed, there was nothing more they could do. Meanwhile, no family members were known to be inbound.

In lieu of a more detailed plan there was only a brief email directive, sent by Tony's estranged younger brother, Christopher, his sole sibling, for the body to be cremated in Strasbourg, the capital of the region, forty-nine miles to the north, and the ashes shipped back to Tony's Italian-born, thirty-nine-year-old wife of eleven years, Ottavia, in New York. (The couple, who had separated two years earlier but at Tony's insistence never divorced, kept in almost daily touch, mostly to discuss his romantic problems but also to work out visits with their daughter, Ariane, though at the time of his death Tony hadn't seen his only child, then eleven years old, in several months.) During the forty-eight hours or so that it took for the coroner to locate a coffin big enough to accommodate a six-foot, four-inch corpse, the morgue remained quiet; no staff members wandered in to ogle the heavily tattooed body of the celebrity chef or sneak a selfie. Reporters and photographers were already streaming into the region from every compass point to cover the stop-the-presses news of Anthony Bourdain's suicide; but unless they could find a tourist to interrogate, their questions drew mostly Gallic shrugs. A moat of local indifference kept the media professionals from the story as they had initially conceived it: shocked shopkeepers, wistful winegrowers, somber sausage makers all expressing their keen French-German grief. As the mayor of Kaysersberg (and coroner of Colmar), Pascal Lohr, said to me when I visited those towns some months later, "Honestly, I felt absolutely no surprise or excitement or sense of loss at the news of his death. I did not recognize his name."

Yes, Anthony Bourdain, God love him, had managed to die in a place where nobody knew who he was. In the spring of 2018, this was no easy accomplishment.

He was a literary man—a reader, a writer, well schooled in life's ambiguities—with a literary, or at any rate a twistier-than-usual, rags-to-riches tale: An angry, upper-middle-class (but nearly penniless), middle-aged, modestly successful (but, yes, somehow penniless) chef, fresh off a methadone taper and known more for his organizational skills than his flair for textures and flavors (in other words, no Ripert, Paul Bocuse, or Thomas Keller, not by a long shot) became not overnight but (even better) gradually and right before our eyes over the course of seventeen TV seasons, a true citizen of the world, hailed just about everywhere he hung his hangover. A tribal chief in Namibia broke out his choicest (meaning most fecal-flecked) warthog rectum for a feast in his honor; the burly coal miners of McDowell County, West Virginia, smiled at the sight of him and slapped his back; the best barmen in Indochina (to borrow a phrase from one of his favorite writers, Graham Greene) knew not just his name and his gin preference (Bombay Sapphire), but, because he was a regular wherever he went and they were the best barmen in Indochina, whether or not it was going to be a martini evening. "His fans are young and old, male and female, straight and queer," Tony's book editor Karen Rinaldi wrote soon after his death, in a piece called "Why Anthony Bourdain Matters." "They are blue and red, east and west, black and white; they are hip and square, adventuresome and timid, paleo and vegan, armchair and inveterate travelers alike. *He was one of the few examples of someone who could piss people off and still maintain their respect in the wake of their rancor.*"

The italics are mine. Rinaldi's observation is incisive, and that she, a close friend, went there—that is, to his increasing obnoxiousness—in the immediate wake of his death is telling, I think. Over his last two years Tony pushed people away or let long-running relationships lapse until by June 2018 there was no one left in his life to play the role of Person Who Plans Your Funeral—or at least no one except a woman whom none of his friends or family would speak to, or even speak *about*, and who would in any case and for various reasons not be up to the task of organizing a proper send-off. Meanwhile, because he was, after all, Tony, he still had (to use Rinaldi's word) the respect, at least, of all who knew him and the love of almost a whole wide world full of people who felt like they did. "There was chaos swirling around him at all times," a veteran TV crewmember said after he died, referring to the personal problems, flight delays, equipment failures and no-show guests that are all part of the slam-bang, 250-days-a-year-on-the-road lifestyle. "But on and off camera Tony lived a magical journey."

* * *

TV is just a business in the end and an especially cold one at that: if you give you get; if you don't you won't, and accounts get settled up pretty quickly. In exchange for a magical journey, Tony performed a minor miracle: he made a cable TV travel show that people actually wanted to watch. It is easy to underestimate how rare and difficult that is. Travel shows would seem to have a built-in appeal. Who isn't curious about faraway places with strange-sounding names? Sit back, relax, take an armchair journey, and all that—sounds fantastic, but the genre is hardly can't-miss. Anyone who remembers Kodak's carousel slide projector knows how bone-chilling the phrase "pictures from our latest trip" can be. And just as uninviting, back in the day, were those chirpily narrated travelogues full of Blarney Stone kissers, rickshaw drivers, and hula dancers that local TV stations once ran during baseball rain delays or at 2:00 a.m., when your dad was just resting his eyes on the couch. Who knows why but human beings don't seem to be wired to care about other people's wanderings, just as absolutely no one really wants to see cell phone pictures of your children or pets. It's one of those aversions that feel universal and eternal; Marco Polo could probably clear a thirteenth-century room. Which of course doesn't mean there hasn't been superlative travel writing or documentary making over the years but that only extraordinary talent for those things can overcome what seems to be a deeply ingrained natural resistance.

The only thing Tony knew about television when he started out was that he didn't want to become a creature of it. Rather than be molded by the network suits into a slick professional presenter, he would gladly hang a U-turn and head back to the kitchen. "Here's my pitch," he said to a cable executive early in his TV career. "I travel around the world, eat a lot of shit, and basically do whatever the fuck I want." That turned out to be a winning formula, and it left Tony with the distinct impression that, as he more than once said, "Not giving a shit is a really fantastic business model for television."

Tony very much did give a shit, though. When he looked at the initial episodes of his first show, *A Cook's Tour*, back in 2001, and saw only "a sort of gonzo travelogue of vérité footage and thrown together voice-overs," he resolved to make it less ordinary but also to stay calm and keep what *was* working. Honing a television show in full view of the public, constantly making it more personal and riskier in terms of the medium's conventions, became his life's work. "The strange and terrible powers of television are really exciting to me," he said in a 2016 interview. From the start, nothing was off-limits for Tony—brief, black-and-white homages to his favorite film directors; animated sequences; dark jokes about suicide (the first episode of *Cook's Tour* featured a shot of Tony lying dead in the shower), cursing and smoking on camera. "A director with an idea . . . *any* new way of telling a story that is likely to cause fear and confusion at the network (and possibly with our audience) . . . is welcome to try," he said back then. "I have enthusiastically supported shows that are . . . anamorphic, told in reverse, shot on deliberately eroded 16-millimeter film stock, dream sequences, animations, shot completely at night, and in places I would otherwise never have gone were it not for the passion of the director. I hate nothing more than a competently shot and edited episode."

Over time elements came and went; the role of food changed from something he sat down to eat and endeavored to describe to a symbol of friendship he accepted with humility and awe from the proud people he happened to be visiting. The show also got less extreme and more grown-up as it proceeded from one iteration to the next. By the end, Tony was no longer testing his mettle with bizarre dishes like the warthog rectum or an Icelandic specialty called hakarl, rotten shark that arrives stinking of ammonia; said Tony, "the single worst, most disgusting, and terrible-tasting thing I've ever eaten," or in Saigon the still-beating heart of a cobra ("like a very athletic, aggressive oyster") or raw blood soup in Thailand. He stopped wanting to eat gross food or dive off vertiginous cliffs into dangerously wine-dark seas with spring break abandon. He was getting tired, for one thing, but he'd also come to realize that the gonzo stuff, while it was good for generating publicity, often got in the way of the storytelling. Startling moments would still occur in the later seasons of *Parts Unknown*, but they'd be more on the order of him quietly observing, as he pushed some eggs around a pan with a spatula in a kitchen in Uruguay, that "making an omelet for someone the morning after is the best thing in the world"—or Barack Obama dropping onto a plastic stool across from Tony in a noodle joint in Hanoi, exhaling meaningfully, then taking a long pull on a cold beer.

One thing that never changed, though, was the central idea of the audience experiencing each destination through the sensibility of one particular person—him. His most basic belief about humanity, he once said, was "the world is filled with people doing the best they can . . . [people] who would like to put on a clean shirt every morning and live their lives with a little dignity." Tony brought to each location "an almost unlimited capacity for empathy," his friend the TV producer David Simon said, "for feeling the lives and loves and hopes of others." His caring but never condescending nature has often been remarked upon, and rightly so. But empathy alone would have made for a soggy series. Two other qualities that often go unmentioned gave the show its irresistible grit and starch. One was Bourdain's work ethic. As a TV personality, he more than made up for all the homework he had sloughed off in high school and college. His goal from the start was to arrive at every stop on the schedule steeped in the history, high on the literature, and hungry for the signature dish he'd heard so much about. Who else on a plane ride to Mexico for a *No Reservations* shoot would reread Malcolm Lowry's alcohol-drenched, Quauhnahuac-set novel *Under the Volcano* for whatever context and perspective it could provide? Tony was one of those perpetually psyched writers who, as Julian Barnes said in his book *Something to Declare*, "pile up research like a compost heap, but then leave it alone, let it sink down, acquire heat, and degrade usefully into fertilizing elements." And Tony expected the same obsessive effort from everyone around him, whether it was the camera and sound people he'd been traveling with for years or the freelancers they picked up for a few days at each stop. Over time the British military slogan "Proper planning and preparation prevents piss-poor performance" became a refrain that he dickishly repeated at the drop of a screwdriver or the sudden swell of background noise that nobody could have possibly foreseen—ever ready to let his loyal compadres know they'd once again disappointed him. "Fun" was not a word that he'd associate with the making of *Parts Unknown*, his most frequently employed director, Tom Vitale, said after Tony's death.

Curiously enough, though, "funny" was. Humor is the other ingredient that gave the show its texture; on and off camera, in and out of boss-from-hell mode, Tony reflexively went for the laugh. "He was a comedian at heart," said Bonnie McFarlane, a veteran standup who once helped Tony book a gig at a Manhattan comedy club so he could tweak his timing. Back in the day it surprised none of his friends that Tony had Elvis Costello's "Alison" on his answering machine ("Sometimes I wish I could stop you from talking/ When I hear the silly things that you say."). "Being funny was extremely important to Tony," his sometimes collaborator Joel Rose said. "He once told me he was reading a book about how to be funny and it said to use a lot of *K* words because *K* words were funnier—and we both thought *that* was kind of funny." The jokes on his show were almost always on Tony and about his size-twelve clay feet. As he hails a taxi in the Montreal episode of his series *The Layover*, his voice-over says, "I rise, I pack, I cough yellow bile into the bidet, and head to the airport." It was comforting for viewers to realize that the coolest-seeming guy in the world didn't actually have life licked. Writing about George Orwell (whose 1933 memoir, *Down and Out in Paris and London*, inspired *Kitchen Confidential*), the critic Lionel Trilling once said that his subject's genius lay precisely in *not* being a genius, and that by "fronting the world with nothing more than one's simple, direct, undeceived intelligence," he occasioned in his readers a sense of relief. So, too, it was with Tony, who constantly reminded us that life is struggle—but that we must press on nevertheless. On another episode of *The Layover*, shot in Hong Kong, he exclaims, "If there wasn't blood in my stool, this would be a perfect morning!"

Might he have laughed at the idea of dying in a place where nobody knew who he was? Possibly. Tony's relationship with celebrity was complicated. Most of the time he enjoyed being famous. His drinking buddies knew all too well that he had a Google Alert for "Anthony Bourdain" set to "as-it-happens" and configured as a push notification on his iPhone. "We'd be sitting at a bar," David McMillan, a cofounder of the Joe Beef restaurant group in Montreal, told me, "and his phone would be going ping-ping-ping every time his name was mentioned somewhere. It was insane. He loved it but it made me feel like a grandpa saying, 'Put that damn thing away!'" When the phone sat silent for too long, Tony would take to social media to say something that might get people talking about him again. One favorite tactic was to knock another TV chef for endorsing a shoddy line of cooking gear or slipping a product plug into his show (things he never did, though it cost him a lot of money). There was, he knew, nothing like a celebrity feud to get his iPhone pinging. "Notoriety to a great extent was a game for him," McMillan said. "He got a real kick out of playing around with his power." A year before Tony killed himself, when he was arguably as famous as anyone in America, he told Patrick Radden Keefe of the *New Yorker*, "If I'm unhappy, it's a failure of imagination."

The story of how he'd reached that point in life is one he never tired of rerunning in his mind—or in front of an audience. Three months before Kaysersberg, while shooting an episode of his CNN series *Parts Unknown* in Kenya, he and his traveling companion of the moment, the comedian and cable host W. Kamau Bell, stood at sunset on a hill in a remote wildlife conservancy, gin and tonics in hand, and talked about their shared bafflement at how far they'd come from the places they'd once assumed they would always be: in Bell's case, Alabama, Boston, and Chicago, where he'd grown up middle-class and middlebrow; in Tony's, the cramped mis en place of one or another New York restaurant kitchen. The two weren't friends yet, you could tell from their body language, but they were getting along in the way that Tony always managed to with his seemingly never-ending stream of on-screen companions. Still, this was not a classic *Parts Unknown* moment; Tony was dead by the time it aired, so it couldn't help feeling a little like a séance, with the star speaking from beyond the grave, an impression bolstered by the dying light and somewhat languid, un-TV-like pace: touches preserved and supplied by his always artful Zero Point Zero production staff.

The conversation begins in earnest with Bell expressing amazement, mixed with gratitude and perhaps a smidgen of guilt, at an unanticipated benefit of show business success: free transportation to still mostly unspoiled places far off the tourist track. How is it possible, he wonders, that he—*he*—is staring out at this stunning African moonscape? After a beat or two, Tony seconds the sentiment, in Tonyese. "As soon as the cameras turn off, and I sit with the crew and have a cocktail, I fucking pinch myself," he says. "I can't believe I get to do this, to *see* this." Another longish pause; the plangent sound of a string being plucked, a cut to giraffes foraging. "I was forty-three years old, dunkin' fries," Tony continues. "I knew with absolute certainty that I would never see *Rome*, much less *this*." The speech is a variation on something he'd said many times on previous shows, in books, in interviews, and in the sold-out talks he gave in theaters and lecture halls across the country. Maybe he was indeed the narcissist he often claimed to be because he couldn't help falling into a reverie at the sound of his own origin myth. Good thing it was a good story. The Kenyan take, while only a partial rendering of the tale, is important to have because it may have been the last time he publicly shook his head in wonderment at his own good fortune. His view of his life was about to change radically—in fact, we know now, was already changing—and soon his precious little story could go fuck itself. "I hate my job, I hate my fans, I hate my life," he would tell his wife, Ottavia, to whom he still confided his most intimate thoughts. But not quite yet.

PART ONE

The road of excess leads to the palace of wisdom.

—WILLIAM BLAKE

At the exclusive Dwight-Englewood School in New Jersey, Bourdain (third from left) hung with a group who called themselves the Cruisers.

Chapter 1

One day about twelve years before he started to smoke and drink, Anthony Bourdain was born. The blessed event occurred on June 25, 1956, the fifty-third birthday of his literary hero George Orwell, already six years gone by then from tuberculosis. Beyond that, the twenty-fifth of June was basically a date adrift in the mid-calendar doldrums, the exact but meaningless halfway station till next Christmas, the unobserved feast of Blessed Jutta of Thuringia, patron saint of Prussia—or at least it was until 2018, when Eric Ripert and José André reimagined it as something else. Now each year on Bourdain Day multitudes take to social media to describe how Tony changed their lives and, just by being his intriguingly weathered, globe-girdling, smart-remark-passing self, somehow got them through stretches of grief, addiction, depression, divorce, and a wide range of physical ailments including eczema and stage four cancer. Many of Tony's former high school buddies are still trying to wrap their minds around the notion that the comic book obsessed nudnik they once shared a joint with has been so quickly canonized. Their skepticism is both natural and laudable; as Orwell himself said (about Mahatma Gandhi), saints should be considered guilty until proven innocent. Indeed, as Jesus said, "Truly I tell you, no man is a prophet in his own land." But Ripert and Andrés conceived Bourdain Day in the first raw rush of worldwide grief, just as CNN's obituary for Tony was rocketing to the top of the most read digital stories list, and those Michelin-starred men know a thing or two about heat—and ventilation. ("The great chefs," Tony once said, "understand human desire.") The idea of Bourdain Day took hold immediately and does not really contradict what the old gang thinks about the teenage Tony. Bourdain Day is above all the celebration of a late bloomer. In addition to being so commendably far from perfect, being a late bloomer was one of the chief reasons Tony could inspire millions of people he never met. *Look at what remains possible, even after youth fades* was, in a way, the pleasing moral of every one of his televised stories. The thing to remember about Bourdain Day, though, is that it is mostly an outlet for his fans' adoration, not a moment to conjure the historical person. You need more than a bottle of champagne to celebrate Bourdain Day; you also need the amnesia that alcohol brings. The inconvenient truth about Tony's feel-good story, after all, is that its protagonist died by suicide. In the end, he was a source of hope for only so long before giving us a lesson in what happens when Emily Dickinson's "thing with feathers" takes flight.

Many of the Bourdain diehards don't want to focus on the messy truth about the bathroom in Kaysersberg or about Tony's last girlfriend, the Italian actress Asia Argento, whom they may see as the villain of the piece or perhaps even, in the more extreme cases, their romantic rival. Which is fine with the keepers of Tony's image—CNN and some of the people close to the Anthony Bourdain estate—for whom a sanitized and inspiring Tony is more valuable than a despairing one when it comes to the continuing business of Bourdain shows, films (like 2021's *Roadrunner*), and books. Those people are hoping that Sarah Bernhardt was right when she said, in her memoir, "Legend is victorious, in spite of history," and that they can add to, while continuing to take a slice of, the decent-sized fortune (despite some misleading news reports, which made it look like he was barely a millionaire at the end) that Tony left mostly to his wife and daughter. In the authorized version of the story, which the marketing minds behind Bourdain, Inc., now tell, references to his death are kept to an absolute minimum. He sometimes seems to have ascended into heaven at the height of his power, making a neat, clean break with his earthly existence. His relationship with Argento, who was at the center of it all at the very end, never gets explained in much depth or detail, and journalists are granted interviews with Bourdain insiders based on their willingness to play along with the myth. "We need to protect the brand!" has, I've been told, been the rallying cry of Tony's intensely loyal agent, Kimberly Witherspoon, and even his good and true friend Ripert has said (out of an excess of protectiveness, not a desire to profit), "I want to control the narrative."

In terms of commercial viability this makes sense: celebratory stuff sells, downer stuff doesn't. Yet when we try to pick and choose the lessons to take from a life, we begin to construct a lie—in this case, a lie about a man singularly devoted to truth and opposed to pretension and public relations. As his friend the *New Yorker* food writer Helen Rosner has observed, Tony "didn't walk through Manhattan with a security detail, or insist on photo approval, or barricade himself behind a battalion of publicists." When traveling for his show, he never dealt with official tourist agencies because he disdained the authorized version of things; he balked at the word "brand" and would surely have hated having a "day" manufactured in his honor. For a while it seemed like half the postings on Facebook's Anthony Bourdain Appreciation Society page were pictures of him giving the finger to, one must assume, the CEOs and senators who think they run the world. "He had a very good sense of what he wanted to stand for," his publisher Daniel Halpern has said, "and what he wouldn't stand for." None of that matters, though, since he's no longer around to defend himself; you can even use AI to have him say whatever you'd like in his own voice, as the maker of the film *Roadrunner* did. One other thing the Anthony Bourdain story teaches us is that when you're dead, they got you by the balls.

The location of Tony's birth was Columbia Presbyterian Hospital in upper Manhattan, but for those inclined to make sense of his life that detail is a red herring. There was never anything upper and for a long time preciously little mid- or lower Manhattan about Anthony Michael Bourdain. Duke Ellington was upper Manhattan. Tony—though his parents may have dipped back into the city so his mother could experience the best Eisenhower era medical care and his father could pace nervously in the same hospital hallways as corporate bigwigs and show business legends, his breast pocket bulging with cigars in the midcentury manner—was basically a bridge-and-tunnel boy from the start. (His bumpkinish veneer survived even his junkie days and is still on display in the early episodes of *A Cook's Tour*.) Twenty-one-year-old Gladys and twenty-six-year-old Pierre Bourdain had eagerly cast their lot with the throngs of upwardly mobile young marrieds just then fleeing the supposed volatility of the urban scene for the supposed safety of suburbia. When Pierre drove his dilating bride eastward over the George Washington Bridge, they already had a cozy little stone house in Leonia, New Jersey, with a nursery waiting. We know that because the Bourdains had barely gotten baby Tony back home when his father, "a resident of 155 Christie Street, Leonia," made the front page of the Hackensack *Record* for knocking over a pedestrian with his car in front of the cooperative grocery store in the heart of the town's bustling business district.

Leonia, a fifteen-minute drive from Manhattan on a decent traffic day, was no Levittown, bristling with identical prefabricated houses. If not quite as prosperous as neighboring Englewood, it was an obviously comfortable community of about 7,500, settled in 1668 by the Dutch and English and passed through by George Washington and his troops on the run from Charles Cornwallis in 1776; a striking seven-foot-tall mural in the town's Anna C. Scott School—which Tony attended from kindergarten until, as one friend saw it, "he got too smart for the public school system in around the sixth grade"—depicts their frostbitten, Valley Forge–bound flight. To stand out for your intelligence in Leonia would seem to be no small feat. A survey done in the 1920s showed 80 percent of the population had attended at least some college, an almost unbelievable statistic for that time; and later 92 percent were said to hold a library card. Over the decades, five Nobel Prize winners, including Enrico Fermi, have lived there, alongside such artistic types as Alan Alda, Freddie Bartholomew, Tony Bennett, Sammy Davis Jr., and Buddy Hackett. When Gladys and Pierre moved a few blocks north in the mid-1960s, they sold their original place to an up-and-coming novelist named Robert Ludlum. You never knew who you'd run into in Leonia. About a year after Pierre knocked over that pedestrian at Broad Avenue and Fort Lee Road, a motorist from Teaneck collided at the same busy intersection with a station wagon driven by Pat Boone.

Yet despite its long and relatively glamorous history, Leonia in the 1950s was in most ways a typical upper-middle-class bedroom community earnestly determined, for the sake of propriety and real estate values, to appear safe, God-fearing, and above all, pleasant. "Most residential streets are lined with maples and oaks that form canopies over the roads," the *New York Times* noted in an admiring 1997 profile, which also mentioned ten churches. The public schools were seen as acceptable, certainly superior to those across the Hudson River, already way too public in Tony's day and getting more so; the police force quietly effective at tamping down almost any sort of excitement. If the town fathers couldn't eliminate sin, they could at least keep it behind closed doors (there were several liquor stores in town but no bars). Citizens of Leonia considered themselves moderately progressive, even if some nearby country clubs were still "restricted" (meaning not open to Jews); and by some weird coincidence almost all the Black residents lived in the same Spring Street neighborhood, literally on the other side of the railroad tracks. The Bergen *Record* was an industrious, better-than-average broadsheet, covering a range of national as well as New Jersey and neighborhood events, but it strove to work in as much happy news as possible amid the ads for girdles, margarine, and forty-nine-cents-a-pound rump roasts down at the Howdy Doody Discount Center. "Park Zoo Gets Tame Monkey" was a typical headline of the times, as was "Nobody Stung as Bees Flee," "Truck Hits Pole But No Blackout," and (on the day after Tony was born) "Hot Dogs Go with Picnics; Can Be Cooked in Various Ways." Of course, suppurating just below this tranquil surface was the vast sea of fear and disappointment on which writers like Cheever, Updike, and later Rick Moody set sail. But sometimes real life in Leonia came close to the tranquilizing myth. Pierre's traffic accident, while it no doubt raised eyebrows, in the end amounted to just another of those forgettable kerfuffles in which the town seemed proud to specialize. His fifty-five-year-old victim suffered only a bruised hip—and readers of the *Record* account probably chuckled over a typo that had Pierre Bourdain being cited for "carless" driving.

Growing up in such a squeaky-clean environment gave the adolescent Tony something to grapple with, especially at a time when young Americans were openly protesting the hypocrisy and complacency of the Establishment. "As kids we both felt that fate had put us in the wrong place," said Dae Bennett, a son of Tony Bennett, now a record producer and back then Tony Bourdain's partner in alienation (and often in detention, for smoking) at the private Englewood School for Boys, which Tony attended from grades seven through eleven. "Just the *whiteness* of the whole scene bothered us." After he got famous, Tony would say repeatedly in books and interviews that he had been an extremely angry adolescent, and it's natural to assume those emotions were somehow connected to the major social and political upheavals of that period—and compounded by his hometown's imperviousness toward the changing times. Tony certainly stood against institutional racism and the Vietnam War, and took part in his share of protests. He wanted to stick it to the Man as much as the next semi-hippie.

But did his rage arise from the meanness and smugness of those in authority or from something more personal? It's hard to say, because when it came to elaborating on the sources of his anger, the writer who would prove so adept at describing the inevitable connection between food and politics, the patent pretentiousness of craft beer, and the vulgar camaraderie of the restaurant kitchen became strangely tongue-tied. In a 2011 interview with Jill Dupleix at the Sydney Writers' Festival, Tony took a stab at saying why he had been so furious back then. His explanation resembled something he'd said many times before—namely, that his frustration was rooted in "a sense of spoiled romanticism, a disappointment with the way things turned out. It was supposed to be far more beautiful and romantic and gentle, and I learned pretty early on that it wasn't going to be like that." Tony was indeed an inveterate romantic to a sometimes ridiculous degree—and he sounds in this case like he's hinting at something not political or societal but psychological and emotional. But what is the antecedent of "it" in that second sentence, and, while we're at it, what is he talking about? Who gave him this idyllic idea of how life was supposed to be? Five years later, in 2016, on NPR's *Fresh Air* with Dave Davies, Tony was still struggling to say why he was so mad. "I think I grew up, you know, as a child of the Kennedy years," he said. "The Summer of Love I missed. I wasn't old enough for everything that was happening with that subculture. So when I became an adolescent, I was disappointed, very disappointed, bitterly disappointed with the way the country was going, with the kind of entertainment and adventures that seemed to be on offer. I seemed to have missed the good times." Sensing that he was flailing like his favorite boxer, "the Bayonne Bleeder" himself, Chuck Wepner (see the serial "disappointeds"), Tony wisely chose to throw in the towel. "For whatever reason," he said to Davies, signaling it was time to abandon this stubborn subject and move along to one for which he had more polished material, "I was definitely a very angry, bitter, nihilistic, destructive, and self-destructive kid."

In the Leonia of memory, Angry Anthony is an elusive figure. Some of his high school friends claimed they saw him in spurts and flashes and always in indirect ways—in the industrious but crude R. Crumbish comic books he drew and in the Hunter S. Thompsonesque writing he submitted in vain to magazines and newspapers, or when he clomped around town with a pair of nunchucks dangling from his belt in an attempt to look badass; most of the old crowd, however, reports no such sightings. The Tony they knew was wildly energetic ("He kind of *popped* when he spoke," one friend said), eager to please, "a joy to have in class" according to his eleventh grade school evaluation, and ultimately just not all that remarkable. The prickliness he did affect on occasion was just that—affected—because, as Jerry Seinfeld has noted, "You can't have comedy without rage," and Tony was even then seriously interested in being funny. "He was intense but not dark intense," David Mansfield, a musician friend of his who left Leonia at eighteen to join Bob Dylan's Rolling Thunder Revue, told me. "It was an us-against-them culture back then, and we had hair down to our shoulders and Tony flipped over the Stooges, Frank Zappa, and all that, but we weren't expressing any deep-seated mental instability. We were just garden-variety neurotics who'd bike around town and kick over the occasional garbage can—that was our idea of being rebellious. After that we'd go home and read [Abbie Hoffman's] *Steal This Book* or *Fear and Loathing in Las Vegas.*" Tony, always a voracious consumer of pop culture, revered Stanley Kubrick's *A Clockwork Orange* and Frank Zappa's *200 Motels*, two of the more surreal movies of the early 1970s, but it was *Fear and Loathing*, Hunter Thompson's "Savage Journey into the Heart of the American Dream," with illustrations by Ralph Steadman, that "blew his mind" said Mansfield, after he discovered it serialized in *Rolling Stone* in 1971. "Tony adopted the language of the book and aspired to the lifestyle," though he always stopped short of the protagonist Raoul Duke's penchant for trashing hotel rooms and totaling cars. "Honestly," said Mansfield, "Tony Bourdain was never terribly fringe. Underneath the posing, he was a smart, sweet, good-looking boy from Leonia, New Jersey."

It's possible of course that Angry Tony was present but outside of his writing and drawing largely unseen. Tony's childhood was marked by a tension between the kid who felt mortified by his idyllic personal circumstances and the one who was thoroughly gobsmacked by them. If he really had been as furious as he seemed to want everyone to believe, it may have been because he was secretly in love with leafy little Leonia and felt ashamed, on some level, of being so sappy. In a school composition written circa tenth grade and titled "Early Morning Whimsy," he wrote of tooling around town on his bike in the cool predawn hour, chatting up milkmen, splashing through puddles, and ogling women who came out on their porches in their nightgowns to pick up the newspaper ("I see you, lady, I see you!" he shouted, sounding a bit like his future bête noire, Jerry Lewis). "This essay lacks the continuity and perception of some of your others," his English teacher, who was no doubt expecting something more scorched-earth, said in a marginal note—but it revealed a tender side that perhaps surprised even him.

Tony didn't just live in Leonia, he reveled in it, a boy leading an old-fashioned boy's life of investigation and adventure, caught up in the small-town rhythms and rituals. "Every winter," said his childhood friend Chris Boyd, "the Leonia police would backflush the swamps to fill up the basketball courts so the kids could go skating and all these bizarre, mutated fish would freeze in the ice—we thought that was very cool." (Tony's fascination with bizarre, mutated things would take a long time to fade; indeed, for a while, he ate such things for a living. As one of his former girlfriends, Paula Froehlich, said to me, "You *do* understand that he never really became a full-fledged adult, right?") On other cold nights, he and Bennett would build a bonfire at the top of a hill at the Englewood Country Club (where Don Rickles and Joey Bishop were members) and sled down the slopes on the back side of the Palisades. Summer Saturdays often meant a trip to Hiram's Roadstand in Fort Lee, home of the Ripper, a hot dog that ruptures when deep fried (the only way you can have it), creating a gaping orifice that aficionados see as a silent scream for chili, cheese, and raw onions.

And then in all seasons there were the comic books, of which he was a most avid student and collector. With Tony, curiosity could easily flare into obsession, as those who, in the early 1980s, watched him morph into a self-styled expert on the JFK assassination and sat through his monologues about Jack Ruby, know all too well. As a kid he had every issue of Zap, the model for the underground comix movement of the 1960s, as well as select rare historic collector specimens of other comics that he kept, Mansfield told me with a chuckle, "in special archival bags." (It's too bad that when Tony later argued that, despite the widespread presumption, he was not at all cool, he didn't think to mention this persuasive evidence.) And he of course could never have enough Supermans or Spider-Mans. A small classified ad he ran in the "Wanted to Buy" section of the *Record* in early June 1971, said: "Comic books—Preferably old but want recent too; Main titles: Marvel and DC; Tony Bourdain, 119 Orchard Place, Leonia." Angry or not, this is the real Tony Bourdain, preserved in agate type. He was fourteen at the time, still a Boy Scout in good standing—and already deeply into drugs, if not yet an addict.

With Tony, as with most people, you have to take the innocent with the illicit. For him and most of his well-off friends, life was, to put it in comic book terms, Zap meets Archie. At the Englewood School for Boys (soon to merge with the neighboring Dwight School for Girls) the clique of twenty or so older kids he hung with called themselves the Cruisers, or sometimes the Crazy Cruisers. They didn't go so far as dressing alike, but they took their club quite seriously and spoke in code words, like "dodowell," which meant, one told me, "everything is chill." (Tony at this time also belonged to another, all-guy group called the Blue Moose Club whose members greeted one another with "G'moose" and had a secret handshake, but they were never his chief tribe.) Around the lush and rolling Dwight and Englewood campuses the Cruisers were considered their own distinct demographic alongside the jocks, the preps, and the nerds. Their name, as far as anyone can recall, came from somebody's car as well as their collective penchant for cruising around North Jersey, going for junk food, and getting high on pot and wasted on illicit pharmaceuticals like quaaludes and amphetamines. (On the Iran episode of *Parts Unknown*, filmed in 2014, Tony says, "I spent my youth pretty much hanging out in a parking lot.") As an adult Tony would grouse that most of his high school friends had more money and less oversight than he did (because their parents were divorced and his weren't), which made it easier for them to get drugs. But Dae Bennett and others remember Tony as one of the heavier users. "He would take anything and a lot of it," Bennett told me. "He and his friends would offer me stuff and I'd say, 'What are you, crazy? You don't even know what that is. They cut their product with fucking Drāno! But he wanted to be that guy that lived out there on the edge." Mansfield remembered an all-too-typical evening when they were fourteen and "barreling down Route 80 with Tony and two or three other friends and everyone was tripping on LSD. I was sober, sitting in the back, and they were screaming about driving through a mushroom cloud of fire."

Yet at other times—times when he was in the company of young women, especially—Tony behaved himself. "We'd cut class and he'd come visit me in my very girly bedroom," Andrea Blickman, then the purple-haired "quaalude queen" and now a nurse, told me. "He'd sit on my canopy bed and we'd just talk for hours" chain-smoking Larks and sometimes less legal cigarettes. He was "obviously vulnerable, very funny, and able to see the world through this twisted Tony lens." Despite his winning personality, the drugs, and Tony's status as "one of the cuter boys" on campus, there was, she said, "nothing remotely flirtatious or sexual" about their marathon chats. "I was a couple of years older than him and he was like my kid brother." Indeed with one notable exception, which we'll get to in a moment, Tony didn't get involved with any of the girls in the group—although he did broach the subject of sex when concealing himself behind what with a stretch we can call art. He once wrote Blickman an obviously fictionalized letter about a road trip he and some friends took to the Catskills, during which he'd "engaged in the old in and out" (a *Clockwork Orange* reference) with "a twenty-year-old exotic contortionist topless dancer named Panama Red," and his graduation gift to Blickman and several other Cruiser girls was an original, hand-drawn, poster-sized comic strip crowded with whips, chains, and giant penises. The recipients said they were not offended—he was such a sweetheart, after all, and sincerely aspired to be a professional illustrator—but one woman noted, "when I later hung one of his drawings in my college dorm room, people got the impression I was perverted."

There was, perhaps not surprisingly, a performative aspect to a great deal of what Tony did in those days. He didn't just draw or write, he also went around acting like an eccentric artist or bohemian author for the entertainment of himself and others. He was experimenting with personalities, he later said, trying them on for size and for the knowledge and stimulation that the pretending provided. It was no different when it came to drugs. He didn't just want to get high, escape reality, take the edge off, or deepen his consciousness—he wanted to take on the trappings of a junkie, right down to the dope sickness, if only to impress those around him. Bennett told me he noticed this dangerous behavior and tried to talk to him about "what can happen when you want to have street cred, but you're from Bergen County and it's kind of hard." The idea of being a pretender was a sensitive subject with Tony (and always would be). "Every time I brought it up," Bennett told me, "he didn't want to hear about it. He'd get pissed off and say, 'What do you care?'" Their friendship soon cooled and they more or less lost touch. But one night nearly forty years later Bennett got a call from his famous father, who said he was in the green room at *Larry King*, "sitting with a guy who says you two spent a lot of time together in detention." He put the other Tony on the phone and Dae—who teared up a little when he told me this story—said, "Hey, man, thanks a *lot*!"

The Cruisers had no formal structure, but they did have a clear-cut leader—Phillip Goldman. Flip, as everyone called him, was a handsome, witty, personable "early adopter of cool stuff," said Blickman, who had a Susan Sontag–like blaze of white in his chestnut hair that seemed to mark him as somebody special. His magnetic pull affected males and females equally, but no one was more in Flip's thrall than Tony, two years his junior, and within days of their meeting his devoted pet. Wherever Flip went, Tony followed, eager to bask in his charisma and do his bidding. At first Flip subjected him to a kind of hazing, just because he could. ("The first Friday of our ski club trips, we made him ride in the luggage rack," he recalled.) As Flip got to know Tony better, though, he came to genuinely like him—and also to think that he might be useful.

Flip's steady girlfriend, it almost went without saying if you were familiar with the Dwight-Englewood social scene, was Nancy Putkoski, a doctor's daughter who was standoffish by nature but blond and beautiful ("in a Polish Catholic sort of way, if that's your thing," one of her female classmates cattily informed me). They made for a dazzling duo, the quick-to-smile Cruiser king and his alluringly expressionless queen. Flip's one problem in the world—or so it seemed—was that Nancy's parents were worried about her getting too serious with anyone at her age and had told their daughter they didn't want him coming around the house so much. Flip thought he could address their concerns by showing up with another friend who might make the visits look more like an innocent group hangout—and Tony, who was still short for his age, had not expressed any particular interest in girls, and always had a few comic books tucked under his arm, seemed like the perfect beard. But then about halfway through the 1973–1974 school year, something happened.

Only the three principals knew the once-coveted details, but it gradually became understood that Flip and Nancy were no longer an item while—much to the surprise of the other Cruisers—*Tony* and Nancy were. (Nancy's only comment to me about this was "High school hi jinks!") What made the situation doubly strange was that nothing was ever explicitly acknowledged. Flip, perhaps out of pride, seemed stoic about losing his girl to an acolyte, and Nancy and Tony carried on publicly almost exactly as before, meaning that they didn't seem to be spending all that much time together. The attachment nevertheless was intense, at least on his part. As soon as Nancy decided to go to Vassar College, Tony, who was a year younger, worked out a plan with his academic adviser to increase his course load and attend summer school so he could finish Englewood early and follow her there. "Clearly, he was devoted to Nancy if not even a little obsessed with her or he would never have left his life in Leonia," Blickman said. You would just never know it from the way they acted. Nancy had always kept her feelings hidden, so you could say she was at least being consistent. But perhaps in his own way Tony was, too. Despite always seeming eager to express himself—with drawing, writing, and verbal humor—he was a boy with well-defined borders and strictly kept secrets. "You want to know what kind of guy young Tony Bourdain was?" Dae Bennett said to me. "He was the kind of guy who, when we were growing up together, came over to my house all the time. But I was never invited over to his house, not even *once.*" Nor did Tony, in any of the abundant yarn spinning he would do about himself in books and interviews, ever give the public more than a quick peek behind the curtains.

Chapter 2

Sometimes a hot dog is just a hot dog. Still, when you consider the bulk of the evidence, it's clear that Tony's first trips to Hiram's Roadstand, undertaken circa age eight with his father, Pierre, were about something more than just his lifelong devotion to what he later liked to call "meat in tubular form." They were a bonding experience. A common love of salty, greasy, sausagey things combined with a certain . . . difficulty with the lady of the house cemented them together permanently into a tight little team. Not that they agreed on absolutely everything, that mirror image pair of animated speakers who fit right into the raucous, masculine atmosphere at the Home of the Ripper. Poor Pierre adored the sarsaparilla soda at Hiram's, while poor Tony favored the birch beer—but that apparently was about as *Long Day's Journey into Night* as those two coconspirators ever got. I call Pierre poor because he died in 1987 at age fifty-seven, alone and overweight; his suburban dream shattered; his marriage long since dead; his career, such as it was, in positively cringeworthy condition. I call Tony poor because when Pierre had his fatal heart attack Tony was, at age thirty, still a crack addict cracking clams at the raw bar of a restaurant in the West Village and feeling like he had failed to make his father proud and now it was too late. "He never saw me complete a book or achieve anything of note,"Tony said later, looking back. "I would have liked to have shared this with him."

Father and son had a tradition of sharing experiences that went back to the days when Tony was still an only child, and they would read *The Wind in the Willows, Winnie-the-Pooh, Doctor Doolittle*, and *Emil and the Detectives* before bedtime. Pierre's French-language copy of the last, looking bedraggled as beloved books do and marked with "doodlings of goofy Nazis and Stuka dive-bombers in the margins," stayed in Tony's possession until the end—which means it survived the sidewalk sales of books and records he conducted when he needed money to buy drugs. Later they would go together to movies like *Dr. Strangelove or: How I Learned to Stop Worrying and Love the Bomb*, which brother Chris was still too young to see and which, truth be told, Tony, at age nine, was also in no way ready for but which Pierre took him to anyway because he couldn't wait to expose him to good films. All Tony would remember about Kubrick's satiric take on nuclear annihilation was his father throwing his head back and laughing.

As Tony approached the stage when children normally start pulling away from their parents and preferring the company of friends, Pierre managed to stay unobtrusively involved in Tony's life, by doing things like chauffeuring him to concerts. In one of the final episodes of *Parts Unknown*, set on the Lower East Side, an otherwise very tired and over-it looking Tony brightens momentarily as he tells Harley Flanagan, the leader, then and still, of a proto-punk band called the Cro-Mags, that when he was about twelve, his father would drive him and a friend or two to the Fillmore East, on Second Avenue near Sixth Street (to see the Mothers of Invention, Ten Years After, or whoever he was excited about at the moment), then, after killing a few hours in a movie house or a bookstore (Pierre wasn't a big drinker), pick them up postconcert and take them home. "Tony's father could make magic happen because he worked at Columbia Records," said Andrea Blickman. "We loved him for that." Once Pierre got tickets for Tony and a bunch of his high school friends to a New York Philharmonic performance of Bach's Toccata and Fugue in D Minor—not because they shared his passion for classical music (they didn't) but because that was the score of the first part of Walt Disney's *Fantasia*, "which if you fancied yourself a member of the psychedelic generation," said Blickman, "was a *very* important movie—we were thrilled!" Later the group (sans Pierre) ventured across Broadway to O'Neal's Baloon, as one did in those days after an evening of high culture at Lincoln Center, and perhaps because their leader, Tony, was so tall they were served alcohol without being asked to produce proof of age. To drink in Manhattan has always been a Jersey kid's dream, and the outing became the stuff of legend, reminisced about enthusiastically more than thirty years later at a reunion held at the home of a graying ex-Cruiser—but not, they couldn't help noticing, by Tony, who sat silently by, as he had for most of the evening, staring blankly into the middle distance and leaving them to wonder why he had come all the way to Englewood if he wasn't going to engage with them, the older, cooler kids he had once tried so hard to impress.

Although their marriage was already showing signs of coming asunder, Pierre and Gladys were not by any means the oddest of couples. Both tall and heavyset to the point of being what Mansfield called "borderline ungainly," they, a secular Catholic and a secular Jew descended from what used to be called hardy peasant stock yet having highbrow tastes in music and books, had somehow found each other (as Catholics, Jews, peasants, highbrows, and wallflowers will in New York) and married in 1954, bringing to a formal conclusion two especially knotty childhoods. Pierre never really knew his father—who for a giddy moment ten years before his birth had made front-page news across the country as "the youngest member of the US Army." To a certain point, it's a charming World War I–era tale. In the summer of 1919, fourteen-year-old Pierre Michel Bourdain was befriended by members of the Fifty-Fourth Coast Artillery when they bivouacked on what one newspaper called his family's "worn-out farm near Maine-et-Loire" in Bordeaux. So smitten were the soldiers with the plucky garçon that when it came time to ship back home, they decided to take him along, supposedly with his parents' permission. The problem was that immediately upon arrival, Pierre Michel was declared a stowaway and returned to France. End of charming story. Seven years later, though, after serving in the army of the Third Republic, Tony's grandfather legally emigrated to the United States, where he took a job as a department store cosmetics clerk in downtown Manhattan and married a French woman named Gabrielle Riousse thirteen years his senior. With help from her income as a dressmaker to the very rich, they moved into a doorman building on West 95th Street and pursued the American dream. Tony's father, their only child, arrived in 1929. All seemed in good order. But on New Year's Eve of 1931, Pierre Michel dropped dead of a heart attack at the age of twenty-six.

The early story of Pierre *fils* is by design a bit blurry. He rarely talked about his boyhood or his bachelor years, making him the opposite of his firstborn child, who seemed afflicted with memoir mania. "My father was, to me, a man of mystery," said Tony, who nevertheless managed to pull together a few biographical details that he passed along to the general public. Pierre, Tony said, grew up speaking French with his single mother at his Upper West Side home and making summer trips to Normandy to see relatives. After graduating from the exclusive Birch Wathen School, Pierre entered Yale in the fall of 1947, at the age of seventeen, but stayed only four semesters. The reason for his early departure is unknown, but he did have a habit of meandering off the path to success. A few years later, after working as an assistant at London Records, Pierre joined the army, where he spent most of his time as a supply sergeant in Germany, doing what exactly it is again hard to say, but probably nothing too interesting. Interesting occupations were not Pierre's métier. For much of his adult life, he held down two pedestrian jobs rather than the one consequential position that defined most Leonia patriarchs. When Tony was born in 1956, Pierre was selling printing by day and working at a Sam Goody record shop at night. Later he sold cameras at the big Willoughby store near Macy's in Herald Square before putting in a half shift at Goody's. No one doubted that he had the requisite intelligence and energy for better things, but he always found it hard to get beyond the outskirts of what interested him. In his 2001 book, *A Cook's Tour*, Tony called him "a shy man with few friends, uncomfortable with confrontation and with large groups, a man who dreaded tie and jacket, unpretentious, amused by hypocrisy, affectation, with a sense for the absurd and ironic [who] took a childlike joy in simple things"—a long way of saying that he didn't interview well.

While entirely American in affect—Tony said he was always surprised when his father suddenly broke into French with Haitian cabdrivers—Pierre had little in common with the fast-talking, sharp-elbowed New Yorkers he often found himself amid. His one professional break came when Tony was about thirteen, and, with the help of a connection from his London Records days, Pierre managed to land an "executive" spot (Tony's kind word; it was more of a midlevel manager position) at Columbia Records. Although his responsibilities involved packaging and not music, which was his passion, he was happy to have the salary, the title (classical merchandising manager), the chance to bring home armfuls of free albums for Tony and Christopher, and (perhaps with help from his journalist wife) to be occasionally quoted in the newspapers about trends in the record industry. (In 1974 he wrongly predicted to the *New York Times* that quadraphonic sound would be the next big thing.) But then something happened or failed to happen and Pierre lost his job at the label of Vladimir Horowitz, Eugene Ormandy, and many of his other long-haired musical heroes. By the time of his death, he was back on the sales floor, dusting and adjusting the plastic cases at an Upper East Side storefront called Orpheus Remarkable Recordings.

Gladys Bourdain, who died in January 2020 at age eighty-five, was never an easy person to please—or to cozy up to—but she was hard not to notice. When I mentioned her to a former colleague at the *New York Times*, where she worked as a copy editor from 1984 to 2008, the woman said, "I never thought anyone would ask me to talk about Gladys Bourdain, though I've spent a fair amount of my life doing exactly that." The general consensus among the nine ex-coworkers I spoke to (seven of them women) was that everyone had a Gladys story. The number of Gladys stories that depicted her as incompetent or ill-informed (or for that matter careless about her appearance) totaled exactly zero. But if I may get a bit Zagaty for a moment, the percentage of those who said that despite her "pristine editorial skills" and "obvious intelligence" she could be "harsh," "difficult," "impossible," "bossy," "challenging," "judgmental," or "imperious" hovered dangerously close to one hundred. She was the sort of person, a former boss of hers at the *Times*, Don

Hecker, told me, who "liked to dominate a conversation and she could not resist giving advice to her colleagues on professional issues like editing and newsroom protocols."

Clearly—and obviously in stark contrast to Pierre—Gladys was the outspoken type, and in part because of what she said when she spoke out and how strongly she said it and how little tolerance she had for anyone who might say something back to her, she rubbed people the wrong way. Her offenses, if you want to call them that, sound paltry when considered apart from the sealed-off Mandarin culture of the *Times* copydesk, but in that context they were legendary. Mostly they concerned the way she carried herself—i.e., as if she were meant to be something better than a copy editor, something higher up on the masthead—but there are also stories about her doing the sort of things that *just were not done* at the paper. Once, for example, after the copydesk was moved to a different location within the building, she was said to have "harassed" managing editor Gene Roberts about the placement of furniture until he had the room rearranged more to her liking. On another occasion, when she thought a coworker had left the remains of a *Times* cafeteria dinner hanging around his work space too long, she waited until he'd stepped away, then scooped up his tray and sent it clattering—real dishes and silverware and all—into a nearby trash bin. Gladys was infamously fastidious; she reacted theatrically to the smell of fish and peanut butter in the office and admonished coworkers for thrusting their hands into a shared bag of popcorn, ordering them to for God's sake go get paper plates. And so on.

Of course, you have to wonder: if she had been a man, would she have been less legendary and perhaps even remembered fondly for her forthrightness and panache? The consensus of my panel of ex-colleagues on that question was "possibly." But to a certain degree at least Gladys seemed to relish her reputation at the *Times* and beyond. "The essence of Gladys Bourdain became clear to me one evening when I went to hear her son Anthony speak at the New York Public Library," Diane Nottle, one of her former colleagues said. "Someone in the audience asked him what it was like to work in a restaurant kitchen, and he said without hesitation, 'If you enjoy lording it over a small group of people in a small place, then a restaurant job might be for you!' I laughed out loud because that was just how Gladys functioned. 'Well,' I said to myself, 'now we know where he got *that*!'"

Gladys hardly mentioned Tony to her *Times* coworkers, even after he became famous—he'd always be too much of a loose cannon for her to publicly associate herself with, and, besides that, she, like Pierre, reflexively took pains to conceal virtually all personal information. In her case, the specific, mundane, and sometimes embarrassing facts of her life (and Tony's) would only have gotten in the way of the image she wished to project—an image of glamour, intrigue, and infinite possibility. " 'Elegance' is the word that comes to mind when I think of Gladys," said Christopher Phillips, who worked alongside her at the copydesk for several years. "Despite being a big, older woman," said Phillips, "she had a way of dressing beautifully but simply, and she always had wonderful skin, lovely green eye shadow, and perfect diction" (all of which, he noted, set her apart from most coworkers, "who came to work looking like slobs"). Apart from the period in the early 1950s that she spent in Paris, working as a correspondent for Agence France-Presse, and falling in love with French culture, Gladys rarely if ever made reference to any past life. "The only time I ever heard her mention her husband," Hecker said, "is when she expressed resentment at his stupidity for not hanging on to a house in France." Phillips, her closest male friend on the copydesk, can't recall her saying a single word about Pierre. "She once let it slip that she'd been a housewife in New Jersey and I was surprised," he said. "You didn't think of her like that. She had a kind of knowledge I associate with cultured Europeans, those people who don't have to study, who just get it from the water. I was shocked when I read in her obituary that she came from modest beginnings in the Bronx."

New York's northernmost borough has never been chic, but it was still the Ogden Nash "No thonks Bronx" and not the Bronx-is-burning Bronx when Gladys Sacksman grew up there in the 1930s and 1940s; the future Supreme Court justice Sonia Sotomayor and her ilk had not yet arrived in sufficient numbers to flush the plebian white population from its perches. University Heights, where Gladys lived, was a bustling neighborhood of corner soda fountains, Hebrew National delis, Loft's candy shops, and Thom McAn shoe stores loosely arranged around the uptown campus of NYU, but the sheer middle-middle-classness of it all, the aggressive nondescriptness, did not necessarily translate into a sense of order and peace.

On April 28, 1949, just after Gladys had left for high school, someone knocked on her door and yelled "Messenger!" When her mother, Martha, opened it, the man produced a knife and robbed her of jewelry valued at $4,600. How Gladys's father, Milton—whose family had arrived penniless from the Ukrainian backwater of Ostroh in the early 1900s and who now ran a part-time one-man "trucking company" when he was not playing poker on the stoop—could have bestowed upon his wife a trove that the New York *Daily News* itemized as "a diamond solitaire, a diamond wedding ring, a cocktail ring, and a cocktail watch" perhaps becomes clearer if you know that Tony's maternal grandfather specialized in the transportation of items that had fallen from other people's trucks. The year before his own home was robbed, Milton Sacksman was arrested, along with two accomplices, for driving around with $60,000 worth of stolen textiles. That crime followed a conviction for selling more than a million stolen cigarette tax stamps—which in turn followed a period of forced confinement for possessing more than four hundred pairs of stolen pants. Milton was in and out of prison (and the tabloids) for most of his daughter's childhood. Gladys may have not yet known what she wanted to be when she grew up, but she knew she didn't want to be a Martha, married to a Milton, not for all the cocktail watches in the world. In the end it is just an inky headshot, taken on the fly, but Gladys looked bright and optimistic—and more than a little pretty—when the *Daily News* "inquiring fotographer," Jimmy Jemail, stopped her outside the Vanderbilt Hotel in Manhattan in mid-November of 1952 and posed the question of the day: Can you spot a married man? If so, how? Gladys's reply showed that at age eighteen her opinion-making machinery was already working overtime. "No," she said. "Intelligent men are more or less alike. If they happen to be married, they can create any impression they wish. That's because most women are gullible and like attention, extravagant or otherwise. The smart men, if they are not too old, remember to take off their wedding rings." Clearly, Ms. Sacksman had a realistic view of the world. No pants-pilferers for her. She would graduate from Hunter College, a good, solid, no-frills city school where smart city girls like her went—and stride into life with her eyes wide open.

Her eventual choice of a husband was not necessarily a mistake—or a surprise if you are a student of human behavior. For an overbearing Francophile like Gladys, the passive Pierre may have been in some symbiotic sense the perfect partner: a French fixer-upper that she could theoretically improve. Their problems would come later. In their early years together the Bourdains were as enthusiastic and as optimistic as any young couple. They lined their walls with the literature they esteemed and on weekends turned their living room into an art house cinema where they projected French and Italian films in 16 millimeter for themselves and sometimes a few friends, using the noisy, hot, and cumbersome state-of-the-art equipment that Pierre borrowed from Willoughby's. When guests came, Gladys sometimes got Julia Child's *Mastering the Art of French Cooking* from atop the refrigerator and made coquilles Saint Jacques. (The sweet smell of the scallops and the muted chatter of the adults wafted into Tony's bedroom—and made him angry, he said, because he was being left out.) Politically Pierre and Gladys were on the same page as well. In 1965 they lent their names to a pledge, drafted by the local Interfaith Council and published in the *Record*, that said they would not discriminate against their neighbors on the basis of race, color, or creed, and would "resist all pressure to sell their home quickly" if a nonwhite family moved in nearby. Leaving no Camelot-era cliché untested, they also acted together in community theater—or at least Pierre appeared in romantic comedies like *Desk Set* and dramas like *Death of a Salesman*, while Gladys (whose domineering manner was perhaps a cover for excessive shyness) worked backstage doing makeup, sound effects, and lighting.

Still, no art form excited them more than classical music, which they went to hear in concert and also listened to at home in the way you were supposed to back then—with an ear cocked for superior stereo separation. "Pierre was the first person I ever met who had a real hi-fi system," said David Mansfield, who was perhaps the only friend Tony ever invited for sleepovers. "He had *big* speakers mounted on his living room walls, Altec 604Es or something, like studio monitors. He also had a Crown two-track tape recorder, where he'd record the weekly broadcasts of the Philharmonic and the Metropolitan Opera—and he'd have the walls lined with his tapes. At the breakfast table he'd be jovial and bright, then he'd sit on the couch, turn up the volume, and just listen to Wagner with his hair flying back."

But while they stayed in touch with their personal interests (as Dr. Benjamin Spock in his bestselling *Common Sense Book of Baby and Child Care* was then advising young parents to do), Pierre and Gladys never abandoned their boys to babysitters or the boob tube. They made trips en famille to France, went most summers together to the Jersey Shore, and regularly piled into their station wagon to eat in Manhattan, sometimes at a Horn & Hardart Automat when they picked up Pierre after work, but just as often in Chinatown, Little Italy, or at the Cuban-Chinese restaurant La Caridad on the Upper West Side. "We just wanted them to be a little more worldly than some of our Leonia neighbors," Gladys, in a rare moment of expansiveness, told the Hackensack *Record* in 2007, "and we loved food of all kinds." From a certain distance—a distance that Tony tried to preserve by almost never inviting friends over—chez Bourdain appeared to be functioning just fine. The family had a working barbecue grill in the backyard, a mixed-breed dog named Puccini, a Wiffle ball and bat in the garage, and a package of chicken cutlets perpetually thawing on the kitchen counter, in accordance with the suburban code. With Gladys's encouragement and direction, preteen Tony baked cookies and gingerbread men at Christmastime; on birthdays, when the boys were allowed to choose whatever they wanted for dinner (and Chris usually picked a piece of cake), Tony requested roast beef with Yorkshire pudding and a chocolate soufflé.

Along with its more agreeable traditions the household also had what seemed to be a larger than average number of strictly enforced rules. Gladys, who fell naturally into the role of bad cop, forbade soda and junk food, constantly corrected everyone's grammar (If Tony asked "Can I have a bowl of cereal?" she would say,

"You *can* but you *may* not!"—though she ultimately gave him any food he asked for because she thought he was far too skinny), and was deadly serious about dental hygiene. "After Tony and Chris brushed their teeth at bedtime," said Mansfield, "their mom would produce these red tablets, which she would make them chew. The tablets stained your teeth to show where you still had plaque." When Tony opened wide so Gladys could make her inspections, he would feel his rage level rising—but really what self-respecting kid wouldn't? And even he had to admit that Gladys, while she may have run an extremely tight ship, was never directly mean or abusive to *him*. "I did not want for love or attention," he wrote in his 2010 book *Medium Raw*. "My parents loved me. Neither of them drank to excess. Nobody beat me. God was never mentioned—so I was annoyed by neither religion nor church nor any notions of sin or damnation. . . . I got the bike I wanted for Christmas." What Tony was ultimately so bent out of shape about, he said, was "the smothering chokehold of love and normalcy in my house."

Enraged by normalcy? As a justification for perpetual anger, this sounds no less suspicious than the previous ones we've seen him proffer. Yet what does seem certain is that the same boy who around his friends played the part of a wisecracking, arm-waving, eyeball-popping entertainer, eager for peer approval in the form of laughs, was indeed a "sullen, moody, difficult little bastard" (his words, in *Kitchen Confidential*) when in the exclusive company of his parents and brother. Tony constantly bullied Chris, refused to apply himself at his expensive prep school, and often showed up for dinner, he said, "late, stoned, and belligerent." If he knew Gladys was having friends over for lunch, he might blithely threaten to wander through the dining room smoking marijuana, just to give her something to worry about. "His teenage years were awful for me," Gladys told the *Record*—but we can see from the opening section of *Kitchen Confidential* that she was understating the case; Tony's dudgeon was already eagle high at age nine, when the family made its initial foray to France.

The Bourdains traveled in style on that first crossing—cabin class on the *Queen Mary*—but, thanks to Tony, not in peace. While there *were* a few things about the trip that he (decades later) had to admit he very much liked—the vichyssoise on board ship (he loved the word as much as the soup), Tintin and Asterix comics, the old Nazi blockhouses that studded the beach in the bleak Normandy resort town where they initially stayed—he mostly played the short-shorts-wearing ugly American *pisseur* who thought the butter cheesy, the cheese pus-like, and the Eiffel Tower only slightly less tedious than what he saw, he said in *Kitchen Confidential*, as the pure hell of pushing "toy sailboats around the fountain in the Jardin de Luxembourg." Gladys and Pierre tried to sweeten his mood with "hundreds of dollars' worth" of supplemental Tintins, which they bought at the English bookstore W. H. Smith, and the tactic did work briefly. But because they wouldn't give him what he'd decided he *really* wanted—permission to smoke cigarettes and to have a glass of watered-down *vin ordinaire* at dinner, like some of his only slightly older French playmates—he sulked and groused his way through the summer. Until the moment he ate the oyster.

While never-order-fish-on-Monday was the most quoted piece of advice in *Kitchen Confidential*, the consumption of that first oyster is perhaps the best-remembered story within the story of Tony's first forty-four years: the slurp that made him a superstar. It's a simple tale—one morning he and his family were taken off the coast of La Teste sur Mer on a small wooden boat to inspect some oyster beds; their guide without preamble reached over the side, pulled up a huge, silt-encrusted specimen, popped it open with a rusty knife, and handed it to Tony (in his telling, the only Bourdain who wasn't rabidly oyster-phobic) to eat. It went down gloriously while his family looked on, aghast, and at first Tony seemed to put the experience in a purely positive light, an "unforgettably sweet" reverse Madeleine moment that "tasted of seawater . . . of brine and flesh . . . and somehow . . . of the future . . ." a moment "still more alive for me than so many of the other 'firsts' that followed—first pussy, first joint, first day in high school, first published book, or any other thing." The oyster changed everything for him, he wrote, because the "glistening, vaguely sexual object, still dripping and nearly alive" brought the realization that "food had *power*" and that life might be chock-full of wonderful and nearly indescribable sensations that, for both better and worse, had to be experienced to be believed. It's such a lovely, startling, and intense passage that you barely notice that the swallowing of the bivalve was, at bottom, a sadistic act.

Or really another in a series of sadistic acts he'd been gleefully inflicting on his family. By the time he made them recoil in horror at La Teste, Tony had been revenge eating his way through France for at least two weeks. The offense for which he was still extracting payback had been perpetrated when they'd visited Vienne, a fair-size city twenty-two miles south of Lyon, and Gladys and Pierre made a lunch reservation in a then world-renowned restaurant called La Pyramide. The booking, however, was for two, not four, something Tony didn't realize until his parents announced, as they pulled into the parking area, that only Mom and Dad would be dining just then. Leaving bratty Tony in the car was like putting Baby in the corner: an undoable deed. He doesn't say in *Kitchen Confidential* that he and Chris were *locked* inside the ritzy Rover they'd rented for their month-long holiday, but he does describe a three-hour, swelteringly hot ordeal that left him furious, even more furious than he surely would have been if his parents had frog-marched him into La Pyramide, forced him to quit whining for a moment, and made him choose something from the hamburger-less menu. "Things changed. *I* changed" outside the restaurant, where, overcome with an urge to "outdo my foodie parents," he wrote, he vowed to become the most adventurous eater they ever saw—to gross them out and cost them a lot of money in the process. "Brains? Stinky, runny cheeses that smelled like dead men's feet? Horsemeat? Sweetbreads? Bring it on!!" His rage, in this case, is more understandable than usual (assuming he wasn't exaggerating about the three-hour imprisonment), but from a literary standpoint the back-to-back epiphanies feel redundant. The trip from "Things changed. *I* changed" to the assertion that "Everything was different now" after the oyster takes only three pages. I wonder if he ever regretted crowding together two supposedly watershed moments or (as long as we're questioning writerly decisions) that double exclamation point. Prose is like hair, Flaubert said, it shines with combing; as a writer and as a man, Tony could be the tousled type.

The Bourdains lived high on the hog—far too high for their own peace of mind. Pierre liked to say, "I am a man of simple needs," and about things like wine and clothing he usually was; but he also yearned for the good life as it was defined in mid-twentieth-century America and had a tendency to indulge his passions without worrying about the price tag. "My father was a dreamer who didn't seem to think or talk about financial things," is how Tony put it in a 2017 interview for *Wealthsimple* magazine in which he danced around an issue that he almost never spoke about. Besides being an audiophile, a traveler, and a foodie, Pierre was also a car buff who for years drove a Rover station wagon that cost about three times as much as an Oldsmobile or Chevy, even though his income was likely a fraction of his Leonia neighbors'. His most expensive habit, though, was saying yes to his wife, who was "far more organized" than he was, Tony said, but whose "aspirations outpaced her ability to pay." The goal for people in their social set was . . . well, whatever the Joneses' goal was; and for a while the Bourdains appeared to be more than keeping up. They took *two* summer vacations some years and bought a bigger house in Leonia just as they moved their boys into private school. They were not savers. When one of Pierre's relatives died in France and they inherited a moderate sum, he and Gladys spent it all immediately on elaborate landscape gardening—"a full build-out; it took years" Tony said—even though they were struggling to pay the boys' tuition. "In retrospect," Tony noted dryly, "maybe we could have done without the shrub pines."

When Tony was approaching high school age Pierre was forced to sell the Rover and afterward drove around town in a dented old clunker that his boys were embarrassed to be seen getting out of; he also had to sell a house they owned in France. "Was I aware of money?" Tony said in the *Wealthsimple* interview. "Yeah. I was aware we didn't have enough sometimes. . . . I was aware that I had far less money at my disposal than just about everyone I went to school with." That was putting it mildly.

Although Tony didn't mention it in the lengthy *Wealthsimple* piece (or anywhere else), when the family was living on Christie Street, Gladys and Pierre once fell so far behind on property taxes that the sheriff put their house up for public auction, with the sale advertised, as by law it had to be, in the Legal Notices section the Hackensack *Record*. The couple was apparently able to scrape together enough and/or negotiate a payment plan that at the last minute allowed them to hold on to their home; but the public humiliation must have been devastating for a family that had prided itself on fitting seamlessly into their cushy suburb. Gladys, for her part, had no doubt about who was to blame for their perpetual financial straits nor any compunction about doing the blaming. "We'll never know exactly what went on inside that house because Tony absolutely refused to talk about it, even to me," his wife, Ottavia, told a friend. "But the first time we ever discussed his mother, he said she was a miserable, bitter woman who had destroyed his father's life. He and his brother watched it happen on a day-to-day basis and both of them wound up carrying the consequences of some kind of trauma. They just expressed it in different ways."

The Bourdains never really changed their spending habits all that much, but after the sheriff came knocking, Gladys did go back to work—initially as a salesperson at a local real estate office and a few years later as a staff writer for the Hackensack *Record.* Under the byline "G. S. Bourdain" she wrote squibs about celebrities, arts and entertainment news, and occasional concert reviews in chatty, workmanlike prose. She seemed to enjoy sniping at big stars like Charles Aznavour and Diana Ross when they came through Radio City Music Hall and other Manhattan venues. Her move to the *New York Times* in 1984 was a testament to her skill with words as well as an early indicator of just how difficult her tenure there would be. Somehow during the interview process, Gladys got the impression, despite the unspectacular salary on offer, that the job under discussion was not just an ordinary spot on the copydesk but the editorship of the Sunday Arts & Leisure section, then one of the most powerful and prestigious positions on the paper. Upon being hired, she went off on a three-week vacation, no doubt spending more than she could afford and figuring she would settle into her well-deserved role as the new queen of the New York cultural scene upon her return. According to *Times* legend, it wasn't until she reported for duty that her expectations were altered with a kind of chiropractic snap. Devastated, but badly in need of a paycheck, she slouched toward the copydesk in defeat. "Getting off on the wrong foot really soured her on the paper," a colleague told me. "She remained in one way or another at war with the *Times* the whole time she was there—but then she was the sort of person who might have been at war with authority figures wherever she was."

The Bourdains of Leonia were by then as past tense as Joyce Carol Oates's Mulvaneys. Long before the final breakup, the family had bifurcated into distinct camps: Tony and his father on one side, Chris and his mother on the other, even when no particular argument was in progress and they were all together in the station wagon or at a restaurant. "Chris basically agreed with his mother's constant message that his father was a weak man with his head in the clouds, a complete loser who was dragging the family down into ruination," a relative told me. Tony meanwhile felt a need to protect Pierre from Gladys, often by getting him out of the house, if only for a few hours. Hence the joint trips to places like Hiram's, to Washington, DC, to march in a protest against the Vietnam War—and, when Tony was fourteen, "the sinister back room of a rundown hotel on 55th Street that some Japanese colleagues had tipped [my father] off to" for their first taste of a new sensation called sushi. Sometimes Chris came along, sometimes he didn't. Pierre could still muster some semblance of parental authority when he needed to—for example, by talking sternly to Tony for not applying himself at school—but Tony in some ways saw him as the brother he wished Chris had turned out to be, and they actively sought each other's company to an unusual extent. When Tony was a junior in high school, Pierre took him as his plus-one to a work-related party at a sylvan estate in New Canaan, Connecticut, where (if the account of the trip he composed for an eleventh grade English class can be trusted) Tony wore dark glasses, hoisted frosty Heinekens, and chatted up "succulent secretaries—all liberal, tits bouncing around freely under expensive blouses," giving them his go-to high school lie about being a writer for *Rolling Stone.* The return trip from an outing like this must have made Tony's stomach clench tighter with each passing mile, for he understood the family dynamic all too well and dreaded his parents' frequent confrontations. He saw that Pierre constantly left himself open to exactly the sort of criticism that Gladys leveled against him in overt and subtle ways, and Tony hated that she hurt her husband just because she so easily could. Why couldn't she (and Chris) love him for what he was and (like Tony) forgive him for what he wasn't? Delicate, vulnerable people didn't need help snuffing out their last few embers of confidence, right?

Some of the explanations Tony provided for his childhood anger work better than others. While he probably was sorry to have missed Woodstock and at times hated the conventional existence he found himself trapped in, what he raged against most virulently was being forced to watch the demolition of his father from a ringside seat. That was almost certainly his primal wound, his paradise lost—what he meant by life not turning out according to his romantic expectations. What's more, his homelife was just too painful and pathetic to talk or write about, making the predicament doubly miserable for a boy who needed more than most to get his version of the truth off his chest.

After he left home for college, Tony was in and out of touch with Gladys over the years (he last spoke to her a few weeks before his death, on Mother's Day 2018); after his TV show became a certified hit, he bought her an apartment near Lincoln Center, so she could walk to the opera, the theater, and the symphony. Whenever interviewers wanted a cozy quote about Mom's home cooking, he talked about how Gladys had taught him, at age six or so, how to make the British sausage and egg dish called toad-in-the-hole and how she inspired his love of carefully prepared food with her date nut bread, pressed jelly sandwiches, meat loaf, and vegetable-barley soup. In the end, though, he could never forgive her for the way she had relentlessly shamed and denigrated Pierre; and when the time came for settling scores Tony cut her out of his will, leaving her upkeep in the last two years of her life to the shocked and resentful Christopher.

The face Tony turned outward during his final year of high school was really a series of masks meant to entertain and divert himself and others but always to keep the conversation in a safe place—what he later called "trying on personalities." The guidance counselor at Englewood School, in his final evaluation of Tony before he left to follow his enigmatic girlfriend to Vassar, put it this way: "Tony is somewhat of an unusual boy, as he has acquired many philosophies during his teenage years. Perhaps this is something of a fad, but I view it as a youngster who is a thinking individual and interested in life and in its possible philosophies." Although his record "is not a spectacular one for a student who hastens toward completion of secondary school [Tony scored 620 and 530 on the verbal and math portions of the SAT and had a B− average for his final semester], there are some real strengths in primarily the field of English. His main interest is journalism and this is coupled with a strong flair for creative writing. Art and films seem to concern Tony a great deal, and he enjoys working in all these media. His teacher of English has found Tony to be a bright, clever, and lively student. He is sometimes full of opinionated views and sweeping generalities, but he is aware and interested in life around him. He is a joy to have in class. In view of Tony's average scholastic record, he is recommended to you on this basis with an understanding that he is more capable than his record reveals."

More capable than his record reveals.

Somewhat of an unusual boy.

A joy to have in class.

If Anthony Bourdain had a headstone, there would be a lot of options.

Chapter 3

"Just one last thing before I let you get back to your day—but first I want to say right now that you've been extremely helpful . . ."

With these words, uttered deep into each of the eighty-five or so interviews I did for his book—either on the phone, Zoom, or in person—I signaled to an interlocutor that we were starting to wrap things up and that if she still had any ore-rich nuggets of information or observations about Anthony Bourdain in her possession, this would be a good time to pass them along. Assuming we hadn't already discussed his death, my final questions usually centered on that topic, which common sense suggested should be broached after we'd bonded a bit. "You must have been shocked," I would say [empathy, flattery], "but I'm wondering if you might have noticed some, I don't know [modesty, faux spontaneity], some seed of self-destruction in the Tony you knew back in the day that eventually caused him to take his own life." Most (including people who had lived with him) responded with some variation on, "No way—he never seemed the least bit depressed." But whenever someone gave the second most popular reply, "Well, he *did* have a dark side," I would press him gently about what he meant. To whatever was said next I would almost always respond with silence (because it was usually something about not being able to quite put his finger on it, that it was just a feeling he had somehow gotten and I wanted to let him know, as politely as possible, that his explanation was inadequate and that he ought to keep searching his memory for something more specific). Sometimes my hackish interview techniques [faux modesty] bore fruit; sometimes they didn't. For better or worse, only one subject veered wildly off script—and that was a not very close friend of Tony's from the two years he spent at the Culinary Institute of America in Hyde Park, New York, whom I'll call Vic. For Vic, my first mention of Tony's death, perhaps because it was combined with the sense that Vic and I were coming to the end of our time together, seemed to trigger a psychotic break.

"No, I was not at all shocked by Tony's suicide," he said without any discernible pause but suddenly in a strikingly steadier and more sonorous vocal register than he'd been employing for the previous ninety or so minutes. "You see, I have telepathic powers and I've been in touch with Tony since he died and have talked to him about it. He had to go to the other side, he told me, because of love." And with that Vic was off to the races, calmly but obsessively spinning tales of space aliens among us and hinting that he was Jesus Christ.

Until then Vic—who obviously prided himself on his association with Tony and tended to pad the stories of his interactions with him—hadn't been the easiest person to keep on topic: an hour and a half is an awfully long time for one of my interviews. But he had certainly stayed this side of sane. Not two minutes before his meltdown he'd been telling me how he, Tony, and some other young scholars from the Culinary Institute had regularly gone skinny-dipping in nearby New Paltz with a bunch of female nursing students from the state university, drinking Genesee beer, smoking pot, and sliding naked down the mossy rocks into the old swimming hole. That didn't sound like something Jesus would do, even on the weekend; and yet that very same Vic would go on to reveal that he had raised himself from the dead "in a cave, at night behind a large stone" which was somehow rolled away at dawn so the world could witness his resurrection. My first inclination was to write him off as a prescription-strength Bourdain obsessive, a subset that includes the worshipper types who get tattoos of Tony and think of him as Saint Anthony, miracle worker, healer, and martyr, as well as the conspiracy theorists who believe that, rather than taking his own life, Tony was killed by agents of the Illuminati on the orders of Harvey Weinstein as payback for his support of the #MeToo movement. While deliberately paced, Vic's spiel was almost pure stream of consciousness, and yet I couldn't help noticing that there was a motif in the madness: the idea that Tony "had to go away because of love." The third or fourth time he circled back to that locution, I posed a question: "Are you talking about romantic love, like his relationship with Asia Argento?" I was surprised he heard it above his own steady babble. But he did, and he responded immediately.

"Nah, that was pain," Vic said. "Pain we can deal with. Tony had to go because he found love—do you know what I'm saying?"

It unsettled me a little that maybe I sort of did.

Friends and relatives of Tony's whom I'd interviewed had told me that seeing up close what had happened to him over the years had driven home what it feels like to be loved intensely by millions of faceless strangers. Or at least it showed them how such a situation could unfold if you were someone with Tony's particular set of pluses and minuses. The main problem of fame for Tony, several of those intimates said, was not the usual complaints: urinal-adjacent autograph seekers, people interrupting his meals in restaurants or prodding him out of a hard-won sleep in a plastic airport seat for the sake of another selfie, and so on. Those things happened regularly, of course, and could sometimes be genuinely annoying, but he had a gift for dealing with overenthusiastic fans. A smile and a bit of banter destined to be blogged about or dined out on for years weren't all that hard to summon for the guy who had a Google Alert set for "Anthony Bourdain" and who most of the time, as I've noted, found being famous kind of fun. He could even get the wannabe groupie types to move along quickly with their pride intact. But the sea of love those individuals personified—*that*, it turned out, was something else again, something much harder to deal with; it was always there, in an ineffable way, and ever ready to pull him under.

The mass audience, in exchange for its love, always wants the same thing: more. Encore, encore! In Tony's case the re-ups came in 250-day portions—roughly the amount of time he would spend on the road each year, getting another season of shows in the can. In the beginning the demands of the public were in one sense the opposite of a problem, because if you're producing a TV show you want the audience to want more. But as he got into his fifties Tony started to run out of gas. The reasons were mostly prosaic—the strains of travel, especially when you have a devoted wife, a young child, and a bad back—but the constant need to find new ways to present superficially similar situations (*Maybe* Peruvian *Patagonia this time? How about* Senegalese *street food?*) and the enervating effects of alcohol were also factors. So what did he do? At first, nothing, for counterbalancing his burnout was his fear about what would happen to all the love he had amassed if he ever just walked away. Such love, he knew, was rare and once lost could never be recaptured, especially at his age. And if such a rupture ever occurred, he also knew, it would be painful for all concerned. "For a while I watched him caught in a kind of cycle," his longtime friend Robert Ruiz told me. "He would be so ready to quit, so close to sending me a text that said, 'I did it. I'm out of there. Let's go have a beer'—and then, pow, he'd get a piece of fan mail from someone who said, 'I went to my local Chinatown for the first time because I watched your show.' Or 'I never thought I'd visit my kid who's a backpacker in Australia but now I'm going because of you.' Or a stranger would come up to him in a bar and say, 'You inspired me to get my first passport!' And all that sentimental horseshit pulled on his heartstrings and he'd turn around and go right back out on the road. It came down to that, really."

Well, maybe not just that. Tony felt additional guilt about the possibility of breaking up with his production crew from Zero Point Zero. He and his core team of techies and directors had done extraordinary work in far-flung and sometimes dangerous places over the course of many years. Together they'd taken chances with their bodies and their ideas; they'd gotten fevers and diarrhea, missed their kids' birthdays and also gotten really good at making television. If something like that doesn't bond you, what does? If Tony pulled the plug, all those good people, who had molded themselves to his work habits and endured his proud dickishness while putting a strain on their own family lives, would be suddenly adrift with no paycheck.

All this weighed on his mind. But really how torn could he be when he knew in his heart that if it ever came down to it, he could never abandon the people who one way or another had helped launch him on his magical journey? Realizing he was incapable of actually making the break with his life as a television personality reduced him to just another trooper in the vast army of humans that psychotherapists call "the worried well." The situation, in other words, was tough but tolerable. And then he met Asia Argento.

Her entrance into his life in mid-2016 changed everything. Almost overnight, his need for an exit strategy from the TV business became urgent. He told his wife, Ottavia (with whom he'd developed a strong if unorthodox postconjugal friendship), that Asia was "the only woman who can love me like I need to be loved," and whatever that meant (Tony was given to grandiose statements that made those in his inner circle roll their eyes), he felt overwhelmed by the desire to be with his new obsession as much as possible. At one point he floated a plan to quit *Parts Unknown* and move to a mountaintop in Tuscany with Asia and her son and daughter and Ottavia and Ariane. That he actually thought he could live in blended-family bliss with a highly temperamental actress and a whip-smart blackbelt in Brazilian jiu-jitsu, both Italian, shows how he could sometimes allow his common sense to be subsumed by romantic impulses. The idea in any case was not received warmly by either Argento or Ottavia when he ran it by them over lunch at what must have already been the tensest table for three that day in New York City.

You might think the advent of Asia would at least settle the matter of whether he would stay or go from TV, but no. His anxiety over abandoning his audience and crew only intensified as the possibility of actually doing so became less of a fantasy and more imaginable. Even if his fans for the most part only loved a not entirely real TV Tony and even if many did so (as the rational part of him understood) out of a need to worship somebody or something, the thought of pushing their love away remained unbearable to him—as unbearable as the idea of not being with Asia Argento. You see the problem.

You need to have a lot of things go right in your life before you can become as miserable as Anthony Bourdain, by his late fifties, found himself—that is, before you can work your way to a position where you have so much to lose. In Tony's case it took decades to reach a height from which falling would matter. The tall, gangly boy whom

Gladys and Pierre hauled from Leonia to Vassar in their beat-up white Volkswagen for freshman orientation gave no indication of being on any path whatsoever that was not the Palisades Interstate Parkway. Although he spoke of the interval nostalgically on his TV show, in *Kitchen Confidential* Tony tells us that the years immediately following his graduation from high school were almost not worth remembering, a crap existence of confused longing. "I spent most of my waking hours drinking, smoking pot, scheming, and doing my best to amuse, outrage, impress, and penetrate anyone silly enough to find me entertaining," he wrote. "Essentially, I treated the world as my ashtray." As for his relationship with Nancy, the beautiful, druggy girl he'd wrenched himself out of high school to follow, they were "unhappily in love" and on-again, off-again even before they arrived at Vassar to enter the class of 1977; he wasn't always sure if she was his girlfriend or not. "The less said about that part of my life the better," he writes in *KC.*

For Gladys and Pierre Bourdain, now inching toward separation and no doubt feeling guilty about the perpetual financial pinch that made them amenable to the idea of Tony leaving the Englewood School a year early, it was also a time to feel no particular optimism about their elder son's future, especially if they noticed him packing his nunchucks for college. Clearly a seventeen-year-old pretend martial artist and aspiring druggie, who'd ranked thirty-first out of forty-eight in his high school class and spent more time in detention than study hall, was not exactly prime college material. But if this period cannot be recollected warmly by Tony and those closest to him, neither should it be given short shrift. For it was in 1973 that he put himself on the twisty path that would eventually take him to Kaysersberg.

* * *

If you study the migratory habits of private school students you'll notice that they occasionally insert a trip abroad between high school and college, or subsequent semesters, especially if their romantic or academic lives have been going poorly. And so it was with Tony, who after graduating in the early summer of 1973 left Englewood School for Italy with a vague idea of becoming a writer—or at least dressing, drinking, and behaving like his rather corny conception of a literary fellow for a while. His goal that summer before college was—as he noted in an unpublished breast-pocket-size diary that has partially survived—to have "a lovely time in Florence living the life of Hemingway." He also planned to bum around Europe a bit, joining what had become by the mid 1970s a perpetual caravan of scruff balls not unlike himself—although the future "hotel slut" who obsessed about thread counts and high-end plumbing already preferred cozy old inns to student hostels. The monthslong trip did seem on the ambitious side for a solo traveler of his tender years but probably doable, if he could get around the problem of being perpetually broke. Tony had put aside money he'd managed to earn as a very bad bicycle messenger in Manhattan (he tended to turn off his pager and go to the movies); his parents had no doubt kicked in a little as a birthday/graduation present; and, to keep expenses down, he planned to stay for a stretch with his relatives in La Teste sur Mer, the wistful little resort town in southwestern France off which he'd eaten that fateful first oyster. It could have been a life-changing or at least a character-building excursion if not for Tony's youthful habit of moving through life chin first. Whenever things went wrong on the road, as they dependably will, he took it hard, processing each mishap as a personal injustice; the diary reads in parts like a primal whine from an adolescent version of his nine-year-old self. Forget Hemingway: within a few weeks he was, he groused, "living on a train, living the life and observing the diet of Gandhi." He had a nasty cold ("Jesus, why did I have to kiss the little bitch?"), a worse stomachache ("I have contributed more shit and more vomit to the Florence sewer system than I do at home in a year"), and yet somehow a gnawing hunger. ("I haven't eaten in two days . . . the sky is my ceiling and my kitchen is the ice cream machine inside the station").

Strange to say but there was a time when Anthony Bourdain just wasn't very good at getting from one place to another. After missing the last train out of Nice on July 19, 1973, he found himself at 1 a.m. "forced to wait an agonizing six and a half hours for an even more agonizing thirteen hours on the train to Bordeaux. I'm tired but have nowhere to sleep. I've considered the old newspapers-on-the-park-bench idea but I don't want to wake up late or worse get arrested." Clearly he felt a little unsafe ("An Italian is across the street lying on a bench. He takes occasional hits on a bottle of cough syrup") as well as envious ("People are getting into taxis heading off to expensive hotels with big beds to fuck and smoke cigarettes, play music and sleep in warmth. Me, my pack is my pillow and the cement my bed. I want to be in the warmth and security of my La Teste home"). With summer not even halfway done, the romance of his European ramble had faded to black. ("I played pool on a broken table at the café across the street from the station. I poured some tea into myself, being the only thing I could keep down, and it was in the midst of a doomed game with myself that the truth came to me, the place I want to be: I WANT TO BE IN FAMILY BILLIARDS IN BERGENFIELD, NEW JERSEY, STONED, LISTENING TO THE QUADRAPHONIC MUZAK AND GETTING BEATEN BY 'LUCKY' GOULD. A HALF-SMOKED LARK IN THE ASHTRAY, SOME OF PETE'S CHEEBA IN HIS PARKED CAR. I WANT OUT.")

Teenage Tony may have lacked the temperamental flexibility to wander free and easy but, as the diary shows, he did have what is probably the single most important quality for a fine travel writer—the outsider's eye. Wherever he went, even in this larval manifestation, he seemed fully present and yet he somehow always hovered simultaneously above the scene, taking in the bird's-eye view, seeing himself and the others as players on a stage, processing incidents as material—for future school assignments, articles submitted on spec to national magazines, or at very least his little diary. Despite his frequent grumpiness Tony was already what Julian Barnes calls "that rare and oxymoronic thing, the wise tourist"—a creature defined a century earlier by Edith Wharton, an extraordinary travel journalist in her own right, as "one eager to give an account of what he sees, and *feels beneath the thing seen*" (the italics and the masculine pronoun are, as Barnes points out, both Wharton's).

This talent didn't kick in only at a certain distance from home, of course; he wasn't merely a travel writer. For him, as for all with the outsider's eye, every locale was in its own way exotic—as we can see from his early unpublished writing about Vassar, just seventy-seven miles up the Hudson River from home. Consider a piece called "It Was When She Said" that he saved in a computer file of juvenilia that was on his laptop when he died. It is the fall of 1973 and the natives are still restless about the presence of men in the dorms and classrooms, it being then only four years into the school's grand coeducational experiment. But—and this is the central point of Tony's piece, which foretells his woke attitude in the wake of the #MeToo movement, forty years later—the Vassar ladies are not man stirred in quite the way that he anticipated or as a traditional red-blooded American male might have preferred them to be.

This was a tempestuous and edifying time to be on the campus of the then 112-year-old institution. The eighty or so men who'd preceded Tony to Vassar divided readily into two distinct types. The first was what Elizabeth A. Daniels, then dean of studies, called "the real individuals and pioneers," high-achieving, self-motivated scholars who as part of their own education wanted to participate in the making of educational history. The other group was comprised of those 1970s-era central-casting psychedelic sorts who seemed to be everywhere in those days but who were drawn most reliably to anything purporting to be new. Writing about that period of Vassar history in 1979, Lucinda Franks of the *New York Times* recalled "characters who swung through the campus like bespangled high-wire artists at a three-ring circus," the most noticeable being a group that "flounced about in glittery shirts, high-heeled boots, and rainbow-colored Afros." Tony didn't fit naturally into either of those original camps but belonged instead to a slightly later and more ordinary wave: the guys who assumed that the lopsided woman-to-man ratio at Vassar would make it easier for them to get laid.

Tony's neatly typed essay is both a confession of stupidity and a dagger of self-blame which, in typical Tony fashion, he eagerly thrusts into his own assumptions. Sitting morosely in the school cafeteria one morning and "poking at my half-eaten plate of cold scrambled eggs" he finds himself jolted out of his mope by a tall blond woman at the next table, who points to a male student standing at the salad bar, and says matter-of-factly to her half-dozen female dining companions, "He's got a cock as big as all outdoors."

What strikes—indeed shocks—Tony is not so much the woman's declaration as her friends' reaction to it: the "sophisticated, attractive, and to me frightening" ladies just to his left seem interested but really not all *that* interested in what was just said. One or two calmly raise or swivel their intimidatingly lovely heads to take in the view. In a tone that suggests semi-bored shoppers, they question the man's ethnicity ("Indian?" "No, half Chinese, half

French") and his potential as a lover ("He moves like a dancer," one says). Another notes that he may be a vegetarian, given the way he is loading up on bean sprouts. Finally they agree that he has "a nice ass," shrug, and move on.

It says something about Tony's sensitivity to the world that he even registered this nonmomentous moment; most guys, if they'd noticed it at all, might have just shaken their heads and smiled. But Tony would always be thin-skinned in a way that served his craft. In his 2010 book, *Medium Raw*, he wrote about how a substandard Johnny Rockets airport hamburger had consigned him for several days to the slough of despond—which allowed him to make a nice point about crappiness being a choice. Here at Vassar he is driven deeper into moroseness by the realization that in terms of the campus sexual dynamic he had "gotten in over my head." He had assumed, he tells us, that being a man at Vassar was going to be "easy and fun, a romp in an all-girl playpen." What that meant exactly in terms of his shaky relationship with Nancy perhaps even he didn't know. But clearly he hadn't envisioned a campus milieu in which formidable women fashioned their own hierarchy of desire. Not that he'd been alone in his naivete. On the very first day of school, a dorm mate we'll call Jerry had stepped out of the shower, "pointed to his dick, and said, 'See this? This is one of only 108 in a very limited series," Tony confesses that had "giggled stupidly" at the remark, thinking he, too, would be seen as part of a "rare and novel species." Now, in light of these overheard comments, that didn't look very likely—and what's more (he simultaneously realized), it was *he* who was vulnerable to the opposite sex or in any case one particular member of it to an embarrassing degree.

"The rather humiliating reality was that I was here at Vassar not out of a daring sense of adventure or out of respect for Vassar's academic traditions," he wrote. "For this and only this reason had I come here—to follow Nancy. A girl I was sure I loved and would always, always love; like it or not. A girl who no longer loved me. The girls at the next table reminded me of this pathetic fact—just being what they were, the way they talked, the way they looked, they reminded me of what I was. Any illusions I had about my 'advantages' of being a New Yorker, a male, a wise guy, a city slicker, they all slipped away at that moment, leaving me scared and gaping."

I wrote "to follow Nancy" in the paragraph above for the sake of clarity, but Tony's original manuscript has it as "to follow Christine." Both the name change and the careful typewriting suggest that "It Was When She Said . . ." was submitted as classwork. If so, it seems to have been one of the few assignments he actually turned in during his freshman year, a time when, says his Leonia buddy Dae Bennett, he routinely blew off school and strode around campus in a dirty trench coat and with those nunchucks dangling from his belt, "trying to project the aura of a tough guy and looking stupid." The members of the old Dwight-Englewood gang were starting to move in different directions at this point, as high school chums will; but some kept in touch with one another and with Tony. Dae Bennett, his brother D'Andrea, and Tony's other friend Dave Mansfield continued to play in a band they'd started a year or two earlier called Quacky Duck and His Barnyard Friends. After graduation they'd signed a deal with Warner Bros. Records, appeared on *The Mike Douglas Show* (the Tony Bennett connection didn't hurt), and during the 1973–74 academic year performed at a couple of outdoor concerts at Vassar. Tony would have been welcome to grab a tambourine and hop on stage with them at any time, but nothing like that ever happened. "He wasn't a musical person, as much as he was into music, and besides that we were too country-rock, too

Eagles for his taste," Dae Bennett told me. "He was all about having that hard edge." Tony on occasion did draw posters advertising the band's appearances, though. They tended to be, like lot of his artwork, studiously weird in an Orwellian sort of way, the work of a wacko wannabe. One poster that Bennett still has hanging in his recording studio shows a giant, sleepy-eyed statue of a duck being pulled along on ropes by a phalanx of grim-faced, drone-like soldiers. The execution is a notch or two below professional and its overall tone seems at odds with a fancifully named country-rock band—but at least it wasn't a profusion of chains and penises.

Tony's extravagant nihilism was more fully on display in an untitled "Kerouac exercise" he handwrote in his impeccable script

Bourdain drew this poster for high school friend Dae Bennett (son of Tony) whose band Quacky Duck and his Barnyard Friends was a local sensation.

on a yellow legal pad, probably during the spring 1974 semester. The multipart piece may have started as a review of Sylvia's Plath's 1963 novel *The Bell Jar* for an English class, but Tony had trouble staying on topic. "I don't want to think too much" about Plath, he said without further explanation. But if that was because she had famously taken her own life a decade earlier it didn't stop him from focusing instead on a self-destructive friend named Bob Harris who was semi-legendary around Leonia for consuming "hero doses" of LSD and going for strolls in highway traffic. Harris was the kind of prematurely burnt out, take-it-to-the-limits guy whom Tony in those days put on a pedestal. "Bob was the sharpest, funniest guy around," he says in the piece. "Thirteen pounds of weed spread over the floor of Bob's attic. Bob was a little crazy. Bob thought he was the son of the devil. Such guilt. He ran away a few times, tried to set himself on fire, drank insecticide. They locked him up. Bob is now in Hartford Institute. Solitary. He hit some people. He never used to do that. He's paranoid. He calls me occasionally." (Harris would die of a few years later at the age of twenty-three.)

The seemingly random, impressionistic, drug-drenched, and barely coherent yellow-paper piece—more James Joyce than Jack Kerouac—may not have pleased Tony's professor (there is no grade on the draft), but it certainly wouldn't have surprised her. Drugs and the young people who got wasted on them were hot topics at Vassar and most other American colleges just then. "1974 is filled with victims of the '60s," Tony wrote. "Drug deformed college students with speech impediments from LSD, canker sores, and scratches from speed, psychotic, neurotic, paranoid, manic-depressive. So many walking dead around, so many freshmen with lines around their eyes, running noses, and burnt-out livers." Abruptly he breaks off for a poem that begins:

Jane twitches
Bob has got the chills
David thinks he's Satan
Joanna's taking pills

The veteran Vassar English professor William W. Gifford once said, "there was a craziness about those years, reminiscent of a carnival in Berlin in the 1930s. One of my students once came to class through the third-floor window." Lucinda Franks recalls that Vassar students "swung from chandeliers in various stages of undress, experimented with multiple drugs and group sex, and held parties straight out of Fellini's *Satyricon.*"

Tony knew all about those dorm-room bacchanals where the punch bowl bore a sign that said "Don't Drink If on Quaaludes." More from his piece: "Went to a party, pretty twisted. Naked, drug-addled boys and girls dancing around a terrace apartment. Jerky, uncoordinated movements to David Bowie. . . . It's night and Nancy and Jane are rolling around on the floor. Rush. Rush. People in the bathtub. Sukie, smack-queen, model, fast mind slicing away through red, drunken eyes.

"Take a bath with me, Tony.

"The prospect of thrashing around in the bathtub with the other puppets in the room was too much for a person in my condition. I declined. But the girl is amazing. *Sad, beautiful, pitiful, brilliant, dramatic, so dramatic . . . I live for people like her.*"

The italics are mine. He would indeed always live for sad, beautiful, pitiful, brilliant, dramatic, so dramatic women—right up until the moment that he stopped living for them.

Chapter 4

While there are no statistics kept on how many young people proceeded from a state of jaded lassitude to culinary school in the mid 1970s, the number must have been very small indeed. Adolescents still living the too-good life on their parents' dime don't often up and decide one day that what they'd really like to do is learn how to slam out 250 nightly covers. There wasn't even back then a coherent "celebrity chef" status to aspire to. For Tony, the distance between Vassar College and the Culinary Institute of America was cab-able but profound. At the former, drifting was permitted, even tacitly encouraged to the degree that it was consistent with the groping and the sampling, the trial and the error, that are thought to be an integral part of a classic American liberal arts education. At the CIA you either showed up for class and did the work—you got your hands burned and calloused and your apron greasy—or you wasted your money.

Chef has always been a mysterious or at any rate an ambiguous profession. Identifying yourself as one might draw a raised eyebrow of interest at a social gathering; but most chef work comes closer to blue-collar drudgery than the supposedly glamorous creative life, and everybody knows that, so the status of any one particular cook remains, at best, suspect. In your checked pants and kitchen whites, with your hair held back rakishly by a rubber band, you might be anything, including a guy who can't afford a haircut. While there were superstar chefs in the mid-1970s—Jacques Pépin, James Beard, and that brilliant amateur Julia Child among them—no one enrolled at a culinary academy with the ultimate goal of having his own TV cooking show, as sometimes happens today. That would have been crazy, not that mental and emotional instability was necessarily a disqualifying factor for a CIA applicant back then. "They were not the cream of the crop, my fellow culinarians," is the way Tony put it in *Kitchen Confidential.* "It was 1975, and the CIA was still getting more than their share of farm boys, bed-wetters, hicks, flunk-outs from community colleges, and a few misfits for whom CIA was preferable to jail or juvenile detention." There was another strain of student there, too, in those days, just as distant from Tony's personal experience: life-hardened middle-aged men who'd spent long years in the military. Given his writerly knack for quick assessment, Tony must have known exactly what he was getting into when he first entered the cool dark hallways of what had once been a Jesuit monastery. But why did he cast his lot with such an unironically motley crew with whom he seemed to have almost nothing in common?

At that point, Gladys and Pierre probably thought nothing their elder son could do would surprise them, but when Tony first brought up the idea of cooking school, he said on the 2014 Massachusetts episode of *Parts Unknown*, "they were as happy as if I'd said I wanted to become an arsonist." Other relatives and friends were just as baffled. The CIA and places like it were in those days, and for the reasons described above, straight shots to the social middle—the cooking middle, too, which in the mid 1970s was still at least a little French, or faux French, but mostly American in the sense of Would you like more cheese on that? For most culinary students there was no shame in that, since being part of the pack was for them a good outcome. Anthony Michael Bourdain, though, was no typical cooking school applicant, being privileged, intellectually adventurous, and (except for what he'd gleaned from novels) utterly unfamiliar with the working-class mindset—in other words, a young man for whom the middle, while it might ultimately be where he'd wind up when the dealing was done, was a step down. You'd have thought someone as romantic and as immature—in both interesting and tedious ways—as Tony would have preferred being down and out (as Orwell was down and out in Paris and London, as the French novelist-vagabond Jean Genet was down and out in prison) to a life of dependable but circumscribed employment in a profession in which, by the way, he had previously expressed zero interest ("No, no, no, no, no, no, no, no, never," his brother, Chris, once said when asked if Tony as a boy had ever talked about being a chef). And beyond that, what about those multiple food epiphanies he'd experienced in France? Why would a well-traveled kid who'd eaten the best stinky cheeses, poulet basquaise, "murky brown soupe de poisson" and fresh-from-the-sea oysters and who'd come, as he tells us in *KC*, to appreciate the awesome power of food, set out to master the kind of mouth-coating midcentury-modern "institutional favorites" the CIA championed in those days: dishes like "chicken Hawaiian, grilled ham steak with pineapple ring, and old-style lumbering classics like beef Wellington," all in preparation for a career likely spent at a "Hilton or Restaurant Associates corporate dining facility"?

On the one hand it made no sense and yet in a crazy kind of Rube Goldbergian way the chain of events that pushed, spun, goosed, and dropkicked him from Poughkeepsie to Hyde Park fit together logically. The precipitating cause, we can see in hindsight, was the final collapse of the myth that he was a student at Vassar in any meaningful sense of the word. Tony had hated college life from the day he moved his drearily predictable collection of guy gear into the "sterile white cubicle in the one modern dormitory on campus" (as he wrote in another piece from his file of unpublished juvenilia). High school for him was a hard act to follow. He missed hanging with the Cruisers and having a formal, well-manicured Establishment framework to push back against (the Englewood School had played the Disapproving Parent role perfectly; Vassar, which put up a rope-a-dope defense to his rebelliousness, had proved to be a no fun foil). But the thing he missed most about Leonia was having a lair; a kid who was always putting on a persona and playing the jokester for the amusement of himself and his friends needed wings on his stage, a darkened out-of-bounds area into which he could retreat for rest and psychic regrouping, a place where he could exhale and let his stage face fall. "Tony was not used to being crowded too close to other people, and he hated everything about that," Dae Bennett told me. At Vassar he had only a fluorescent-lit dorm room in which it was impossible to disappear—or even lie down in bed without spilling beyond his allotted space.

Living in such close quarters may have made Tony more self-conscious about his height, which was often the first thing people noticed about him. (When they met in 2000, Lydia Tenaglia, later a leader of Zero Point Zero Production, thought, "He's very tall. We're going to be looking up his nose a lot with our cameras." The TV writer David Simon said that hugging Tony was like "embracing a cathedral.") When he started high school Tony had been, if anything, a bit undersized, but he had gained, by some accounts, eight to ten inches between the ninth and twelfth grades. He took no particular pride in his size and found it embarrassing to have people constantly registering it. Chris Boyd, a childhood friend from Leonia who is six feet eight—four inches taller than Tony—told me, "Tony and I would get stared at a lot and occasionally fucked with by the little Napoleon types. Like a lot of big guys, we had to learn to defuse situations, to break the tension." If Tony was going to be judged, he wrote around this time, he wanted it to be not by his size but by "the cream of my record collection," which upon arrival at Vassar he had carefully arranged on a shelf above his bed, knowing that "in those first weeks the albums would provide crucial hints about my identity to potential friends." (As if every other male freshman wasn't laboring under the delusion that his precious yard of vinyl proffered the key to his much speculated upon personality.) Say this much about Tony: he earnestly gave dorm life his best shot, taping his Bruce Lee poster to the wall above his headboard, tacking his picture of Alex from *A Clockwork Orange* to the foot of the bed, and stapling his poster of Beethoven to the window shade. But even with his beloved stereo and the last-minute addition of that then-newfangled dorm-room amenity, the mini-fridge ("which I'd convinced my parents was a necessity"), the space fell short of feeling homey, and he stayed there as little as possible.

During those frequent periods when he was on the outs with Nancy—who lived in Cushing House, a few dorms away—and felt too far behind on his assigned reading to show up for class, he spent most of his time either wandering the campus or working on a piece of writing, which may or may not have been part of his coursework, in one of the school libraries. No matter what else was going on in his life, Tony never stopped scribbling short stories, essays, and the occasional one-act play (a typical theater piece that he reworked several times from high school to college was called "Invasion of the Glands"). Still, the lack of any real retreat left him feeling permanently out of sorts—"dickish," he said, falling back on a variation of one of his favorite words—and turned him, or so he insisted in *KC*, into a pathetic cadger of free drinks and stealer of drugs, "a spoiled, miserable, narcissistic, self-destructive, and thoughtless young lout, badly in need of a good ass-kicking."

Could he really have been that much of a misanthrope? It seems unlikely. Tony was always unfairly hard on himself—a tendency that research has shown to be a common trait among people who take their own lives. In reality he seems to have had a normal number of friends, both holdovers from high school and newly made Vassar buddies including a dependable drug connection named Gordon Howard who would become his first literary agent (He sometimes wrote Howard's course papers in exchange for quaaludes or pot). When toward the end of Tony's freshman year a mixed group of Dwight-Englewood and college friends invited him to go in on a summer-long beachfront rental in Provincetown, Massachusetts, he said yes immediately. Why not? He was unhappily adrift and the days when the Bourdains went to France en famille were by then, because of hard times and harder feelings, a thing of the past. Meanwhile, could fate have come up with a more appropriate getaway for a wannabe misfit than a town so closely associated with the creative, the cold-shouldered, and the proudly queer? Provincetown—three miles long, two blocks wide, and set on the outermost end of Cape Cod—was a finger of sand curled in a come-hither gesture that he could never have resisted.

Perhaps all you need to know about how things went there in the summer of 1974 is that Tony brought Provincetown on stage in *Kitchen Confidential* in a chapter called "Food Is Sex." His unsteady steady Nancy was one of his housemates and nude sunbathing was how he and his pals got through most hungover P-town mornings, but for Tony, who was seventeen and given to "sensual inclinations" when the idyll started, everything—the streets "clogged with . . . slutty chicks, dopers . . . and thousands upon thousands of energetically cruising gay men," even the murky, salty, chorizo-spiked

Portuguese squid stew they ladled out at every chowder house in town—tilted toward the erotic. Even the people who made the stew struck him as sexy when he observed them up close for the first time as coworkers in a place called the Flagship (the Dreadnaught in *KC*)—and why wouldn't they, given their "big, badass" knives and filthy/funny lingo, their tattered headbands, metal wrist cuffs, ivory scrimshawed rings, and gold hoop earrings? If Tony had entered the restaurant business anyplace else, he might have taken his colleagues for granted and treated the job as temporary drudgery—but in Provincetown he found himself plate scraping and pot scrubbing among . . . if not actual pirates then people who seemed only a parrot away. How could a kid who'd always been drawn to outsiders and outlaws, who'd wanted to smoke and drink wine at the dinner table at age nine, manage not to have his timbers shivered by the sight of genuine ne'er-do-wells threatening one another with anal rape as they danced around the kitchen shucking Wellfleets and frying flounder?

Tony had the restaurant business forced on him by another summer housemate named Nancy Poole, who'd noticed he was the only member of their commune who both didn't have a job and hadn't paid his rent, and so more or less ordered him to apply for a dishwasher spot at the parodic Cape Cod fish house where she worked. Tony initially balked at being a lowly "suds buster" who was also expected to peel potatoes and clean shrimp. But once he tied on an apron and got a gander at the tattooed brutes who guzzled the owners' booze, "screwed their way through the floor staff, bar customers, and casual visitors like nothing I'd even seen or imagined," and could sky-hook a dirty sauté pan into his pot sink like kitchen-bound Kareems, he fell in love. From the start it felt like the real thing, not just a summer romance, but then one midweek afternoon about a month later a large wedding party pulled into the Flagship and sealed the deal. The bride, he tells us, was blond, beautiful, and still wearing her virginal white gown when she first laid eyes on Tony's boss, the swaggering, rippling, part-time construction worker Chef Bobby. Fade out, fade in to the serving of the batter-encrusted main course—during which both bride and Bobby disappeared from their respective stations only to materialize in the restaurant's backyard, having stand-up sex while Tony and his colleagues cheered them on through an open window. But for a few small clockwork movements—the rhythmic thrusts of chef Bobby, the backward eye-rolling of the bride—it was an R. Crumb tableaux vivant. Seeing the newlywed get "an impromptu send-off" into married life "from a total stranger" while bent over a fifty-five-gallon drum, Tony realized afresh that America is a great country and that he'd been wasting his time at Vassar.

"And I knew then, dear reader, for the first time: I wanted to be a chef."

The Tale of the Bawdy Bride, let's call it, is almost too good to be true (more on that in a moment), and yet by itself it didn't pack quite enough wallop to pull Tony out of college and propel him into the restaurant business. Not immediately, anyway; there is only so much, after all, that even a titillating epiphany can accomplish. Despite his tenuous connection to Vassar—his report card was a veritable festival of D-minuses and incompletes—stepping off the bachelor-of-arts train was a very big deal in those days, when it was still expected that every generation would do better than the one before. Dropping out meant you were going against the American tide, retreating to the social status that your Depression-forged parents had worked so hard—in the case of Gladys and Pierre it might also be said so heedlessly—to escape. Even a rebellious, impulsive person like Tony had to hesitate before making such a leap. And so it was back to Poughkeepsie for one last shot at a life in which other people do the cooking.

Tony did make one adjustment that seemed sincerely intended to help him stick it out in regular college: he moved off campus into an apartment with several roommates, as a lot of Vassar students did in their sophomore year. In hindsight we can see that in doing so he was attempting what in AA is known as the "geographical cure"—a sarcastic term because it never works. In short, it is the belief that a change in venue will lead to a fundamental change of mindset. For Tony, moving out of the dorms did not even temporarily do the trick. He may have had a tad more privacy in his dumpy little apartment in downtown Poughkeepsie, but he was still the same chemically enhanced truant he'd been the year before. Dae Bennett remembers visiting him in the new place on two occasions, once during a party at which the guest of honor was a welding tank full of nitrous oxide ("I walked in and everyone was sucking on this hose") and then again on a random afternoon when Tony was "sitting in the living room listening to music, watching TV, and reading a book all at the same time—which was very much in line with his personality in those days."

About the only other change he made during his second and final year at Vassar was of the sartorial sort: a samurai sword now dangled decoratively from his belt, next to the nunchucks, sending out a clear message to all who gazed upon it that no matter how tall the wearer was, he was not yet fully grown. As far as anyone can remember, he unsheathed the weapon only once, to "chop down about an acre of Vassar's lilacs . . . so I could fill my girlfriend's room with the blossoms." Although he doesn't mention it in *KC*, Tony by doing this was in a rough way re-creating a stunt that Joe DiMaggio had once pulled (with roses) for the benefit of Marilyn

Monroe. Was it a conscious homage? When you say it with flowers, of course, there's only so many ways you can say it, but Tony—a lifelong Yankees fan and an avid student of popular culture (and a man prone to homages, as he would later demonstrate on his TV show)—might well have known the story of what Joe did for Marilyn that time she was in the hospital in LA and been inspired by it. What we do know is that both the student and the ballplayer, besides sharing a predilection for the grand gesture, knew what it felt like to have love buckle into obsession. After he and Monroe divorced, the great DiMaggio would sometimes chain-smoke in the shadows across the street from her New York City apartment house, waiting to see who might be paying her a visit. Tony felt very strongly about Nancy in those days, but he would hit bottom on account of another woman who at the time now under discussion had not been born.

Tony's performance during the 1974–75 school year was bad enough to briefly reunite Gladys and Pierre as a functioning parental couple. One day with the fifteen-year-old Chris in tow they drove north to lay down the law. "Our parents did not have a lot of money, and I definitely remember, we went to some restaurant in Putnam County, New York, on Route 22, where our parents had a massive, huge fucking argument with Tony," Chris told *GQ* in late 2018. " 'Why are we paying for Vassar? You're fucking up there!' Which he was. The upshot of that was that he did not go back to Vassar. After that, he ended up working out of Provincetown, Massachusetts, down at the restaurant there."

Cutting that final spring semester short, Tony arrived back in Provincetown in April 1975, sporting a powder-blue seersucker Pierre Cardin suit that he thought would be just the thing to wear when strutting proudly down Commercial Street that summer. He'd made it all the way from dishwasher to part-time broilerman during his first stint at the Flagship, and he'd expected to keep climbing the ladder all the way to full-time broilerman, a position of no slight prestige. He also expected, as he had when he first came to Vassar, that he would bedazzle the locals with his alluring/intimidating cosmopolitan vibe. But nothing in P-town was as he'd imagined it would be. The Flagship had been sold in the off-season to the owner of a nearby spaghetti house who was not automatically hiring back the old staff. Everyone had to try out for a spot. Those who'd already passed the test by the time Tony arrived comprised a unique demographic: physically intimidating Black men who spoke only Italian, at least in the kitchen—a bunch of un-jolly Rogers who worked in a seeming chaos of leaping flames and flying fusilli as they banged out four hundred covers on a busy evening. *You gonna stand there all day, Mr. Bluesuit, or are you gonna put on that apron?*

Tony's audition was going poorly even before he stupidly barehanded a hot sauté pan filled with osso bucco Milanese and immediately dropped it to the pasta-covered floor. He then compounded his error by asking his boss, Tyrone, if there might be some burn cream and a Band-Aid in the vicinity. In Tony's memory his question caused the cacophonous kitchen to suddenly go silent as the staff watched Tyrone glower, savoring the moment. By the time they knocked off for the evening, the crew had christened him "Mel," short for *mal carne*, which is Italian for "bad meat." The owner, Sal (he's called Mario in *KC*), said that based on his shaky performance the best he could do for him was a job as a prep, which was one step up from pearl diver, which is restaurant slang for dishwasher.

Here *KC* gets . . . let's say schematic. Having been pinged over to Provincetown by the collapse of his Vassar experiment, Tony now had to get ponged back to Dutchess County, New York, so he could enlist at the CIA because, well, that's what happened in real life. But why did that happen? Why didn't he simply go straight into the restaurant business, like the vast majority of aspiring chefs? In *KC*, Tony says it was all about getting revenge on the coworkers who'd made him feel foolish. Slinking off to his little room above the Spiritus Pizza parlor, he said he "began to formulate a plan, a way to get back at my tormentors," the gist of which was that he would attend the Culinary Institute of America ("they were the best in the country," he somehow knew) and then upon graduation apprentice in France where he'd "let sadistic, bucket-headed French sous-chefs work him like a Sherpa" until he could cook those P-town pirates under the table. "I'd show them!" he rather melodramatically vowed. It's easy to imagine him—or this character he has created—shaking his fist at the sky. But the more you think about him in his lonely garret, coming up with a scheme that will take at least three years to show any results, the more his depiction of events strains credulity. A much likelier explanation for how things worked out was that feeling a tug toward the kitchen but still desperately wanting to stay close to Nancy, he took a course of action that would position him, for the next couple of years at least, at a cooking academy just five and a half miles up the road from her dorm. But because that motive makes the protagonist sound less than heroic—and his storytelling instincts nudged him toward the revenge business (which might, with a very big stretch, be said to be based in reality)—he got a bit artistic with the truth.

It's fair to ask if this manipulation of the facts is strictly kosher in a book of nonfiction. It is certainly not unusual. In memoirs as in novels, characters sometimes need to be moved into or out of rooms or across state lines—or in Tony's case, out of a Seven Sisters college and into a trade school—to keep the plotline unspooling smoothly. In the process, motivations may be oversimplified or wishfully brought into being. (His hero Orwell said that "autobiography is only to be trusted when it reveals something disgraceful.") Still, when the author is Anthony Bourdain, a man widely perceived—and beloved—as the ultimate straight shooter, you do wonder if the audience should expect a higher standard, namely nothing but the painstakingly fact-checkable truth. The modification under discussion here happens to pertain to a relatively small issue. Yet if Tony tinkered with reality in this one instance, might he have done it elsewhere in the book, too?

He did do it elsewhere in the book and to varying degrees. Christopher Bourdain has more or less pooh-poohed the seminal oyster-eating incident, saying (although he would have been only about seven at the time) that he doesn't remember any such thing ever happening or being talked about within the family at a later date. Then there's the bawdy bride story. That hit a kind of narrative trifecta—deftly underscoring Tony's take on the sexual magnetism of his fellow workers at the Flagship while setting up his metamorphosis from rudderless child to wannabe chef *and* giving the reader a good chuckle about the institution of holy matrimony along the way. But how true to history is it? In an interview Tony did with the journalist David Blum in 2013 he suggests by his hesitations and grudging semi-walk backs that the best answer is probably "mostly" or "somewhat." Tony was rarely if ever asked about the bawdy bride, an episode that I suppose people thought too good to question, so he may have been caught off guard by Blum's inquiries. But when his interlocutor broached the subject twice (not to question the story's veracity but to say something about "the seductive power of food") Tony batted him away and then batted him away again, as if he didn't want to talk about it. (Tony was typically so honest in interviews that there is much to be mined, I think, from his occasional evasions.) Finally, he seemed to admit that it wasn't really the romance of the restaurant world that the woman was grasping at as she went over the waterfall into wifedom; she was merely indulging a personal fetish. "I think she just liked rough trade," Tony told Blum. "She just wanted to have sex with someone nasty and dirty, in a grating situation." More power to her, but if it didn't matter that the bride's ravisher was a chef, then the incident loses at least some of its oomph as a pivotal moment in the life of the author. Here again we can see how Tony nudged and fudged the facts to create a "better" version of events—how, like most memoirists, he gave aesthetic form to reality.

And while we're on the subject of honesty, what of TV Tony? How true to life was that attractively patinaed and preternaturally curious pilgrim whom we followed obediently to Hong Kong, Brooklyn, and Antarctica? David Remnick, the editor of the *New Yorker*, spoke rather accusatorily on this subject—and right to Tony's face—in a 2017 podcast. "You invented this character of you," Remnick began, bluntly laying out a take on Tony that must have made his eyebrows rise. "It was partly reality, partly you were drawing on your somewhat misbegotten past, the drugs and the booze and all the rest of it, and you created a larger-than-life presence on television, which is very much, I imagine, part you and part something—" As Remnick seemed poised to pronounce the word "fictional," Tony interjected "maybe aspire to, I think"—and then abruptly changed the subject.

Nice move, AB. Even a great editor needs an editor. Remnick may have been the man who "discovered" Tony (and may also have been a little ticked off at him just then for something that was going on behind the scenes—more on both of those things ahead), but "fiction" is far too strong a word for what Tony, either on the screen and on the page, was up to.

Who among us does not prefer a little varnish on her truth? Arrangement, emphasis, enhancement—these are the difference between a crafted work of memoir and an unreadable data dump. Only those who never get their nose near a book demand "just the facts"—which in any case must be delivered in an order that reflects bias and affects their interpretation. After spending two years talking to people who appeared in *Kitchen Confidential* either under their real names or pseudonyms and who knew Tony on and off camera, I do not have the sense that we were misled. Not all of those friends and associates are happy with Tony. A few of them complain that they were unceremoniously cut from his life when he no longer needed them, and some say his suicide was hideously wasteful and selfish, especially in regard to his daughter. But no one, however angry they were or remain, told me Tony had misrepresented their time together. The consensus was that he was always true to his reader in his fashion—or as Tim Ryan, a contemporary of his at the CIA and since 2001 that institution's president, told me, "Tony's goal was always accuracy, even if he achieved it sometimes by exaggeration." I believe Tony would plead guilty to that. ("I think when you use hyperbole as much as I do," he told the journalist Jessica Bennett in 2003, "a constant mea culpa is required") He never pretended to be a journalist ("I don't feel qualified. . . . I don't want to feel restrained by that title," he said in 2016); he always defined himself in a looser way—as a "storyteller-essayist"—and yet he took commendably little advantage of the wiggle room that distinction provided. On his various cable shows he eschewed the traditional TV phoniness, refusing (like Sinatra) to do retakes or participate in shots of himself saying hello or goodbye to people he wasn't actually meeting or leaving. Such artifice "really takes the air out of the whole enterprise," he said in that later interview. And he consistently spoke, in print and on TV, in the key of self-criticism. Compare him to another bridge-and-tunnel boy who rode to fame on the same two-stage rocket—bestselling memoir, then popular TV show. Donald Trump's self-mythologizing involved only puffery and magnification. The persona Tony perpetuated was not a soufflé but a reduction, an attempt to intensify rather than inflate, a simmering down of personal history into a vivid and stickier essence. Tony's fundamental message—his überjoke—was that the greatest job in the world had fallen to a deeply flawed former steak frites cook who'd already given up on happiness and was sitting high on American Express's 10 Most Wanted list when fortune struck.

Chapter 5

At Vassar, Tony had goofed off nonstop, consumed all the drugs he could stuff into his nose and his mouth (he wasn't shooting up yet), and was probably as miserable as he'd ever been. At the Culinary Institute he tried something different—the work-hard-play-hard approach—and had a much better experience for it.

Why he chose a different tack at the CIA is hard to say. A little older now, he may have at last realized how difficult it was for Gladys and Pierre to scrape together his tuition and wanted to be more respectful of their efforts. Or, more likely (since adolescents don't think all that much about other people, and Tony was at this stage of his life still very much an adolescent), he may have felt that he had found at last the "controlled environment" that school counselors had always told his parents he needed, and immediately went all in, as he was inclined to do with anything that truly caught his fancy. "I like the regimentation. You either fuck up or you don't," he would say years later to an interviewer who asked what first drew him to the professional kitchen. "For an undisciplined, dysfunctional guy like me it's a world of absolutes." It probably also helped that, with the exception of a class taught by a certain sadistic, soufflé-obsessed septuagenarian he called Chef Bernard ("You are a shit chef! . . . You *dare* call this cuisine?"), he found the first year's course work extremely easy ("This is the chef's knife. This is the handle. This is the blade"), especially after working a full summer at the frantic Flagship. The more he immersed himself in the curriculum of the CIA, the more he enjoyed it. After his experiences at Englewood and Vassar, he could barely believe that the hours spent in a classroom—in this case wearing a buttoned-up chef's jacket, checked polyester pants, and a nerdy neckerchief—could be so much fun, and not just when his meat instructor made hand puppets out of veal breast or put on a "lamb demo/sexual puppet show." Or when the Chinese teacher of Oriental Cookery (as it was then still called) went off on a politically incorrect rant, extolling the virtues of Szechuan and Cantonese cuisine while deriding sushi and sashimi as crimes against seafood perpetrated by a degenerate Japanese culture. Or when, as Tony's classmate Nick Valhouli told me, the pastry professor bragged (yet again) about having made Vito Corleone's daughter's wedding cake for the movie *The Godfather.* Or when Tony put one over on his teachers by sneaking a little glassine envelope of Minor's chicken or lobster base into one of his stock pots, injecting an instant flavor boost that could mean the difference between a B+ and an A in that arcane offshoot of academia.

Not that it didn't pain him a little to deceive those poor old cranks. In *Kitchen Confidential* he admits to being slightly besotted with the "Euro-geezers" who dominated the faculty, even though they taught antiquated techniques (like thickening sauce with the combination of flour and fat called roux) and, with their focus on dishes like cauliflower in Mornay sauce and lobster Thermidor, represented "the last of a dying style." Working with chefs who'd learned their trade in Lyon or Paris between the wars only whetted Tony's appetite for the ad hoc postgraduate period he still theoretically planned to spend in France, apprenticing at the sharp elbow of some mercurial master (or two) before returning to plot his own rise.

Nor did Tony hide his newfound lightness of being under a bushel. When the school bell rang each day, the boy who'd once swung between fashionable glumness and comedic outrage (he would always resemble that character in the novel *Homeland Elegies*, of whom the omniscient narrator says, "Cheery pessimism. Or weary optimism. Take your pick") returned anew to a state of raucous celebration. A Hollywood movie montage meant to illustrate this period would show him cannonballing off cliffs into deep blue mountain pools at a nearby granite quarry; flinging Frisbees like the archetypical 1970s freshman, tapping kegs and smoking pot on the rolling riverside grounds of the Vanderbilt Mansion in Hyde Park—and, as previously noted, sliding down slippery rocks into swimming holes roiling with naked nurses all while Carly Simon sings "These are the good old days" on the soundtrack.

Even when Tony and his friends worked the weekend jobs that were posted on the bulletin board in the placement office, hilarity ensued, like the time they got to see a rich Long Island bar mitzvah boy and his pals ride into a reception hall on a trunk-to-tail train of baby elephants. He would not be this happy again until thirty-something years later, when he was married to the lovely Ottavia and had a healthy baby daughter (and he was moved to end a 2009 episode of *No Reservations* set in Sardinia by saying "What do you do when all of your dreams come true?"). For a guy who smoked, drank, and more than just dabbled in drugs, Tony was a hale and hearty-looking specimen at age twenty, handsome of face despite a slightly goofy gap-toothed smile (though not as appealing as he'd be when his light brown eyes achieved a watery sadness and the wrinkles set in), with shoulder-length brown hair that he parted in the middle and sometimes pulled back into a man bun. This was a much more confident Tony than the one we've seen at Englewood School, the perpetual Cruiser-in-training, the fawning acolyte of Flip Goldman, the tall kid who tried hard not to tower. Here he stepped up and became (by virtue of his having worked in a restaurant and having had sex with a woman) the leader of chef wannabes, the organizer of all those crazy-fun field trips, the central figure in a clique whose swaggering presence defined Dutchess County, New York, cool. "Tony had a kind of aura that you noticed right away," Vic, his CIA classmate said, before he went psycho on me. "People were drawn to him. I'm not ashamed to say I was, too."

But where was Nancy Putkoski in all this? The short answer: Tony's Polish-Catholic hot girlfriend was still running hot and cold as she finished up her last two years at nearby Vassar. The meaning of her frequent absences could only be guessed at. Theirs would always be a difficult relationship to peg, since they were so unalike in several basic ways and were rarely together in public, even during the "on" portions of their romance. Friends on the level of Vic or Tim Ryan—that is, casual, cooking-school friends—never saw her or heard Tony say her name during his two years at the CIA; if she ever went with Tony to the famous Friday night blowouts held at the former mental hospital on Route 9, and now a CIA dorm, no one can recall a sighting. "He didn't pretend he was single," Dae Bennett told me. "He just never brought her around. I always had the sense that he was faithful to her through all the ups and downs. I never saw him with anyone else. I just never saw him with *her* and I sometimes wondered why."

In hindsight we can see that Nancy after an initial hesitation was blossoming slowly but surely into a state of full commitment. For the next quarter of a century she and Tony would be, as he wrote in *Medium Raw*, "a Great Couple," and sometimes, literally, "partners in crime." They would get on and off heroin together, an experience that Tony sometimes cast in romantic terms, comparing it to the 1989 Gus Van Sant film *Drugstore Cowboy*, in which addicts, played by Matt Dillon and Kelly Lynch, rob a pharmacy to feed their habit. ("That kind of love and codependency and sense of adventure—we were criminals together," he told the *New Yorker* writer Patrick Radden Keefe in 2017. "A lot of our life was built around that and happily so.") In 2000—fifteen years after their surprisingly traditional wedding—he would dedicate *Kitchen Confidential* to her and describe her as the woman "whom I adore, and with whom I've been stealing horses since high school." (It was the third consecutive book he dedicated to her, after his two mystery novels; a fourth "For Nancy" was still to come.) The fissures in their relationship didn't become obvious until *KC* roared onto the bestseller lists in 2000, and she let him know that she had no interest in the social and publicity functions that flowed from celebrity. Staying home and watching *Simpsons* reruns twice each evening, as they both had been doing for years at that point, was just peachy with her, she told him in both direct and indirect ways. By then, you could say, Nancy knew who she was and who she wasn't, but her strong aversion to the spotlight may have first reared its head circa 1975, as Tony was stepping up and becoming cock of the walk at the CIA.

Not everyone at the school was a Bourdain fan, though. In the course of a good education you inevitably learn as much about yourself as your course material, and one thing Tony discovered at the CIA was that he was a zealot on the subject of not suffering fools—a quality that, as you may have noticed in your travels, fools tend to dislike. Was this really a trait he inherited from his mother, Gladys, an infamous enforcer of standards, you might say, especially in her area of professional expertise? That's not a question I would have asked Chef Tony when he was holding a meat cleaver, but he would in fact always seem happy to teach you a hard lesson or two about staying alert, applying yourself fully to things that were worth doing, and being at all times a professional.

The key word here is "happy"; he actually appeared to *like* being tough on people. *Proper planning and preparation prevents piss-poor performance.* "I do not need to be adored," he once said. "I'd much rather be, like, Meyer Lansky famous." Another favorite saying of his that surfaced during his TV years was "Only pet the baby when it's sleeping," meaning that you should keep your underlings striving for compliments by never actually doling any out. The Emperor of Empathy, insiders knew, could come off as exceedingly cold, but his attitude was really no secret. In a chapter of *KC* called "Department of Human Resources" Tony tells the story of an unnamed chef friend who fired a malfeasant cook, only to have the man (who had been "behaving insolently and fomenting dissent among his coworkers") go home and hang himself. How did Tony console the distraught boss, who said that he'd suspected the troublemaker might resort to suicide if he let him go? By assuring him he'd done the right thing and that in the end it was no great loss. The head chef couldn't let someone walk all over him or extort him with threats of self-harm while keeping the kitchen in a state of dysfunction. That was a form of emotional blackmail that Tony wouldn't tolerate. "Fuck him," Tony wrote. "We're on a lifeboat, baby. The weak? The dangerous? The infirm? They go *over the side.*" He did say in the next breath that he was exaggerating a little, but in fact this was more than just rhetoric. His judgments were harsh and final. "If he thought you worthy of friendship, he liked you; if he didn't he didn't," a business associate of Tony's told me, "and he never changed his mind about his preferences."

Tony's bare-knuckled philosophy of human relations evidenced itself at the CIA in various ways. The rubes and newbies there annoyed him with their naivete about life in general, and because he couldn't put them on the bus back to Podunk, he punished them by playing practical jokes. For example, the school had a rolling admissions policy at that time, which meant that a fresh crop of innocents would arrive every three months. On orientation day, Tony and his friends would greet the newcomers with an offer of discounted passes to the student lounge. It was a good deal, too—$50 for a stack of 50 passes—or it would have been if the student lounge had charged admission. In the end the scam wasn't so much about enriching himself as it was about busting chops and having a laugh, though Tony did make a few bucks along the way. "The suckers were usually too embarrassed to ask for their money back," Nick Valhouli told me, with a chuckle.

Tony doesn't mention this particular prank in *KC*, but he does boast that he basically supported himself by cheating his schoolmates at card games like poker and acey-deucey and selling them "beat drugs" at exorbitant prices. And he did this with a clear conscience, he insists, because all of his victims were on the verge of entering the restaurant business and so they "might as well learn sooner or later." But exactly *what* they might learn from being cheated—or how his justification tracks with what he writes elsewhere in the book, about restaurant workers being basically decent folk who live by their own code of honor among outcasts—he doesn't say. The larger point here, I think, is that besides being a stickler for astuteness, Tony was at bottom very much a Jersey boy, with Jersey boy values and ways—which, for one thing, meant that being a dick was what you felt honor bound to do when the opportunity presented itself. It once was and maybe still is an unwritten law, and not just in Jersey, for a certain kind of boisterous male in a way that being an asshole wasn't. Tony hated assholes and later would have what he called a No Asshole policy when it came to doing business with people. An asshole is a dick who doesn't care if his behavior has any educational or entertainment value as long as he is getting something he wants. Assholes are fundamentally evil people who lack any joie de vivre, like Donald Trump. True dicks are in it at least partly for the laughs; and the chance to be one must, like any worthwhile opportunity, be seized without hesitation. In a way it's like what Gore Vidal said about having sex and appearing on television: it would be perverse to pass up the chance.

In one of the last episodes of *Parts Unknown*, a lively compilation of scenes and outtakes from past shows broadcast after his death in 2018 under the title "Bourdain's Impact," Tony proudly proclaims himself to be the "same dick I was thirteen years ago"—but really that number could have just as easily been thirty or forty. By the end it was an unconscious choice for him, an automatic way of being. If you were charismatic enough, he had long since discovered, you could, if you were so disposed, conduct what was essentially a constant, low-grade hazing ritual that kept people discomfited while simultaneously making them feel like they were on the verge of being admitted to a very exclusive club. And people, being people, would love you for doing that to them.

By the mid 1970s, Tony had found a good rhythm. That second summer in Provincetown had set him up for a strong start at the CIA, which in turn made his next summer on the Cape an entirely different and much more satisfying experience. Now he had something the other P-town cooks didn't: a formal education in cooking, even if it was only one year's worth and he still had a lot to learn. This time instead of a seersucker suit he packed *The Professional Chef* and *Larousse Gastronomique.* Instead of having a chip on his shoulder about being a cosmopolitan sort, he had a self-assuredness bred of genuine Manhattan restaurant experience. As he notes in *KC*, he had picked up more than a few useful culinary techniques on his weekend gigs in the city, where he learned to work a station, as he modestly put it, "without embarrassing myself." He had moves. Sal, the owner of the Flagship, noticed the difference in him right away, and, more important for Tony's ego, so did the man he called Dimitri. Alexej Getmanov, the German-born pasta specialist at Sal's other place, Siro and Sal's, was already a veteran of the restaurant business, eight years Tony's senior; fluent in several languages; steeped in literature; and a connoisseur of art, gambling, military jargon, fly-fishing, vodka, and gardening—the sort of Renaissance guy who could do the Sunday *Times* crossword puzzle in half an hour if his hangover permitted. He was also the only chef for miles around who'd also been to cooking school, though the Swiss hotel academy he attended had expelled him for doing the twist in the dining room. The previous summer he'd been a figure of fascination to Tony but someone too high on the command chain to acknowledge a mere dishwasher, or *plongeur.* Now he gave himself permission to engage with this interesting kid, and the two fell into a friendship that would last until the early '90s before it ended abruptly. By the time *Kitchen Confidential* came out, he had forever stopped speaking to Tony.

This was, of course, the exact opposite of what usually happened when Tony started popping up on *Letterman* and other shows to promote his bestselling "Adventures in the Culinary Underbelly" several decades later. Fame brought Tony, as it does for most people, more old friends than he remembered ever having, and many of them came bearing invitations, sob stories, investment opportunities, and other annoyances. Getmanov's singular reaction was not lost on Tony, and ten years after the book made its splash, and with the silence still ongoing, he expressed bafflement in *Medium Raw* over "Vladimir's" complete disappearance. Perhaps Tony had forgotten what he'd said about him in *KC* (just as he'd forgotten that he'd called him Dimitri in the earlier book, not Vladimir). Some of his descriptions of Getmanov would strike the average reader as surprisingly unkind. While he'd written glowingly of his friend's intellect and attention to detail in culinary matters—and cited his admirable lack of restraint when it came to alcohol, cocaine, and amphetamines—he had also said that he was fat, a mama's boy, and a loner who lived year-round on the tip of Cape Cod because he feared the outside world. On the other hand, maybe such frank description wasn't meant to be so insulting. Tony was always fascinated by the flawed people who were drawn to the restaurant business—the crazies, criminals, substance abusers, and other wounded souls whom we pay to feed us—and he honestly thought your imperfections made you more interesting. He was of course admirably unsparing about his own foibles and faults. But that was Tony's take on the world. Getmanov, who probably had a more conventional definition of slander, seemed unappeased by the adjacent praise that included Tony's calling him "the second great influence in my career." He not only stopped talking to Tony, he also stopped talking about him, at least publicly. "Alex is a hard no," I was told by a mutual friend when I requested an interview, twenty years after *KC* came out.

But wait: the *second* great influence of his career? Tony no doubt sent a lot of readers flipping backward through the pages with that line. Did we miss something? Who was the first? As near as I can tell he is referring to Howard Mitcham, a quintessential P-town character sort of known sort of widely in 2000 for his still-popular cookbooks *The Provincetown Seafood Cookbook* and *Creole Gumbo and All That Jazz*. Tony gives Mitcham an enthusiastic page and a half of description two chapters before he introduces us to Getmanov, though he doesn't say explicitly that he was an influence. Mitcham, deceased by the time *KC* appeared, was a heavy-drinking head chef at various P-town places who careened around town shouting incoherently (partly because he was deaf) and probably scaring small children with his giant shock of "unruly white hair" and gin-blossomed features. Tony would have admired him merely for that, but the native of Winona, Mississippi, had somehow developed a way with seafood that, if Mitcham himself hadn't been such a supple writer, might have been said to defy description. Tony thought of him as "a juju man, an oracle who spoke in tongues" and who had a mysterious, almost mystical connection to the native clam, or quahog, a normally tough customer that he scattered generously in soups, fritters, spaghetti sauce, and pies. Despite the impression Tony gives in *KC*, he never actually met the then fifty-something Mitcham, but he revered him from afar as the still-living legend who lovingly tended the gleaming new trash cans that bubbled with lobsters, crabs, quahogs, and corn at Provincetown's annual John J. Gaspie Memorial Clambake—and who encouraged the local kitchen lackies to forget all the New England cooking clichés, get beyond fried fish, and let the chips fall where they may.

Tony in some ways would never get beyond Howard Mitcham. Tony's go-to dish whenever he was asked to cook something on a TV talk show would be a variation on the master's Portuguese squid soup. He made it so often that Eric Ripert teased him about it; he made it for Ottavia and Ariane at home. In a 2006 *New York Times* piece that asked food celebrities to write a brief essay about their favorite out-of-print cookbooks, Tony said that the *Provincetown Seafood Cookbook* took him back "to the . . . days before the glamorization of chefs, stacked food, artsy presentations, and pomposity. Mitcham . . . was something of an inspiration to ragtag part-timers like me." But for Tony, the wild man of Provincetown would remain a distant demigod—at least compared to Getmanov, who became first his daily postwork drinking buddy and then a business partner in a little catering company they started.

Moonlight Menus, as they called it on the business cards they printed up and personally distributed all over town, spun out of an assignment they got from their boss, Sal, who selected them to prepare the food for the casual-seeming but socially significant garden party he hosted at his home each summer. They weren't his highest-ranking or longest-tenured cooks, but he saw something in them as well as something happening *between* them, and he gave them free rein to express their inner Paul Bocuses using the kind of "pâté en croute or galantines in aspic, or elaborate chaudfroid presentations" that no one else in those breezy, sandy environs had ever heard of. Their imaginations almost got the best of them; Tony said in *KC* that he had to physically restrain Getmanov from using finely cut vegetables, egg whites, and olives to create a tableau of Moses parting the Red Sea on the side of a striped bass that he, Tony, had suggested in jest. If it wasn't for the cocaine, they would have collapsed from exhaustion and perhaps died in Sal's walk-in freezer. But the garden party was such a success that by the end of the season they'd struck out on their own and were fashioning edible Towers of Babel, Space Needles, and Parthenons for the kind of P-town players who didn't mind being campily pretentious. As Tony would later write in an unpublished piece of fiction based on this period, "Every old fag, every coke dealer, every ex-wife on the Cape was shoveling the bucks" at the Moonlight Menus boys, him and Getmanov. But it wouldn't be a Tony story if he didn't also mention a few failures. Not every one of their edible *essais* turned out well. They overcooked and overspiced some dishes and obscenely overdid the blue food coloring in a wedding cake—but together they had more hits than misses and decided that, a year down the road, after Tony graduated from the CIA and Getmanov mustered the courage to finally move out of his mother's place and face the world beyond Provincetown, they would take their culinary act to New York City.

This seemed like a good idea at the time.

PART TWO

Death was the only absolute value in my world. Lose life and one would lose nothing again for ever. I envied those who believe in a God and I distrusted them. I felt they were keeping their courage up with a fable of the changeless and the permanent. Death was far more certain than God, and with death there would be no longer the daily possibility of love dying.

—GRAHAM GREENE IN *THE QUIET AMERICAN*

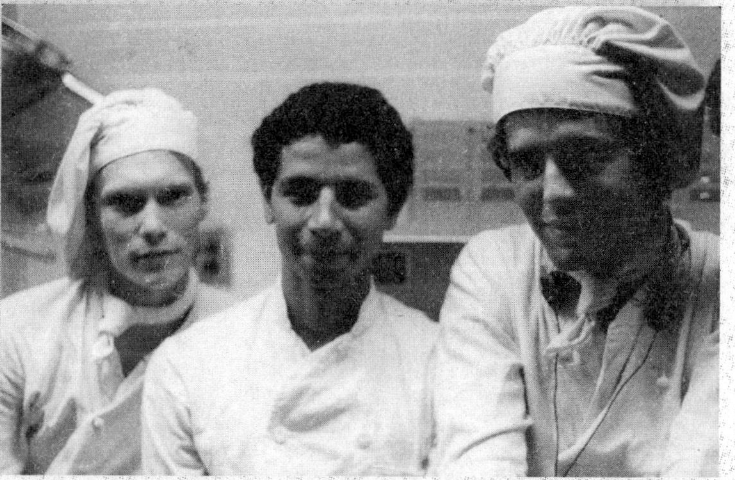

Now a retired Episcopal priest, Michael Schnatterly (left, with Bourdain and an unidentified dishwasher at Chuck Howard's restaurant in the early 1980s) said that Tony "believed when he was twenty-something that the world would someday know his name—and that cooking and writing would be the way that happened."

Chapter 6

When Anthony Bourdain awoke early on the morning of April 12, 1999, in his sixth-floor apartment on Riverside Drive and West 116th Street, he was every bit the flat-out American failure that his mother and father (by then twelve years dead) had always feared he would grow up to be—but he was a particular flavor of failure that his parents might have found uncomfortably familiar. While Pierre and Gladys Bourdain had owned a lovely split-level home in the suburbs that they couldn't afford, Tony lived in a cavernous apartment—"an old-fashioned classic six," said a female coworker who house-sat for him when he and Nancy took their occasional trips to the Caribbean, to sit on a beach and drink margaritas, "to this day the biggest New York apartment I've ever seen"—on which he was dependably three months in arrears on the rent. Nor was that the only obligation of his left flapping in the breeze. American Express was attempting to collect the thousands in debt he'd accrued before they'd canceled his credit card; and the IRS, he sensed, would soon come down hard for ten years of unfiled returns and thousands more in unpaid taxes. The agency's extended silence felt to him like the silence of the invisible, no longer drum-beating Indians in the old cowboy movies.

Some deadbeats don't work, don't pay their bills, and don't give a damn what anyone thinks about them—but that wasn't Tony. He was a functional failure, a variation on the kind of normal-seeming creature Joan Didion (in *The White Album*, one of his favorite books) described herself as being circa 1967: "a competent enough member of some community or another, a signer of contracts and Air Travel cards, a citizen" for whom life wasn't working out as planned. It was not easy to see from the outside how bad off he was. When you went to his and Nancy's place premovie or preconcert, say, you might be served shots of vodka in exquisite crystal glasses lined up on a silver tray (wedding presents, but still). You might wonder at their vast collection of books. On the day under consideration, Tony had recently returned from a business trip to Japan and that morning he would make a stop at jury duty on his way to the restaurant where he worked as head chef—all further signs of societal stability. His secure job at Les Halles, the famously not great but not bad brasserie (everyone said the same thing about it) on Park Avenue South, paid something like $85,000 a year, decent money. It was true that Nancy, though she spoke vaguely sometimes about becoming a shoe designer, did not really look for work and spent most of her days on the couch watching Court TV and *Judge Judy*; but she did have a modest income from her parents, and a few years earlier she and Tony had monumentally reduced their monthly nut by getting off heroin. They weren't broke, exactly (Tony usually had about $800 in the bank), and they weren't particularly extravagant, materialistic, or hell-bent on impressing their neighbors, as Tony's parents had been. Tony always said he knew that "no sports car was ever going to cure my ills." So why did they fall so short of solvency; what made them so unable to keep pace? Their basic problem, it seems, was a common one, especially for creative types, but taken to extremes. Tony and Nancy were impulsive, messy people (or at least Tony was messy outside of the kitchen), spectacularly poor at the part of adulthood that involves making your income last until the end of the month. That was all, oddly enough, but that was enough.

Coming from the home they did, it probably makes some kind of psychological sense that one of the Bourdain boys, Christopher, turned out to be a financial adviser and the other a financial disaster. Tony was glumly resigned to his failings in this area yet at the same time made anxious by them. His dalliances with bohemianism notwithstanding, it particularly scared him to be without health insurance. Except for one emergency visit to a dentist in "a filthy-looking office on the ground floor of a housing project" who would accept payment in installments, Tony hadn't had (or, thankfully, needed) medical care in at least a dozen years. Nancy's father was no doubt footing her doctor bills, but what if Tony's luck ran out and he came down with something serious? Bourdain men, he knew, did not exactly exude longevity. And what if the IRS suddenly hauled him into court? How could he possibly pay for a lawyer? He had no car to sell. Thank goodness he was also a functioning alcoholic and could medicate himself on the cheap. "On the rare occasion when I went to bed sober," he wrote in the 2010 follow-up to *Kitchen Confidential, Medium Raw*, "I'd lie there in terror, my heart pounding in my ears, trying desperately to not think the unthinkable: that at any time, either landlord or government or the long-ignored but very much still-there folks at AmEx could take everything, everything away."

Twenty-five years of arriving early and working hard—twenty-six since he vowed to try his luck in New York with Alexej Getmanov as soon as he graduated from the Culinary Institute of America—and this tattered excuse for a middle-class existence was all he had to show. Not even those (bargain-rate) Caribbean vacations were as carefree as they might sound. Nancy loved the convenience of hopping on a plane and hopping off someplace warmer a few hours later; which sovereign nation she was sinking her toes into really didn't matter. But Tony yearned to see the wider world that he'd so far experienced mostly in books and in movies. "I have a rampaging curiosity about things, and she was content, I think, to be with me. To go to the Caribbean once a year," he said. "There were things I wanted, and I was willing to really hurt someone to have them." Well, maybe. Those friends who remain loyal to Nancy will tell you that Tony did indeed break her heart, but during their last year or so together it was difficult to say who was pulling away from whom; she refused to allow him to touch her, and as he told one girlfriend, he had yearned very strongly to be touched. What does seem certain is that on April 12, 1999, when they were still very much a married couple sleeping in the same bed, he felt sad knowing that he would likely need to abandon his "little-boy dreams of travel and adventure."

More money is of course the best-known balm for poor money management, but standing in the way of an income surge in the Bourdain household were the twin barriers of Nancy and Tony. Nancy's refusal to work probably had more to do with extreme shyness or mild agoraphobia than indolence, but her position was nonnegotiable—and Tony, partly out of a belief that she had a moral obligation to exercise her keen intelligence and that she would generally feel better about life (and smoke less dope) if she pushed herself out into the world a little more, found her inaction in the face of their dire need downright appalling. In a shockingly frank (and decidedly out-of-character) passage in *Medium Raw* (written several years into his next marriage) he revisits the rage which "consumed me out of all proportion" at what he describes as Nancy's two-plus decades of frittering away her days watching television ("I was angry with my wife—very angry, a long-festering and deep-seated resentment . . ."). It wasn't like him to be publicly as hard on other people as he was on himself, but in this case, perhaps because he was a bit ticked off about paying her alimony, he didn't hold back. All of Nancy's TV watching wasn't in vain, though. Her interest in the law led her to explore the intricacies of New York City's housing codes, where she discovered enough loopholes to help them forestall eviction. He did thank her for that.

Besides having his back against the wall, Anthony Bourdain at this juncture also had his head against the ceiling. Oddly, a few years before, when he'd been making regular visits to the methadone clinic and cooking in, or applying for positions at, what were essentially misguided notions with kitchens (the movie *Casablanca* may have been a plausible if corny theme for a restaurant, but Marla Maples? . . . *The Ed Sullivan Show*?), he had not been as bad off as he was on that April morning. That was because his problems back then, as awful as they were, all seemed fixable, and anyone who has read *People* magazine has heard stories about lost souls who went from the wrong track to the right track and became superstars. What's more, Tony in those more distant days had only recently started a side career as a writer of mobbed-up, noirish mystery novels—and while very few strike it rich in the fiction business (his advances were minuscule and there was no budget for a book tour)—this, too, was a situation with a theoretical upside as well as an ego-soothing sound to it in the present. With his literary reputation technically still in play, he would bound out of bed at 5:00 a.m. and on three or four hours of sleep craft another chapter or two about murder and mayhem in the world of Mafia-controlled chophouses and watering holes. True, the publishing industry journal *Kirkus Reviews* had not been kind to either *Bone in the Throat* (calling it "a catalog of first-novel mistakes" with flabby dialogue) or its follow-up *Gone Bamboo* ("a sorry, soggy mess of a stew"); and the Cleveland *Plain Dealer* had run a mixed review of *Bone* under the headline "Stock Ingredients Simmer in Authentic Chef's Plot." But other critics had been more receptive to the author with the striking book jacket photo and the interesting backstory, so for a few years Tony could tell himself that he was still a taste capable of being acquired, an ember waiting for Oprah to exhale on.

Now, a few years on, though, things seemed more settled, in a bad way. His publishing connections had stopped saying his mystery novels "were not selling" and started saying they "had not sold," and he had sculpted a too-cozy spot for himself at a place he could never graduate from without being instantly out of his league. Les Halles was his velvet prison; there he was the supreme boss and had the blessings of the management to do pretty much whatever he wanted in terms of the menu. For both better and worse, Tony *was* Less Halles, to the point where the owners sent him to their struggling Tokyo satellite to help make the place a little less Japanese and more like their bustling New York flagship. But just beyond the front door of the original restaurant, on the same Park Avenue South sidewalk where people would one day line up to mourn his passing, his was, in 1999, a different and sorrier story—or, worse yet, really not a story at all.

If the pre-fame part of Tony's life is a lesson in anything, it is a lesson in the pitfalls of persistence. "He believed when he was twenty-something that the world would someday know his name—and that cooking and writing would be the way that happened," Michael Schnatterly, who worked with Tony in the early 1980s at the restaurant W.P.A., told me. Tony kept his eyes on those dual prizes, like everyone said you're supposed to when you "find your passion." In a narrow, literal sense things did work out the way he'd always thought they would: he did in fact become a celebrity chef with a runaway bestseller. But the greater truth was that he had for years misjudged both his culinary and fiction-writing talents and as a result wound up investing a lot of time and hope in pursuits at which he turned out to be not terribly good.

Opinions on Tony's cooking skills vary and, not surprisingly, tend to rise and fall depending on the state of his relationship with the opinion giver. Steven Tempel, Tony's longtime sous-chef and one of the more aggressively colorful and finely drawn characters in *Kitchen Confidential* ("My evil twin, my doppelganger, my director of clandestine services . . . my closest and most trusted friend and associate") told me, "Look, Tony was an amazing writer and an amazing speaker—when he started talking around the bar, you just sat back and listened—but the guy couldn't cook to save his life." His statement should be taken with caution, though, since Tempel, by all accounts an excellent cook despite some bizarre and/or disgusting habits that he was happy to have Tony immortalize in *KC*, followed him for years from restaurant to restaurant, seemingly happy to play the wacky sidekick. More likely Tempel, who died in a car accident in February of 2022, had let anger or hurt at being dropped as a friend in the years after *KC* color his assessment. Fame, he told me, turned Tony into "a pompous, arrogant douche." He said that anyone who knew him back then could see that just by the cocky way Tony carried himself on TV, but he offered evidence from personal experience, too. "I once called him all excited and said, 'Dude, I just had a baby,' and Tony said, 'That's cool, I'm in the Sahara four wheeling with Ozzy Osbourne.' I thought, really, Tony? Fuck you." As outrageous as Tempel can be—and he *was* known for simultaneously powdering his testicles with cornstarch and singing Elton John songs while working the line—it obviously stung him when Tony moved on.

Dennis Mullally, a veteran bartender, provided a more level-headed critique of the chef he worked with at a place in the West Village called Formerly Joe's in the late 1980s and early 1990s, even though he, too, has issues with Tony. Or an issue, anyway: he thinks it was reprehensible for "Flaco" (Spanish for "thin"—and what everyone at Formerly Joe's called Tony) not to have considered the effect of his suicide on his then-eleven-year-old daughter, Ariane. "If he was standing in front of me right now," Mullally told me, "I would punch him in the face." In their three or so years as colleagues, though, he and Tony never progressed beyond a polite acquaintanceship, and I don't think his opinion of Tony's cooking, formed long ago, has been contaminated by subsequent events. "In the kitchen, Flaco was a solid performer," he said. "His food came out when it was supposed to, it looked good, it had a good flavor profile. Did I think of him as some form of culinary genius? No."

Formerly Joe's barback Robert Ruiz, an enthusiastic supporter of Bourdain the man, was much more effusive about Tony's culinary skills. "He made the best crab cake I ever had, the best lamb shoulder I ever had, and the best eel dish I ever had," Ruiz said, rattling off examples as if he defended his old friend for a living. And then there is Eric Ripert, who met Tony after *KC* made him famous but who loved him well enough to speak honestly. "I have cooked side by side with him," Ripert said. "He has the speed. He has the precision. He has the skill. He has the flavor. The food tastes good. *Creativity*-wise . . . I don't know."

Tony had once thought that even if he wasn't the greatest chef, he could still be a very successful one by virtue of his organizational skills, his familiarity with certain fundamental dishes that might be called French comfort food, and his overall culinary vision—his sense of what would come next. Several decades in professional kitchens, however, had made him more realistic about his limitations, to the point where he might lose respect for someone who praised his cooking too extravagantly. Those people either knew nothing about food or they were trying to ingratiate themselves with someone famous. "He was much happier when people complimented him on the way he cut a show or wrote a script," Ottavia has said to friends. "He knew that's what he was especially good at." By the late 1990s, Tony understood that he had become what in team sports is known as a role player, and he was at peace with that. "It's not Super chef talking to you here,"Tony wrote in *KC.* His was, he said, the number that restaurant owners called when their first choice turned out to be a homicidal alcoholic—and given the nature of the business that happened more often than you might think. His good friend and coauthor of graphic novels, Joel Rose, who claims to have eaten in every place Tony ever cooked (and who comes at the subject as the son of a Carnegie Deli waiter), told me, "He was never a top-line chef; he was what's known as a *fixer.* He would be brought into restaurants that were in trouble. He had a great crew. He wasn't going to make it into a two-star Michelin restaurant, but he was going to do a really good job of making it into a decent place to eat."

Did Tony ultimately lack some innate magical something the best chefs possess? Well, he had a chance to be great, or at least extra special. No one is born with a Michelin star. A so-called natural talent for cooking actually needs to be nurtured and imagined into existence over the course of many years (with the pupil doing all the self-nurturing and imagining while, traditionally, the master teaches mostly by example and the occasional physical assault). Tony, with his very first step out of cooking school, veered from the path he'd so theatrically vowed to take back in Provincetown, when, after retiring to that apartment above the pizza parlor to plot his revenge for professional humiliation (or whatever), he'd promised himself that he would do his postgraduate work in France, slaving for a few francs a week in the kitchens of sadistic geniuses, suffering for his art, he'd said—just as Ripert and Gordon Ramsey had subjected themselves to the relentless perfectionism of the immortal Joel Robuchon; just as Scott Bryan, the brilliant Boston-born "chef's chef" who became his friend (and got his own chapter in *KC*), had for years bounced around Europe and many top American restaurants of that era, "getting my ass kicked" and elevating his game. David McMillan, one of the chef-owners of the Joe Beef restaurants in Montreal and a good friend of Tony's, told me, "When I was a young cook I worked in a restaurant for thirty hours a week, and then I went to France, where they made me work for one hundred hours a week for five years. When I came back to North America and worked only eighty hours a week it seemed relatively easy." This would never be the Bourdain way. Instead of paying his dues in the brutal, time-honored fashion, Tony made what in retrospect seems like a very uncharacteristic and shortsighted but entirely conscious decision. As he often said, when explaining why only a relatively few industry insiders had heard of him when he burst onto the scene with a memoir about his thirty-odd years in the restaurant business, "I went for the money."

For Tony, taking jobs that paid something resembling a living wage, in places that were not, say, Brendan Walsh's Arizona 206 or some other avant restaurant of that era made all the difference in how far up the ladder he would eventually travel. "I talk to my cooks sometimes about the choices that Tony made," David Kinch, the three-Michelin-star chef behind Manresa (in Los Gatos, California) told me. "I warn them to think at least twice about the kind of lateral move that will probably mean reaching the end of their learning curve instead of continuing to build the foundation of their cooking." Tony himself called the abandonment of his plan "my favorite mistake," though he put "mistake" in quotes when he wrote that in 2010 because back then he thought everything had turned out for the best, and anyway he was at peace with his reasons for taking the easier, more-traveled path. For one thing, he was going with the flow of history. A. J. Liebling wrote in 1959 that "It is harder every year to recruit boys of superior, or even of subnormal, intelligence for the long, hard, dirty apprenticeship, at nominal pay—or none, in the early years—that makes a cook." No longer being a boy was also a factor. Having reached the age of twenty-one, Tony felt that it would have been unrealistic if not even a little unseemly to belatedly assume the role of the browbeaten apprentice.

Ripert, after all, had been a barely teenage culinary student when he'd shared "a hot, dank, windowless box" of a room (should he call it a hellhole or a shithole? he wondered while composing his memoir, *32 Yolks*) with two other restaurant interns, one of whom got drunk and vomited into his cot each night, a few inches from his head. Later he endured a middle-aged sous-chef who beat him about the shoulders almost every morning "with all his might" while asking his hardworking and, of course, stupendously promising young pupil, "What atrocities will you commit today, Ripert?" The pressure from Robuchon, over the course of one of the eighteen-hour days you put in for him at his restaurant, Jamin, was no less intense but strictly mental, or at least it worked out that way for Ripert. Gordon Ramsey was once hit in the head by a plate of hot ravioli flung by the enraged master. "I was twenty-five," Ramsey wrote, "but I was taking shit like a fifteen-year-old." A fifteen-year-old in a Dickens novel, maybe. With sizzling cream sauce in his ear and burns on his face, Ramsey meekly apologized to Robuchon, as he knew he was expected to.

Tony, who later joked that he was already living, like a divorcée, in a style to which he'd become accustomed, did not, when the time came, so much reject this sniveling existence as forget it was even a possibility. Instead, he grabbed the first job that came along via the bulletin board in the placement office at the CIA—in this case, sixty-four floors up at 30 Rock. He would start at the top and see where you went from there. The bumpy journey had begun.

Chapter 7

The Rainbow Room, opened in 1934, was by the late 1970s already a dinosaur of a dining establishment that had virtually nothing to offer a fledgling chef in the way of education, unless it was the old culinary saw about an ounce of sauce covering a multitude of sins. No restaurant in New York was grander in its physical proportions—the Room was actually a large, open main area; a substantial grill; and several adjoining banquet halls which together sat about five hundred diners, done up in an authentic art deco style and featuring heady views of Manhattan that could get you humming *Rhapsody in Blue*—but neither could you find a more vivid example of the hypocritical high-end, big-city restaurant experience, with only a few sets of swinging doors separating a throbbing hive of sweaty, cynical, underpaid, mostly foreign-born workers from a symbiotic mix of tycoons and tourists who enjoyed getting dressed up and, as Tony said, "eating garbage at the top of the world."

For a young troublemaker destined to someday rip the lid off the inner workings of the restaurant business, though, the Rainbow Room, as operated by its ownership in those days, was a godsend, a cornucopia of crimes against gastronomy, starting in the cavernous kitchen, so poorly ventilated in certain inglenooks that rough-and-ready crew members regularly fainted where they stood. Tony's first assignment there in 1978 was to prepare the daily lunch buffet, or as it might more honestly have been known, last night's main course leftovers, now tarted up comically with French names like Salade de Boeuf en Vinaigrette and Tongue en Madère and served by the future TV star himself wearing one of those chef's hats that looks like a coffee filter and a menacingly broad smile. (Whatever didn't get eaten would be saved for the *next* day's exclusive Luncheon Club buffet.) Later, as he wrote in *Medium Raw*, he spent a six-month stretch there doing almost nothing but turning out leathery soufflés made from "cement-like béchamel, cheap flavorings, and meringue." Soul-sucking work? Indubitably, but also muckraking gold. (As Philip Roth said, "Nothing bad can happen to a writer. Everything is material.")

And what of Tony's willingness to swap learning for earning? How was that panning out? More good news for the future author of a book modeled on another called *Down and Out* (Tony would get the germ of the idea for what became *Kitchen Confidential* about a year later). Although he eagerly succumbed to the pressure from management to work a double shift—meaning that he started at 7:30 a.m. and didn't peel off his sweat-soaked polyester whites till midnight—and the room was theoretically a union shop, he still was taking home less than $200 per week, which even in the late 1970s was borderline slave wages. And during those hours he might, in addition to preparing the buffet, sear a hundred beef Wellingtons for a sit-down banquet and peel seventy-five pounds of shrimp. He was also absorbing abuse on a regular basis—although not, alas, from anyone who, if in a better frame of mind, could have shown him precisely when to add a splash of sherry vinegar to a seafood buillion so the acid doesn't stop the tenderization of the already simmering carrots. His nemesis, rather, was "a big, ugly Puerto

Rican with a ruined face named Luis," who after consuming half a bottle of cooking brandy would come up behind Tony and aggressively grope his buttocks through his checked pants. Tony more or less tolerated these assaults for a while because Luis outranked him in the kitchen and because it was the sort of thing that happened all the time behind the scenes at the glamorous Rainbow Room. But then one day while making crepe filling with a big meat fork, he saw Luis homing in and, timing his thrust precisely, drove the long twin tines into the man's knuckles "with a satisfying crunch." Luis howled like "a burning wolverine." No one dared bother the young line cook again.

It has been a long time since Tony Bourdain made his bones at the Rainbow Room, a long time even since he sat down to remember his late-adolescent adventures there for his memoir. When he held that job he was already more than dabbling in drugs and drink and smoking something like four packs of cigarettes a day—and yet there was a corner he still hadn't quite turned in terms of freshness and innocence. He was still walking around with what some of his older friends recognize as his original smile (a distinctly goofy, slightly bucktoothed grin that would keep evolving until, by the end, he had worked his way back to the same greenish beam of nonjoy he had used on the buffet line). Someone just now coming to his most famous book, and knowing what ultimately became of Tony, may feel their stomach clench when he describes in *KC* how, during his fifteen-minute work breaks, he would often sit on a ledge of the RCA building with his long legs dangling sixty-four floors above West 49th Street, "smoking weed with the dishwashers." And yet all that young guy—the pre-heroin Tony—was doing back then was surveying a world of possibilities. *Look*—someday all those people down there will be my customers or my readers. Or so he hoped and dreamed. His still-untattooed arm clung tightly to the window sash. This kid wasn't going anywhere but up.

Another reason Tony's Rainbow Room stint seems so far in the past is the way he talks about his coworkers—which is, more often than not, in terms of ethnicity. Luis, as we've seen, was an ugly Puerto Rican. What more do you need to know? We also meet a "beefy German sous-chef"; a smattering of Irish waitresses; a "taciturn Swiss"; an Austrian; a Dominican; two Basques; an "ex-Wehrmacht corporal" who said "zey" for "they"; a "just-off-the-boat Italian with a heavy accent"; two additional Italians with heavy accents, as well as another "blue-eyed Italian"; and a "kindly Neapolitan chef." No real names, just nationalities are given, and together, he tells us, they comprise a "motley assortment" of crewmates. (Black coworkers don't get mentioned, perhaps because they barely existed. Women employees he generalizes about in terms of their appearance, writing that most "looked like whichever was the uglier of Cagney and Lacey [the later episodes when they bulked up to cruiser weights].") Today this is embarrassing to read, but of course a lot of people still talked this way circa 2000, when, having secured an advance of $50,000 from Bloomsbury, he was churning out *KC* as quickly as he could in his apartment on Riverside Drive. Twenty-odd years ago it was still widely believed that ethnic and racial stereotypes, like word clichés, existed for a reason and that citing someone's national origin was an efficient way of conveying a set of roughly accurate characteristics while retaining plausible deniability. *Hey, all I said was that the guy was Italian.* It was a slightly naughty habit, perhaps, but also, in this view, street-smart and slightly funny. And there was something else it was, too—it was "very Andy," as those who worked at Formerly Joe's used to say when a phrase or an occurrence reminded them of the restaurant's owner, Andy Menschel. Menschel was the kind of New York guy who talked that way all the time.

Andy Menschel died, childless and nearly friendless, of cancer, a few months after Tony in 2018. He was for most of his seventy-something years, like Gladys Bourdain, a physically large, socially awkward, and highly opinionated person about whom people told stories. Tony wouldn't work for Menschel full-time until he was more than ten years into his culinary career—that is, in the late nineties—but when he took the job at the Rainbow Room he had already crossed paths with and been deeply affected by the manipulative, micromanaging, strikingly generous, and often very mean man he called Bigfoot in *KC*. Tony was also by that time already a true believer in what he called the Bigfoot System. Indeed, apart from his parents, Menschel—a native Long Islander about fifteen years his senior seems to have briefly played basketball at Syracuse University, worked in construction, ran various restaurants in Lower Manhattan in the 1970s, 1980s, and 1990s without ever learning very much about cooking per se, and who described himself as just "a big, fat, red-faced balding Jewboy"—was probably the single most important influence on Anthony Bourdain's life.

Why Tony settled on the soubriquet of Bigfoot is hard to say. It's not especially witty or ironic in the usual Bourdain way (or even in the Three Stooges way: bald guy = Curly). Menschel was a heavyset man who stood about six foot four with hands so large they made people nervous. Bigfoot had big feet. Beyond that, Tony tells us, everyone south of 14th Street would know who he was referring to anyway. But was that really the case? Menschel's places were strictly of the small-scale bistro or faux-roadhouse sort, and their radius of influence usually extended no more than a few blocks in any direction. Was he really the restaurant legend that Tony made him out to be? When I put that question to Edie Falco, another Formerly Joe's veteran who'd been a waitress there before her acting career kicked in, she laugh-snorted. "Andy Menschel was a lot of things, but I'll tell you what *I'd* call him," she said. "I'd call him a big fat bully." I don't believe Tony would have disagreed with her—and yet he understood that he was hopelessly in thrall to a highly imperfect role model, a mercurial mass of humanity who nevertheless had something to offer an ambitious but rudderless young cook. The things Menschel taught him—or it would probably be better to say, the qualities that Menschel *brought out* in Tony—remained deeply important to him his entire life and, I believe, figured very strongly in his final decision in that hotel room.

Tony stumbled onto the Bigfoot System in 1975, when he was still in his first year at the Culinary Institute of America and his old high school buddy Flip (who by then had renamed himself Sam) Goldman gave him a call that changed his life. Sam had drifted into the cooking racket after earning a film degree at Boston University, and as adept as he was at seemingly everything he tried, and as charismatic as he couldn't help being, he had gone far fast, landing the executive chef job at a bustling Menschel-owned roadhouse-style restaurant called Montana Eve at the ridiculous age of twenty-two. Since dazzling the owner at his job interview, though, Goldman, who was not really qualified for the position, had regularly fallen out of favor, getting caught in the typical Menschel cycle of rejection and sporadic approval. He was criticized constantly and fired and rehired so often—while simultaneously being slipped court- and ringside-seat tickets at Madison Square Garden by the boss—that he was confused not only about his employment status but also about his worth as a chef and maybe even as a human being. This is how it tended to work with Menschel, who was famous among his employees for showing up unannounced at their mother's hospital bedside or their father's wake—and then firing them not too much later for giving a regular customer a free cup of coffee. "Slow night?" he'd say to a waitress, and if she said yes he'd peel a twenty off the wad in his pocket and give it to her. But when she finally left his employment, on either good or bad terms, he'd yank out one of his scary gray ledger books and show her a record of every twenty he'd ever given her—not because he wanted his money back but just to remind her of his power. Keeping his employees off-balance and beholden to him were among his main objectives, it seemed, every bit as important as pleasing his customers. Tony himself was not immune to these psychological games and in fact got enmeshed in the Montana Eve drama as soon as he started the job that Goldman had called to offer him in late 1977—a standing gig as an omelet man for weekend brunch.

On his very first day, after Tony knocked out three hundred meals in the tiny Montana Eve kitchen and was slouching toward the door utterly spent and probably wondering whether his work had been up to sophisticated Manhattan standards, someone tapped him on the shoulder and said, "Andy wants to see you in his office." Since he'd already been told that the owner had a volcanic temper and had once killed a man in a bar fight (the story about Menschel that everyone heard first), Tony was not expecting happy talk. But Menschel that night greeted him with a smile; praised his grace under pressure; and, after they'd toasted with cognac, christened him Flaco (there was already a Tony on the staff) and pronounced him part of the team. Bigfoot "purchased my soul for two snifters of Spanish brandy," Tony wrote in *KC*, exaggerating only a little.

The Bigfoot System was three different things, mainly. It was dumb, it was weird, and it was inspiring. Menschel was a mad scientist of casual dining. He had pondered long and deeply the subject of watering hole management and had developed theories about almost anything you could think of pertaining to personnel, menu, supplies, equipment, and workplace psychology on that particular level of the restaurant business. We'll get to the more interesting theories in a moment. First it must be said that Menschel was in many ways a typical white male child of the early 1940s, who displayed all the predictable prejudices (he was also no killer, the colorful tale notwithstanding). At his places, Hispanic men were busboys and barbacks and nothing else; the waitstaff and hosts were white females; bartenders were white males. As far as anyone can remember only one Black person ever worked for him, briefly. Menschel was also, despite being Jewish, rabidly anti-Semitic, not just in his hiring practices but in his routine speech if not also in his heart. None of this is terribly unusual, of course; self-haters abound and his hiring practices mirrored the New York City restaurant business as a whole. His feelings about chefs, though, were at least more unusual if not more enlightened. Peek into any of Menschel's kitchens and you'd likely see four or five Chinese men slinging his brand of slightly French hash (and swigging Heinekens). Although he sometimes also hired Caucasian men as cooks when he had a gut feeling about a particular individual, he firmly believed that the Chinese possessed the best knife skills on the planet and so could extract the greatest yield from any piece of fish. Where he got this peculiar notion (a Fu Manchu novel?) nobody knows, but success for Menschel was always measured in seconds saved and ounces rendered, all of which he kept track of in his ledgers. There was a right way and a less right way to do everything, he believed, so why settle for second best? Even the beer he served his Chinese cooks was part of the overall philosophy. We'll get to that presently.

It's not that Tony countenanced Menschel's theories of racial and ethnic aptitude (or lack of same) even if he sometimes rudely parroted Menschel's politically incorrect speech. This part of the system—the dumb part—was not what intrigued Tony, and the fact that Menschel went far beyond merely calling a Swede a Swede may have been one reason why the two, despite their strong underlying connection, sometimes clashed loudly during working hours and never evolved into anything resembling friends. What Tony—a highly disorganized man away from the kitchen, let us not forget—liked far better about the system was the sense of order it imposed, and how it played into the notion (preached and personified by his mother, the *New York Times* copy editor) that if something is worth doing, it is worth doing well. Menschel (no neatnik himself, in droopy jeans and untucked T-shirt) had figured out "best ways" to handle virtually all things bistro—how the liquor bottles should be arranged, how far apart the snack bowls should be placed on the bar (two and a half feet); what kind of pens the staff should use (Parker, fine point); what color ink should be in those pens (blue only; checks written in black would earn you the dreaded "come see me in my office," which at Formerly Joe's was a brick-lined chamber with a foot-thick titanium door). Edie Falco remembers getting pulled aside for a lecture by Menschel after she committed the sin of walking from one part of Formerly Joe's to another empty-handed. "In a restaurant," Menschel told her, "there is always something that needs to be carried. Don't waste a trip!" This was the weird part of the system—not because his rules were illogical or entirely arbitrary ("I have to admit," Falco said, "Andy, with all his little tips and bits of advice, made me a better waitress") but because they were so numerous and, even though the worst he could do was fire you, seemed so life-and-death to all who were caught up in the never-ending task of keeping Mount Menschel from erupting.

Tony liked the way the system focused more on management

than on cooking, an area in which he didn't think he needed the boss's help. Menschel had thought through all the nitty-gritty stuff—the behind-the-bar plumbing, which in his places always featured a perfectly positioned hot-water hose so the bartender could easily melt down ice at the end of the night; the inventory sheets, laid out carefully in clockwise, geographical order to save footsteps; the way he dealt with purveyors, making sure to pay them promptly on the first of the month so he'd have leverage in any dispute; the way he curried loyalty among his employees by giving all his workers an unheard-of *two* free shift drinks, premium brands included, and (in contrast to owners who served the help a thrown-together "family meal") the choice of anything on the menu except the steak or the lobster special. Yet there was more to it than that. At some point on the system's spectrum, being a better restaurant worker started to shade into being a better human being—and this (what you might call the inspiring part) is where Menschel had Tony, and at least few others, by the heartstrings or maybe it was the soul. For Menschel, character was everything. The world, he would happily tell you, contained only two kinds of people: those who did what they said they were going to do and those who didn't. The former deserved to be treated decently, the latter punished severely.

"Andy didn't care whether you were a millionaire or had twenty-five cents in your pocket," Formerly Joe's barback Robert Ruiz, another true believer, told me. "The only thing that mattered to him was your integrity." Character cannot be taught (something else he often said), and so, like Montaigne, whom he probably never heard of, Menschel was constantly on the prowl for people who could be depended upon. A job interview at Formerly Joe's, at least for a while, consisted of four questions, gruffly posed: Are your parents still together? Did you graduate from college? Are you currently employed, and, if so, when can you start? The first was meant to see if you'd ever been exposed to a long-term commitment; the second pertained to your likelihood of finishing what you'd started; and the third and fourth were a trap. If you said you had a job but were willing to leave it with less than two weeks' notice, he wouldn't hire you because he figured you'd someday do the same thing to him.

Menschel's priorities played out especially starkly in his rules about lateness. Basically, it worked like this: if you were on time too often, Menschel fired you. That's because, as Claudine Ohayon, an ex-waitress and now a voice-over actress, explained to me, "In Andy's world, on time was late. If your shift started at 4:00 and you got there at any time after 3:45, he'd send you home and call in someone else. If you were running late for work, the only way to possibly save yourself was to call ahead and let Andy know. This was before cell phones, of course, so if I was stuck on the subway and not going to be fifteen minutes early I'd get off at the next stop, scramble up to the street, find a pay phone, and then run back down and catch the next train. The whole time I'd be shaking." Which was fine with Andy. Even if you couldn't teach character, you could, Menschel believed, flush it out into the open with a well-timed blast of fear.

Some people—like Ohayon, Edie Falco, and Sam Goldman—took what they liked from the Bigfoot System and left the rest. Looking back, Ohayon said that although "Andy had a stare that could turn your blood to ice," she was "forever grateful to him for making me realize how important it was to be on time." And we've already seen how Falco, though she ultimately tilted negative on the man, saw at least a little something of value in his rants. Yet to others—usually young men in search of something to believe in—Menschel could be much more than just a colorful if difficult character you met along the way; he could be, as Ohayon put it, "not just a father figure but almost a godlike figure."

Ruiz and Tony were two employees who chose to brush aside the weirdness, the bullying, and the bigotry and instead focus zealously on Menschel the mensch. In *KC*, Tony called him "the most stand-up guy I ever worked for" and spent a good-sized chapter arguing for his primitive brilliance. What others may have seen as somewhat trite maxims—the business about the world being divided into bullshitters and straight shooters, and the warhorse about anything worth doing being worth doing well—Ruiz and Tony heard as a rallying cry in the ongoing struggle to address Montaigne's perennial question: How to live? What made them feel that way?

Ruiz's devotion to Menschel is not hard to fathom. When they first met in the mid-1980s, Ruiz was, owing to the recent deaths of both parents, a newly minted sixteen-year-old orphan in need of work. Menschel made him a busboy; got him an apartment; and, over the years, taught him how to talk to customers and suppliers; coached him on handwriting and even bought him a penmanship practice book, the sort of $1.50 favor that is remembered forever. Many years later, when Menschel was terminally ill, Ruiz moved in with him and became his caretaker; for years he lived in Vietnam with his wife and a diminishing stash of Menschel's ashes which he occasionally scattered on one or another remote beach. Tony, meanwhile, had his own reasons for falling hard for the system, and the man behind it, starting with his lifelong inclination to be what chef Scott Bryan called "the all-in guy" who always went quickly from "intrigued by" to "obsessed with," no matter if the subject was comic books or the JFK assassination. Beyond that, though, both he and Ruiz illustrate the consequences of what social psychologists call "confirmation bias" and "authority bias" combining forces to create something like a cult. Both men no doubt believed in personal integrity before they met Menschel, but without thinking too much about it, without making it a religion. It's not exactly a controversial theory. What Menschel did—by publicly proclaiming the importance of integrity and promoting the idea that the principles he espoused needed to be defended from an army of pathetic excuse makers, promise breakers, and miscellaneous flakes who threatened to make the world a crappier place—was to turn their passive assumptions into a cause worth fighting for. He took a point of view and made it a way of life; he gave his acolytes a hill to die on, and for that bequeathment of unreal real estate they were forever grateful.

Tony carried Menschel with him in a no less meaningful way than Ruiz did. The chippiness he exhibited about never becoming a TV phony? His willingness to spurn lucrative endorsement deals for products and services he thought second-rate? That was Menschelism in action. "Proper planning and preparation prevents piss-poor performance"—and all the other dickish-boss stuff he pulled during his seventeen years on TV? Tony's Zero Point Zero Production crew, without ever actually meeting Andy Menschel, has met Andy Menschel many times. Nor are Menschel's appearances in *KC* confined to the Bigfoot chapter; when Tony writes, "Somebody who wakes up with a scratchy throat and a slight fever and thinks it's okay to call in sick is not what I'm looking for" in a line cook, he is once again channeling his old boss. Menschel even shaped Tony's formidable online persona. "Tony was the Big Brother of social media," the Montreal chef David McMillan told me. "He insisted that any chef in any restaurant, any maître d', any waiter—they had to not just be dedicated to good food, they had to be a good person on top of everything else. If he caught you doing something fishy to customers or your fellow employees, you'd get completely *destroyed* by him on Facebook, Twitter, or Instagram in a way that only he could do. And no one would complain because he was almost always right."

Long after he became famous Tony's eyes would snap open at 6:00 a.m. no matter where in the world he was or how long he'd been sleeping—a flashback from the days he'd worked day shifts for Menschel, he said. Business associates often said that if they arrived at a meeting with Tony twenty minutes early, perhaps because they were nervous about meeting the great Anthony Bourdain for the first time, they would find him sitting alone in the waiting room, reading a book. Call him weird or say he overindulged the eccentricities of the artiste, at least he had figured out who he was: a man who thought that on time was late and for whom lateness was a sign of capitulation to the great leveling force of the universe, the thing that made you just another mealymouthed schlub. He often said in later life that he wasn't concerned with other people's punctuality—that he didn't care when *you* got someplace, only when he did, but that wasn't true.

Tony could be very judgmental. Ask Rachael Ray and Emeril and Alice Waters and Guy Fieri and the other celebrity chefs he publicly took to task for in one way or another being lazy or fake or just ridiculous. He especially wanted to demonstrate to the world that you could be rich and famous without being a craven asshole who cared only about being rich and famous. He refused even to socialize with people who he thought had fallen into that trap and would turn on his heel and stalk out of a party if he saw someone in the crowd whom he'd come to disrespect for the way they'd handled success. He would proselytize about integrity with a Menschel-like fervor to an audience of one at an airport bar or to millions on TV. Then one day he looked up and saw what he had become.

Tony brought the Bigfoot System with him from Montana Eve (where he worked weekends while still at the CIA) to the Rainbow

Room, but since he didn't have any autonomy there he couldn't do anything with it. And so it remained, for the year and a half he spent there reheating leftovers and constructing Naugahyde soufflés, a kind of arrow in his quiver, as was, in a way, his friend Alexej Getmanov, whom he finally coaxed out of Provincetown and maneuvered into an equally bad job beside him on the line. In retrospect we can see the ambitious young Tony marshaling his assets, husbanding his resources, getting ready for the next move.

Before he left the Rainbow Room, though, he did try to put his mark on the place by running for union shop steward. If he couldn't improve the dining experience, maybe he could help make the working conditions slightly more humane, or at least shake up the power structure, in whatever time he had left there. Campaigning on the promise to lower the heat in the kitchen and lessen the pressure to work double shifts, he easily won the election, beating his nemesis, the *culo*-clutching Luis. But then something strange happened: the loser took the news with a sly smile. What was up with that? When a representative of management dropped by Tony's station to praise Luis's past work for the union and say that he sincerely hoped the new shop steward would stay healthy and live long, Tony got the message. In short order he and Getmanov were down the sixty-four stories and out the door. It was time to leave and, besides, the irresistible Sam Goldman was once more beckoning.

Chapter 8

When I talked to him in early 2021, Sam Goldman, the former king of the Cruisers, was a pale and pixieish man in his mid-sixties, smoking his way through stage four lung cancer and grateful for having been sent to federal prison for several years in the early 2000s on drug charges—"It saved my life," he said, coughing—but four decades before he was still far too golden boyish for his own good and people kept lavishing him with opportunities that he was, by his own admission (then and now), unfit to handle. We've already seen what happened at the roadhouse called Montana Eve, but the more full-fledged restaurant known as W.P.A.—which Tony called Work Progress in *Kitchen Confidential*—is an even more striking case in point. When a trio of B-list theatrical producers bought Montana Eve from Menschel and his partners in 1980, the buyers might have seen the transition as an opportunity to ease out the overmatched Goldman as executive chef with the excuse that they were starting afresh, as new owners will, but alas those poor impresarios were as in over their heads as he was, and so, smitten with the sight of Sammy sporting a jaunty chef's neckerchief and brandishing a shiny saucepan, they invited him to occupy the same exalted spot at the much more ambitious place they were now adding to their ill-fated little restaurant empire. "I was in no way prepared for the top job at W.P.A.," Goldman told me during the course of a two-hour Zoom chat from his home in Pasadena. "And I didn't waste any time in calling in my friends Tony and Alex [Getmanov] so they could do all the work and I could get all the credit."

All the credit would never amount to much, but then there are different ways to measure success and Tony did wind up calling his chapter on his W.P.A. experience "The Happy Time." Michael Schnatterly, a young line cook at the restaurant who went on to become an Episcopal priest, told me, "I would not trade those days for anything—I could not have had a better life at that moment." And that only makes sense given that he, Goldman, Tony, and Getmanov had camaraderie; creative freedom; cocaine; and, after a certain point, heroin to enjoy in considerable portions. Their comeuppance was on the horizon, to be sure, as alas it always is in cases of excess, but in the meantime they were all working hard and hovering in the sweet spot that you sometimes hear speakers reference ruefully at Narcotics Anonymous meetings.

"All the problems that go along with drugs came later," Goldman, who'd become a confirmed Twelve Stepper, told me. "We may not have been as focused on our work as we should have been, or as kind and loving to other people in our lives, but our key relationships were still more or less intact and we still had money. There was no downside to heroin yet." As William S. Burroughs tells us time and again (in books that Tony—who always strained to see the literary side of drug addiction—constantly pressed upon Goldman), if you want to be a junkie, you've got to put in the effort. Until you start to feel a little dope sick, and then keep going, and then keep going some more—until then, for better and worse, friends + freedom + fairy dust = fun, fun, fun.

What Goldman was taking charge of in 1980 was the second iteration of W.P.A. When the place first opened on Spring Street about four years earlier, it struck an off note as an ultraexpensive restaurant that would somehow pay homage to a New Deal agency dedicated to creating infrastructure jobs for Americans rendered destitute by the Great Depression. Or maybe it was *mocking* the Works Progress Administration rather than paying homage to it; probably even its founders didn't have a grip on just how ironic and decadent they were trying to be. Wunderkind designer Ron Doud—who would later help create Studio 54—hung the interior walls with ersatz versions of the epic murals that the FDR administration had commissioned to honor manual laborers and which still adorn the lobbies and terminals of banks and railroads. Before these grim, Gothic scenes of heaving and hoeing would sit the kind of diners that one newspaper critic described as a "snooty, pretentious nightmare of tuxedoed new money artsy elegance" poking desultorily, by candlelight, at their small plates of extremely tall food. W.P.A. opened with a blast of paid-for publicity and, four years later, closed so abruptly that it's a wonder Liza Minnelli and Halston weren't trapped inside. The gates had been down for several months when Goldman was asked to come in and create a Second Coming worthy of the trendy, upscale neighborhood that SoHo in those days was turning out to be.

The entire restaurant business just then stood on the verge of sea change, as Tony was the first of his friends to discover. The day he showed up at W.P.A. for the three amigos' initial strategy session he had a suitcase in one hand, a five-ounce tin of caviar in the other, and some barely containable news on his lips. He'd come straight from the airport after spending a week in France with his parents, making the familiar rounds of the relatives and throwing in a few side excursions, just like in the old days, although this trip, a belated present for graduating from the Culinary Institute of America, had the bittersweet feel of a last waltz. Gladys and Pierre would soon separate, sending both their sons into what seemed to some people like a tailspin of despair, which was odd considering their advanced age and the many years of marital tension that had preceded the more formal split. For the time being, though, Tony was excited about the astounding things he'd seen happening in France and, via TV and print journalism, throughout Europe. "You won't believe this," Goldman recalls him saying, while still getting himself and his bag through the W.P.A. entryway. "Over there they're treating chefs like *fucking rock stars*! They're like gods in France and all over Europe. Chefs—*fucking chefs!*—are on every station, in every newspaper; they endorse products, they give interviews, people ask for their autographs!"

This is old news now, the chefs-as-rock-stars thing, but Tony's discovery came at a time when the foodie revolution hadn't quite happened in America yet and future sensations like the San Franciscan Jan Birnbaum would still avoid traveling to work in their uniform "or anything that made me look like a cook," because they were more than slightly ashamed of their profession. If an attractive woman asked what he did for a living back then, Alain Sailhac, who would later become the head chef at Le Cirque in New York City, told her he was a head waiter, because he knew that sounded more impressive than the reality. "Chefs were not renowned or celebrated," the food writer Andrew Friedman said in his highly entertaining history of the era, *Chefs, Drugs and Rock & Roll*. "At best, they were regarded as craftsmen." In a 2016 *Eater Upsell* podcast with Amanda Kludt and Daniel Geneen, Tony said that "there were no chefs anyone wanted to fuck before Jeremiah [Tower] and Marco [Pierre White]" came along and changed the whole perception of what a chef should look like and behave like. Before them, he said, "our image of the chef was this servile, dumpy, Italian probably, twirling his mustache, who would appear obsequiously at the table with a popping gesture. 'What would you like, signore? Signore, I will do anything for you. Your *speecy-spicy* meatballs.' And the last person whose opinion you wanted was the chef's. They were the backstage help."

To Goldman (who admitted he still doesn't get the phenomenon), Tony's effusions simply made no sense. "I remember turning to Alex Getmanov and saying, 'This is crazy talk. I think this boy has bumped his head.' I mean, it was as if we were an office full of accountants and he's telling us that in another country across the sea accountants are superstars and they're making competition shows and reality TV shows about accountants. That would have been just as believable."

But even if Tony wasn't exaggerating or once again being the overly enthusiastic all-in guy, what did this development mean for him and his compadres? His excitement seemed to suggest that he thought their lives were about to take a turn for the better because of what he'd seen in France—but who was going to treat *them* like rock stars? Could chefs actually cook themselves into a state of Jim Morrison– or Mick Jagger–like celebrity? How exactly did this phenomenon work? Tony himself had no immediate answers, only a vague and somewhat vain idea that he'd been carrying around for a while—that he wanted, for personal and professional reasons, to be more than just the speecy-spicy meatball man; he wanted to be a kind of chef plus—more precisely, the chef who gave new meaning to the term "potboilers." Writing had long been, at the very least, his avocation, and turning out novels and short stories had seemed like a logical way to both satisfy his creative urges and distinguish himself from the crowd of cooks constantly pouring on to the job market, if only for the sake of his own self-image. If his literary efforts brought in some royalties, and his reputation as a chef-writer attracted a few curious customers to his restaurant of the moment, so much the better.

But what he'd seen happening in France made him rethink all that. If people were going to put cooks in the same category as guitar gods, it might be more in keeping with the zeitgeist, as well as more fun, he reasoned, to set writing aside for a while and instead hitch his wagon to another of his longstanding passions: rock and roll. But how would *that* work, since he played no musical instrument and could not carry a tune? Without thinking it all the way through, or even half the way through, he came up with a plan, or really more of an intention, to perform a kind of alchemy that would somehow meld cooking with the twangy-angry punk music he held so dear. In his mind's eye he could just see the fans lining up outside his place of business, like they did at CBGB and the Mudd Club, even if he couldn't quite complete that vision by imaging what might be happening inside those venues to justify everyone's excitement. Cooking and music can happen simultaneously, of course—at the first version of W.P.A. they'd played "Brother, Can You Spare a Dime?" and other Depression-era ditties over the sound system while people ate $10 slices of apple pie à la mode—but common sense tells us that cooking and music combine about as readily as cooking and hockey or hockey and existentialism or Spanish literature and your mama. How could you possibly become the culinary equivalent of the Ramones?

The fact that you couldn't didn't stop Tony from trying and urging his partners to do the same. As they went around town, recruiting help for W.P.A., they told Schnatterly and others that they were assembling an all-star group of kitchen workers, "kind of like Blind Faith," who would revolutionize the New York City restaurant scene. "Their vision of the place," Schnatterly said, with

Protestant understatement, "was somewhat grandiose." For better or worse they believed their own bullshit, not just about rock and roll cooking but about their innovative oomph. The three principals saw themselves, Goldman said, "as the next generation of cooks who would create dishes no one had dreamed of, food that would take us to the future." Or as Tony said in *KC*, "We fancied ourselves the most knowledgeable and experienced young Turks in town."

That they agreed on even that much seems startling, since they squabbled about almost everything else, especially the rather central question of what they would serve. Goldman remembered how, "We'd be all fucked up on alcohol and drugs and we'd have these loud arguments about what kind of food we'd have, and how to make each dish the correct way. Each of us would be holding on to a different one of Escoffier's books, which we'd brandish like a weapon as we insisted that the *real* recipe for what we were fighting about was in *here*!" Their battles never got too personal, though, or, God forbid, physical; the boys could always be brought together again, by even the most tentative suggestion or inquiry from one of the restaurant's owners, for a tension-relieving group eye roll. In the end, though, the self-styled hotshots didn't come up with anything that could be called groundbreaking in a good way.

In a 2007 episode of *No Reservations* set in Los Angeles, Goldman, fresh out of prison and working as a door-to-door meat salesman, reminisced with Tony about the good/bad old days and recalled the pretentious and anything-but-cutting-edge hodgepodge that was W.P.A.'s grand reopening night menu: steak Rossini (a beef, foie-gras, and truffle concoction attributed to the chef Marie-Antoine Carême, who died in 1833); pasta with trail mix and anchovies; and veal scallopini with calvados ("which *New York* magazine tore up"). Eventually the bill of fare would become what Tony in *Kitchen Confidential* called "the Greatest Hits of Our Checkered Careers So Far," which in his case was the Portuguese squid stew he learned to make in Provincetown, his aunt's tomato salad, and "my mom's crème renversée." Anything that was innovative and actually tasted good at W.P.A. was probably stolen from another restaurant or a cookbook.

Goldman and Tony were both first-rate technical cooks (with the former generally acknowledged as the superior), but neither had much of a culinary imagination. "Frankly, I was surprised that, given how good he turned out to be at nonfiction writing and television, Tony was so lacking in creativity as a chef," Goldman said. It would be hard to say what was more detrimental to the restaurant's success—Tony's frequent fallow periods or his occasional brainstorms. Among their low points was a group invention they called lobster Neapolitan, which was really an adaptation of a dish popularized by Patrick Clark, the brilliant chef at Odeon on West Broadway: lobster in vanilla sauce. "Patrick's version was delicious," Goldman said, "just a hint of vanilla in the butter sauce, a classic idea coming out of nouvelle cuisine in France. But it led us to think, you know, if vanilla is so good why not also chocolate and strawberry—and all at once? We were sure everyone would talk about it and that it would get us in all the newspapers. In the end, it turned out that we got just one review in which the guy said, 'Worst idea ever,' and he was right."

Well, maybe he was and maybe he wasn't; at W.P.A., the competition for that title was stiff. Consider a spin-off venture that Tony tried to launch at just around the time the restaurant was opening—a kind of rock and roll catering company that he called Kitchen Confidential (it was his first use of the name). In the previously mentioned file of juvenilia that he kept on his laptop, I found this (manually) typewritten credo:

Kitchen Confidential is not a secret society for hungry private eyes, although in the words of its ringleader, Anthony Bourdain, it is a conspiracy.

Picture this anomalous situation if you can: Anthony Bourdain, a chef of considerable merit, emerges from the kitchen. He is twenty-five and sports a Walkman which is blasting largely atonal music into his skull. As the driving force behind Kitchen Confidential, he sets the tone, which he would describe as "a shady alliance of high-priced freelance talent planning to change forever the widely held opinion that chefs are old, ugly, drunken, and not of this continent."

The plan: in addition to creating fine food at the restaurants where the Kitchen Confidential members are currently reigning with "iron fists," K.C. has plans to go into a club, or a press reception, and for a preset sum of money offer a "completely outrageous" banquet; "elegant" luncheon; 19th-century traditional feast, or an apocalyptic event of sheer gastronomic excess.

Why rock and roll clubs? Because these young men find this kind of environment to be one they like and understand the best. As the working hours of a chef leave these heroes out on the street looking for fun just about the time that the rock and roll clubs are starting to hop, it seems quite logical that they might spend their time propped up at the bar of the Mudd, Danceteria, or the Ritz unwinding and soaking up the atmosphere. After all, when not in their chef's whites they not only understand this undernourished crowd, they blend in with it. It didn't take more before their enterprising minds realized they have a skill that could enhance what these already fine clubs are doing to keep America's youth off the streets and out of the slammer.

Special talents identified:

Anthony Bourdain: heavy conceptual organizer. Fast volume cooking, any station. Specialty, classical French, American regional, banquet pro.

Alexej Getmanov: million dollar hands. Serious French, German, Italian, and Russian culinary background. Phenomenal garde-manger. Ten years on Cape Cod. Educated in Bavarian Hotel School.

Sam Goldman: gives great phone. Finds the products needed. Good at nouvelle, French, American/New England. Labor racketeer.

Michael Schnatterly: garde-manger, sauté. Jack of all stations. Premier slicer of cold food in New York.

John Verga: hotshot saucier. No available information.

Variations of this message appeared on handbills that the principals distributed at downtown clubs and pasted over stenciled warnings to Post No Bills. Tony also decided that he, Goldman, and Getmanov should each kick in $200 so they could hire a photographer from *Rolling Stone* to shoot a portfolio of glamorous album-cover-style group portraits of them in their chef's togs, to be included in a slick press kit. They did at least get some decent pictures for their money, one of which Tony used twenty years later on the cover of the first international edition of the book *Kitchen Confidential.* But back in the day even his closest W.P.A. compadres had a hard time grasping his vision as outlined in the handbill. "I think we did the photo shoot just to shut him the fuck up," Goldman told me. As for the bars, clubs, and other music venues that were their potential customers, either they, too, didn't understand what he was getting at with the rock and roll catering thing or they were turned off by the promotional material's cocky tone.

In any case, Kitchen Confidential the catering service never got its first customer.

Business at the restaurant wasn't so bad, though, at least at the beginning, despite the shortage of appealing menu options and less-than-enthusiastic press (Goldman remembered Mimi Sheraton of the *New York Times* writing "something about young New York chefs using bluster to cover up a lack of skill—which I took as a reference to us"). Perhaps some members of the dining public felt drawn to the strange energy then emanating from the W.P.A. kitchen. In *KC* Tony recalled how they would begin each evening shift by blaring the soundtrack of *Apocalypse Now*, one of Tony's all-time favorite movies, over the speaker system. And when Jim Morrison started singing, "This is the end, my brand-new friend . . . the end," someone would toss a match on the brandy-soaked range top, "causing a huge, napalm-like fireball to rush up into the hoods." While they still weren't managing to merge music and, say, oysters Mitcham, a dish of their invention that they'd named after Provincetown's widely lamented sultan of seafood, they *were* enjoying themselves.

"We all worked while wearing cassette tape Walkmen turned up very loud," Schnatterly said. "The Ramones and the Ventures were very big for Tony, and if a song came on in the middle of the rush that was really cranking him, he'd pull out the plug from my headphones and put them in his Walkman, so I could experience the same song. There was very little verbal communication because if you wanted to talk to someone you had to go pull their headphones off, so we did a lot of gesturing and pointing." Now and then Tony would come as close as he would ever get to public dancing. "The idea," Schnatterly told me, "was always to get as much joy out of this day as you can and then, well, tomorrow's another day."

It wasn't *just* one big party, though, thanks primarily to the lessons Tony had learned from the Bigfoot System. "I remember

Tony sitting down with me early on and saying how the restaurant business is just that, a business with a capital B, and we had to remember that we couldn't get careless," Goldman said. "That was all stuff he got from Andy Menschel." Everyone who worked there got the message that the resurrected W.P.A., as studiously louche as it may have appeared to be, had rules and standards that you could get fired for violating. Employees had to arrive for work at least forty-five minutes before the doors opened and all the cooks had to maintain a tidy mise en place. "It was about being neat and clean and well stocked through the nightly rush," Schnatterly said. If a purveyor tried to stick them with wilted produce or less-than-pristine fish, Tony pulled the same retaliative tactic that Menschel used in such situations: he let the driver unload the entire order and carry it all the way inside before telling him to pick it up and take it all back where it came from. They never got screwed twice by the same supplier.

Still, on the whole, "discipline" did not have the same meaning at W.P.A. as it did elsewhere. With the full knowledge and consent of management (meaning basically Tony and Sam), most of the kitchen staff spent their busy working hours washing down illegal pills and potions with tumblers of straight vodka. The challenge, as Tony once explained, was to "work through" the feeling of inebriation to show that they could do what had to be done under less than ideal conditions. If you are not young, male, and stupid, you might not understand that, but it made perfect sense to them. "Through the fog of the drugs," Schnatterly said to me, a few days after he'd retired as a parish priest, "I think we did an amazing job."

And *after* work? That was when the bosses broke out the Cristal champagne and the coke and, along with some of the female help, found a way to let their hair down even further. Schnatterly believes that cocaine at least initially was viewed as having putative medicinal purposes. "We were really tired all the time and that was the drug we thought was enhancing our ability to keep things straight and keep cranking out the food." Before long, though, they realized they needed something to take the edge off the cocaine, so they could manage at least a couple of hours' sleep after they'd stumbled home at dawn. And so began their heroin journey.

Or at least so began Schnatterly's. Although they started at almost exactly the same time, each member of the W.P.A. crew who got involved with the drug approached it from a different perspective. Schnatterly was the sweet, hapless hippie who'd come from Ohio to have an acting career and who managed to get mugged every few weeks on the streets of lower Manhattan; he never progressed beyond occasionally snorting heroin and thus had a more benign experience than Sam and Tony, who before long started to inject it. Goldman said that for him "junk was part of a logical progression"—a matter merely of time and opportunity, a development as inevitable as dusk. As for Tony, he had also been moving up the scale of increasingly stronger and more exotic substances; but for him, an aspiring addict who had always wanted to go the furthest the fastest, getting hooked on heroin was the fulfillment of an almost lifelong dream. It meant he had at last summoned the courage to join the fraternity of the strung-out-seeming idols—like Burroughs, Lou Reed, Iggy Pop, Chet Baker, and Hunter Thompson, to name a few—that he'd been emulating one way or another since grade school. His overriding emotion when he arrived at a state of junkie-ness, he confessed on at least one occasion, was not fear or excitement but pride. "I'll tell you something shameful," he said in 2014, when he joined a support-group meeting for the Massachusetts episode of *Parts Unknown*. "The first time I felt [dope sick], I looked into the mirror and I smiled."

Cue the Ramones. It wouldn't be terribly off the mark to

think of Tony's life as a performance. He often said he hated the word "authentic"—his nearly two decades of world traveling having taught him the futility of striving for the unalloyed version of anything—but on a personal level, authenticity, in the sense of being the real thing and not a pretender, was his lifelong preoccupation. He wanted to show the world not who he was at bottom but rather who he preferred to be: the slightly (as Lady Caroline Lamb said about Lord Byron) "mad, bad, and dangerous to know" dude from downtown; the guy who on the Hong Kong episode of *The Layover* tells his tailor, "Make me a suit my mother would hate"; a genuine battle-scarred badass. Hence, in his twenties, the hard drugs and, in late middle age, the multitude of tattoos. Hence the inability to disengage himself from the television juggernaut that had turned him into Anthony Bourdain. Sure he said, in so many words, "I'm not really cool" and mocked himself in a way that might seem to undercut his toughness, but isn't that exactly what a self-possessed renegade would do?

Goldman remembers, if somewhat imperfectly, how they came to cross the border into the land of heroin—which was, as it turned out, pretty much the same way that young numbskulls with New Jersey license plates have been doing it for decades. "It was after closing and we were all going out to a bar and someone said, 'Let's go get heroin.' We went cruising around the Lower East Side in my little red VW Rabbit but we didn't know where to go, didn't know where to look, so we gave up and went home and wound up not getting it until a couple of days later." Long pause while Chef Sam stared at the ceiling. A condition he called "chemo brain" had been making it hard to focus. "I think it might have been raining."

Chapter 9

A chilly, dark night, you say? A rain-smeared windshield? Shadowy figures in tenement doorways? *Perfect!* This is how Tony, in 1981, wanted to lose his heroin virginity—as if he were in an early blaxploitation flick with Curtis Mayfield or Bobby Womack sermonizing on the soundtrack. If you could have bought smack at Macy's, he would never have gotten hooked. He was in it mostly for the atmospherics, hoping someone would notice him out there on the wet asphalt, through the fog. That was his way. "Tony had this *thing* where he liked to pretend he was living scenes out of movies," the Montreal chef Fred Morin, who appeared in one episode of *No Reservations* and two of *Parts Unknown*, told me. "He was obsessed with movies and inserted a million movie references in his TV shows, more than anyone could ever catch, but what a lot of people don't know is that he also designed them into his actual life. He'd imagine he was the main actor, but at the same time he was, in his mind, a kind of set director who wanted to curate all the details of a scene—what everyone ate, the furniture, the clothing, the music they were listening to."

Morin was talking about Tony circa 2007, a time when he would invite a carefully considered bunch of friends down to Miami; put them all up at the campy, art deco Raleigh Hotel; and then arrange a poolside party the way a Hollywood production designer might. When he'd decided everything was just the way he wanted it to be, he'd stride into the scene—which was his way of saying "Action!" and which signaled that all the "extras" could then start lounging around in their vintage bathing suits while smoking cigarettes and drinking beer and chatting. It was a little weird, but fun. Tony loved everything about the Raleigh Hotel—that it was a crumbling heap of faded tropical glory, that the concierge was named Crispy. By then this was a rich and famous man's fetish that he could afford to indulge. But Tony's obsessive interest in movies and his desire to live inside them (not so odd if you think of what every child in a darkened theater is thinking) were no less fervent when he was in his late twenties and forced to take his backdrops as they came. The Lower East Side—with its ultra-urban scenery (Richard Price in his novel *Lush Life*: "falafel joint, jazz joint, gyro joint, corner. Schoolyard, crêperie, realtor, corner. Tenement, tenement, tenement museum, corner")—excited Tony's inner location scout.

After he and Goldman failed to make a connection on their first foray, Tony was delighted to return several times that same week to search further for people who'd sell him Body Bag or Toilet or one of the many other "brands" of heroin packaged specifically for giddy white boys like him. Ultimately, Tony would take his first snort of the drug on his own, in a bombed-out tenement on Rivington (the street that, as a cinephile, he probably knew figured prominently in *A Hatful of Rain*, a 1957 movie about a morphine addict), but within a few days he and Goldman were both using and within a few weeks they had progressed to injecting, brothers in track-marked arms.

"I don't think I gave Tony his first heroin, but let's just say we did a lot of it together early on," Goldman told me. Dependence on the drug was just as William S. Burroughs had promised it would be: junk was not a "kick" as much as it was "a way of life" they soon enough learned, a twice or thrice daily task to be checked off their to-do list, another brick in their backpacks. "Our restaurant life between 5:00 p.m. and the beginning of the dinner service involved scrounging up money and finding out what busboy or dishwasher you could send across town, so you could get through the dinner shift," Goldman told me. He meant get through the dinner shift without throwing up. Burroughs also advised in his book *Junky* that heroin affected its users in sometimes surprising ways—and both Nancy Putkoski, who began using the drug at the same time Tony did, and Goldman have said that for them, addiction was, at least in the stages just beyond the previously mentioned sweet spot, a pain in the ass but not the end of the world.

"It does look pretty bleak in the rearview mirror," Putkoski said, "but, when you're living it, it's just your life. You struggle through." Goldman told me that "people are always surprised when I tell them that I did my best work, that I got my stars from the *New York Times*, while on heroin. But I react differently to drugs than most other people—differently, for example, than Tony did."

Tony definitely did not do his best work while on heroin. While he romanticized it till the end—in the last regular episode of *Parts Unknown*, the singer-poet Lydia Lunch feels obliged to interrupt his nostalgic reverie about the Lower East Side in the early 1980s to point out, "Tony, those were the *bad* old days"—he had to admit in later years that hard drugs had affected his professional judgment, and maybe that of his colleagues, too, just a teeny bit more than they liked to admit. "We behaved like a cult of maniacs," Tony said in 2015, when asked about the W.P.A. time. "We thought we were creative geniuses and created a very chef-centric menu that was not what the dining public wanted. We were cooking out of our league. It was not a professional operation. . . . I liked the life that went with being a chef. I was getting laid, I was getting high, I was having fun. I had no self-control. I denied myself nothing. I had no moral compass. . . . We helped bankrupt the place in short order." Actually, it wasn't all that short an order in which W.P.A. succumbed. Because the owners had tons of money to waste, the second iteration lasted almost four years—though about eighteen months into the venture the boys debuted a weekend New Orleans–style brunch complete with Dixieland band that is universally recognized in the restaurant business as the white flag of surrender. Tony would make his exit shortly after that, leaving Goldman and Getmanov to soldier on without him, or at least without his daily presence—he stayed very much in touch.

Tony would reconsider what the W.P.A. experience meant to him several times as it receded into the past. He started out quite positive on the place; as has been noted, his chapter about "Works Progress" in *Kitchen Confidential* was called "The Happy Time." But in 2013, when Ecco Press published the Insider's Edition of the book that allowed him to insert marginalia, he wrote on the opening page of that same supposedly upbeat episode, "This is where it all started to go wrong in a lot of ways." It isn't hard to see why, upon further reflection, he felt that way: W.P.A. for him was a gateway to a long period of drug dependence and, because substance abuse tends to flatten one's career trajectory, what might generously be called professional drift. But his mulling didn't stop there; and a few years later he flip-flopped again, saying his W.P.A. adventure had been a good thing after all—and precisely *because of* the sorry path it had put him on. "Had I not known what it was like to fuck up—*really* fuck up—and spend years cooking brunches in bullshit no-star joints around town," he wrote in *Medium Raw*, "that obnoxious but wildly successful memoir I wrote wouldn't have been half as interesting." Quite possibly—but by suggesting that everything in the end had turned out for the best, Tony made the same mistake that Willie Shoemaker made aboard Gallant Man in the 1957 Kentucky Derby: he stood up in the irons too soon. Tony wasn't at the end yet when he wrote that in 2010. At the age of fifty-five he still had plenty of time to fuck up royally, and when a half dozen years later he did exactly that, he still had time to fuck up further by thinking he had fucked up irrevocably—a misperception that caused him to seek a permanent solution to what might well have been regarded as a temporary problem. At least Shoemaker misjudged the finish line only that once.

One genuinely positive thing that happened at W.P.A., in spite of everything, was that Tony finally grew up a bit. He certainly started to grow nicely into his large, craggy features and gangly limbs and became, when you also consider his ability to make heads swivel at a bar (as he held forth about things that had happened and thoughts that had occurred to him in the last twenty-four hours), every bit the commanding presence that Goldman ever was. When the place opened, "Sam was still the guy you wanted to be," Schnatterly told me. "He was the better chef and he had the girlfriends. I certainly didn't want to be Tony Bourdain." But by the time Tony moved on to Chuck Howard's, the theater-district boîte, where he got his first job as executive chef in 1982 (it's called Tom H's in *KC*), the subterranean shift had occurred and Schnatterly (and eventually Getmanov) went with him.

Tony, while still at W.P.A., also finally untangled his thoughts about music, and how it might and might not be employed in juxtaposition with food. By the time the New Orleans brunch rolled around, Louis Armstrong and Crab Louie, po' boys and Pet Shop Boys—these things remained discrete concepts in his mind. In time he grew ashamed of how he'd once gotten music and food so muddled. He made no reference to Kitchen Confidential, the rock and roll catering company, in the book of the same name or in interviews afterward—and in 2016, during that *Eater Upsell* podcast conversation, went so far as to denounce some of his fellow chefs for thinking far more clearly about the possibilities of celebrity than he once had. "[Cooks] were never rock stars," he said. "I think anyone who took that seriously is really in peril. . . . If any of us thought we could have been rock stars, or if any one of us could play guitar, we sure as shit wouldn't have cooked. We cook because there was nothing else for us, more often than not." Pooh-poohing a recent resurgence of the notion, he spoke of "delusional behavior" that ignored "the very nature of the business, which is grinding repetition. And if you cannot submit to a life where the first requirement is consistency in grinding repetition, then you're gonna be a shitty chef." Tony, despite his hyperactive brain and low threshold of tolerance for boredom, never had trouble handling the repetitive nature of cooking and was happy to be known as the cool-handed hired gun who could bring consistency to the most disorderly kitchen. But, for reasons of self-esteem, he could never be just that. Which is why, when he saw his connection to music for what it was, he returned without hesitation to the idea of pursuing a side career as a writer—and not just any old ink-stained factmonger, mind you, but a writer of fiction, which in those days was still clearly the higher calling for anyone who messed around with words. The beauty of this goal, compared to the musical one, was that it was theoretically attainable—although in reality there was one small problem.

From an unpublished mid-1980s story of Tony's titled "Ace Woke Up":

Ace woke up in a room with white walls, a watercooler, a movie screen, and two cages. In one cage was a man. In one cage was a cat. A voice came from behind the screen.

"Ace, this is the Master Gland. Please pay attention to the two restraining compartments in front of you."

Gas filled the cage. The man inside started shitting and pissing and then he puked and puked and rolled around uncontrollably in the mess, making funny noises. Then he got an erection and died. Gas filled the cage with the cat in it. It started screeching, then seemed to go to sleep, and then it died.

"And now watch this!" said the voice. On the screen flashed slow motion reruns of what Ace had just seen, over and over.

DING, DING, DING

From an untitled, unpublished short story written by Tony around the same time:

She met him at the door in a fantasy ensemble of pastel pink lingerie, garters, corset, the whole bit. This fabulous-looking woman, long black hair, men's magazine body, classic cheekbones, stood there, resplendent in undies that he knew were intended to inflame and endear. Certainly it seemed any normal male would have pinched himself to see if he was dreaming. Undeniably, Kathy turned heads whenever she walked in a room. Yet somehow (and it wasn't the dope) the gesture had the opposite effect. He felt . . . offended . . . offended that she would think him moved to passion by such ubiquitous stimuli. Embarrassed, guilty about his visible lack of enthusiasm, he lied. Sliding a hand around the base of her spine.

"You look delicious."

"So do you." She always said stuff like that.

Tony's early fiction writing was not always this awful, and sometimes it was actually okay, but it seldom broke the plane of mediocre. Writer Joel Rose still remembers being initially underwhelmed by what slid out of the manila envelope that bore the rubber-stamped return address of one Anthony Bourdain: a manuscript of what today would be called a graphic novel but back then was still a comic book. Rose and his then-wife, Catherine Texier, shared a fourth-floor walk-up on East Seventh Street in those days; and in addition to the novels and poetry they wrote, they were partners in editing a literary quarterly they'd started in 1983 called *Between C & D*, after the avenues that bordered their Lower East Side block. The magazine, which competed with such titles as *Bomb*, *Redtape*, and *Benzene*, published rising young edge dwellers like Kathy Acker, Gary Indiana, Emily Carter, and Tama Janowitz and became, Rose said to me when I visited his current apartment in early 2020, "an immediate sensation." He meant a sensation by homemade literary quarterly standards. Instead of the seventy-five copies they initially intended to produce on Rose's scrappy little dot matrix printer, he and Texier were soon selling six hundred, and dealing with a burgeoning amount of submissions. In their statement of purpose, published in the first issue, the couple had promised to serve up content that was "gritty, urban, sometimes ironic, sometimes gutsy, erotic, violent, or deadpan, unsentimental rather than 'sensitive' or 'psychological.'" In short, *Between C & D* seemed made to order for the writer Tony Bourdain wanted to be.

Tony's comic book was about what a lot of his youthful fiction was about: a young chef desperately searching for drugs on the streets of downtown Manhattan. His short pieces in those days tended to be either blatantly autobiographical or set on Pluto in the far distant future, whatever it took to get published—not that any of these early pieces ever did. "To put it to you quite simply," Tony said in his cover note to Rose, "my lust for print knows no bounds. Though I do not reside on the Lower East Side," he noted, "I have in the recent past enjoyed an intimate though debilitating familiarity with its points of interest." (Had he lately been reading A. J. Liebling, one of his all-time favorite authors? It sounds like it.) Rose had no idea who Anthony Bourdain was and thought the artwork "sucked" but that the writing was relatively promising—"Tony was from the start a gifted storyteller," he assured me—and Rose wrote back to Bourdain to convey his more positive reactions. A week later the buzzer in his apartment rang, he skittered downstairs, and found at his front door a very tall young man in chef's whites who was obviously high. "I'm Tony," said the caller, offering a shaky hand and an apologetic smile, "the comic book guy." Rose, who'd done a lot of drugs himself in the 1970s, was not judgmental and, being a writer as well as an editor, probably eager to procrastinate. He invited Tony upstairs, and they talked for nearly three hours in his kitchen about literature and life, both of which Tony was having trouble with at that juncture.

Rose said that he immediately detected in Tony a distinct feeling of unworthiness: "He was *sooo* insecure. He wanted so much to be a writer but he lacked the confidence. He didn't know any writers and believed he didn't belong in that world." Tony's hesitation came down to what for him it so often did: the original sin of being born suburban. Despite ample evidence to the contrary, literature, he believed, was not by rights the bailiwick of ordinary bridge-and-tunnel boys like him. What Tony didn't realize was that he was hardly alone in his insecurity and that most serious young writers—no matter how many lawns they'd mowed in their day (or, conversely, how many dirty-water hot dogs they'd eaten)—suffered, one way or another, from what the critic Harold Bloom called "the anxiety of influence," meaning that they felt intimidated by the masters who had hacked out a path and thrown down a gauntlet, daring future generations to find new and better ways of making something out of language. Tony himself was a textbook case of anxiety of influence. Among his unpublished college writings I found a poem called "The Impossibility of Doing Anything."

The seeming impossibility
Of saying
Of writing
Anything new

I have been preceded
By such talent
Nurtured on such
Extremes

That no extremity
It would appear
Has not been
Visited previously

The class of '77
So bombarded by
Information
Up to date
Out of date
And otherwise

What to do
That's new?

The requirements for genius
These days
are unreasonable

You can't get by anymore
Just being clever
Or even desperate

No, that's not terribly good, either. A poet I showed it to for her evaluation called it "a poem trying too hard to be a poem." But Rose had taken an immediate liking to Tony the man and felt moved to help him get better. Together they reworked a semi-fictional sketch of Tony's—about a twenty-something chef who gets turned away by drug dealers because they can't make out the track marks on his arm and therefore think he may be an undercover cop—into something publishable. "FAO," as the story came to be called for obscure but no doubt valid artistic reasons when it appeared in *Between C & D*, marked Tony's first foray into print. He wasn't kidding himself, though. He knew he had a lot to learn about the craft of fiction, and because he always read a lot about writer's lives—how, when, and where they worked; their relationships with their editors; their favorite cocktails; and so on—he thought he knew just the literary guru he might learn it from, the guy everyone said was the best. In a letter to Rose, he said he looked forward to "life after Lish," when doors both real and metaphorical would swing open before him.

Poor Tony. Gordon Lish was, like Andy Menschel, a force to reckon with from Hewlett, Long Island. At *Esquire* magazine and later the publishing house Alfred A. Knopf, he'd forged a reputation as a sometimes brilliant but often overly aggressive editor who injected too much of himself into the work of Raymond Carver, Richard Ford, Cynthia Ozick, Barry Hannah, Amy Hempel, and Don DeLillo. Or tried to. Some authors pushed back against his brash blue-penciling, while others, because they were more easily cowed or sincerely believed he had improved their writing, let his changes stand. It would later emerge that Lish had taken the liberty of transforming Carver into the pioneering minimalist that many came to admire by making massive cuts and changing his endings and titles ("What We Talk About When We Talk About Love" had originally been called "Beginners"). Even Carver had to admit that his stories were often better for being made leaner and somehow more mysterious—and they certainly were better read than previously. But Lish ultimately alienated too many influential authors and agents, and after he was eased out at Knopf, he picked up the thread of a teaching career at Yale and, later, Columbia, conducting seminars in fiction writing at the homes of trembling students.

The heartbreaking thing was that not all of his acolytes trembled with fear—at least at the start of each seminar. Some trembled with excitement and anticipation as they settled in with eager faces and sharpened pencils among the classmates who, it soon became clear, were there mostly to have their emotional resilience pushed to its limits. Captain Fiction (as Lish called himself) liked to demonstrate early and often that the put-downs he'd scribbled on manuscripts at *Esquire* and Knopf paled in comparison to what he was happy to tell a fledgling writer to her face, with a full complement of peers watching. A *Chicago* magazine journalist who took his seminar described Lish's method as "a mélange of technique honed from boot camp, est, the brainwashing scene in *The Manchurian Candidate*, and shock treatment," and said he was "arrogant, egocentric, and megalomaniacal." When another Chicago journalist ran those adjectives by Lish and asked for a reaction, he for once had no edits to offer. "I am all of the above," he said.

Rose was not opposed to a young writer going the academic route; he'd gotten an MFA at Columbia himself. Still, he tried his best to discourage Tony from taking the seminar. "Lish was too self-involved to deal with the people and the issues that were in front of him," he told me. "Tony went to him because he was desperate for validation. I continuously encouraged him and told him to trust his natural voice, but he was looking for more. He enrolled, was accepted, and was absolutely thrilled to learn that the class this time would be held at Lish's own apartment. But Lish did a bait and switch on him, a sort of a gaslight thing. He encouraged him as a writer at first and then crushed him." We don't know what Lish said to Tony because Tony never talked about the seminar, and Lish, now in his late eighties, doesn't remember anything about him other than that he was a tall, charming lad in chef's clothing. Other survivors have testified that when Captain Fiction was in attack mode, his favorite words were "boring," "inconsequential," "dishonest," and "unnecessary." Whatever he said, though, by first praising Tony's work and then dismissing it, Lish was only increasing the leverage with which he twisted the dagger. "Tony was shaken and hurt like I've never seen him," Rose said. "This was not the best period in Tony's life and his perceived failure with Lish stuck with him for some time to come."

The Lish debacle came when Tony was in the midst of a commendable, if not exactly all-out, effort to get his life back into some semblance of order. As he approached the age of thirty he had several interconnected self-improvement projects on his plate. Besides the writing seminar, which had been intended to help turn an avocation into a paying sideline, he also wanted to finally make an honest woman out of Nancy, his partner in crime and one and only for the last ten or so years. Their wedding, in the Lady Chapel of Saint Patrick's Cathedral on September 10, 1985, was on the small side, and on a Tuesday, but otherwise deluxe and traditional in every way, right down to the parchment scroll certifying a blessing from Pope John Paul II. The tone for the occasion was set by Nancy's well-to-do parents, who were writing the checks, but the bride and groom—eager to be more normal and less fringe, for a change—put up no resistance. When, at the reception at the Vanderbilt Mansion in Manhattan, Sam Goldman felt overcome with dope sickness and stepped outside to vomit, it only underscored the gap that was starting to open between him and the couple who were by then at least several months past their break with heroin addiction. You have to feel for Tony. Despite setbacks within setbacks, he was not without hope—or grit. Filling out the form for the wedding announcement that ran in the *New York Times*, he'd given his profession as "chef and short story writer." In other words, fuck you, Captain Fiction.

Toning down his drug use was the mid-1980s überpriority of Tony's from which all the other projects flowed. He was still in recovery in quotation marks, because while he was now staying away from heroin one day at a time, he had entered a methadone program and he continued to drink steadily and sometimes heavily and to sniff or smoke cocaine—a pattern of behavior that Twelve Steppers would hardly see as consistent with getting sober. Tony had hit bottom in classic, almost cliché fashion. One otherwise normal day in 1984, after nearly a half dozen years of regular heroin use, he looked in the mirror and "saw someone worth saving—or someone at least I wanted to try real hard to save," and said, you know what? *Basta!* "Vanity," he explained in typical self-deprecating fashion, had been his primary motivation for getting clean(er): he felt he was too smart, too *special* to be toying with death. He didn't think *someone like him* should be getting ripped off by brutish, bottom-level drug dealers (who sometimes just took his money and then sauntered away) and hassled by the police.

But if Tony had bottomed out in textbook fashion, his approach to his problem was, to put it kindly, unconventional—and in a strikingly old-fashioned way. There'd be no going away to rehab for Tony (or Nancy), no working his way through the Steps, no getting a sponsor. "He thought AA was for idiots," chef David McMillan, who got sober in 2017, said to me. "He thought you had to do it on your own—you have to white-knuckle it." Tony actually believed that his problems with drugs and alcohol stemmed from a "character flaw," a term that for the last eighty years or so has usually been used to explain what a predilection toward addiction *isn't.* At the unidentified support group meeting that he dropped in on in the 2014 Massachusetts episode of *Parts Unknown*, he said, "There was some dark genie inside me that I very much hesitate to call a disease that led me to dope." The dark genie theory of drug dependency went out with the bubonic plague—but Tony was stubborn. He had always balked at being told what to do, especially when it involved accepting the conventional wisdom.

Over the years he did show up now and then at Narcotics Anonymous meetings, but his behavior there could be distracting. A woman friend of his who accompanied him to several NA meetings in New York City told me, "When he got up to speak, he always sucked the oxygen out of the room. Partly that was because he was famous by then, but part of it was because instead of baring his soul the way that other speakers did, he would challenge what was being said. He certainly didn't want to hear talk about alcohol and how it related to drug addiction—he felt very strongly that drinking was a separate issue. Tony didn't have the humility and gratitude part down. There was always a feeling of thinly veiled anger whenever he spoke—and in the program you often hear that behind anger there is fear."

Tony's bullshit detector would later become almost as famous as he did—but having such a good one is both a blessing and a curse. What may have made him so agitated in and outside of meetings was the fear that he was telling himself a lie when he insisted that he knew better than some smoke-filled roomful of addicts how drugs and alcohol might or might not be making his life unmanageable. He would live with this internal conflict for the rest of his life, but the realization that he was bullshitting himself about addiction, I suspect, may have started to nag him in the mid-1980s after he'd given up heroin but was still (he couldn't have helped but notice) crawling around the floor of his apartment, picking up dust and paint chips and hopefully some spilled cocaine and desperately stuffing it all into his crack pipe. Or it may have occurred to him that most other people did not, like him, travel to a brightly lit room several times each week to pee into one kind of container or another while a bored-looking man stood by watching.

Also from the juvenilia file:

First he makes me piss in a test tube. Then he tells me to roll up my sleeves so he can examine my arms. We go to his office, where my file, a biography in milligrams and pay stubs, is laid open on his desk, next to my wife's.

He asks me if the methadone is holding. His eyes are what my father would call "glass-bunny eyes." He smiles, an insincere, stupid-Buddha grin, and assures me that should I become "uncomfortable," an increase in dosage would be no problem.

My wife is at the head of the line. She is being medicated, stirring the bright orange jungle juice in her clear plastic cup with a wood swizzle stick. She opens her bottles and tops them off with more orange drink from a pitcher on the counter.

My legs hurt and I'm late for work but I don't mind waiting. My wife waits for me in a chair by the "urine desk." I watch, as one at a time, the punctured, bruised, and puffy bodies ahead of me step to the counter and lick and slurp down every drop of sweet, chalky narcotic from their cups. Most will sell their bottles on the street, and join other lines, for preferred brands.

The nurse doesn't look at me as she hands me the clipboard. She doesn't like me, or my wife; all those wasted advantages. Mostly the clothes. My wife is wearing her pearls; and, today, armed for a morning sales meeting, she's in a tweed suit from Sak's.

I sign the clipboard and the nurse gives me my thirty milligrams. She shows me the diskettes in the bottom of the cup and adds the boiling water. The orange tabs swell up. For a second, they look like those Japanese pills, the ones that turn into animals or flowers.

I don't add any juice to my bottles. I like how they feel, warm and comforting in my pocket. My wife and I walk to the subway. We smirk and giggle like naughty children.

When I finish work I walk over to 49th and 9th. It's not the heroin I want. I just like to sit for a while on my stoop and watch.

My counselor calls it "drug-seeking behavior." But he admits I've been good.

Today, I sit, presently unpunctured, stabilized by the state, but hungry still. Hungry now.

There is beauty in this secret choreography. There is music for me in the whistles, the cries, the whispered Spanish.

I alone, the exiled prince on my stoop, can hear them. Protected by the bottles in my pocket, exempt from the call to prayer that tugs my players on.

These are my treasures. These sounds, this endless dance, is for me alone. You can't see it. You couldn't afford it. You wouldn't. My former colleagues are a very exclusive group.

I watch Aztec faces and jailhouse smiles, the handoff, the score, the baiting and switching, the dropping of dimes, dummy bags for dumb customers, the whines, the fear, the realization, as another one goes over the roof.

Better, right? This is a hyrid sketch that mixes eras—Tony was already off methadone and separated from Nancy when he was living on West 49th Street—but otherwise seems to stay close to the facts. Nonfiction would always be his strong suit.

Chapter 10

As we work our way back around to April 12, 1999—the last day Tony woke up in his big, dusty Riverside Drive apartment wondering, as he smoked a Marlboro and stared at the ceiling, as was his early-morning wont, which massive chunk of capitalism would sooner or later come crashing down on him: the health care system, the credit card industry, or the federal government—I should tell you about a conversation I had with Pino Luongo, a prominent New York restaurateur of a generation or so ago, in the course of researching this book. I reached out to Luongo because he had hired and fired Tony in 1996 and partly for doing so had been awarded a chapter of his own in *Kitchen Confidential*, seventeen somewhat fraught pages in which I thought you could see Tony working out some things about himself. Would Luongo mind talking to me a bit about his old and now departed friend (for they had in fact remained on good terms despite what must have been for Tony an especially ego-bruising dismissal)? I asked in an email. Luongo's response was quick and positive. He'd be happy to meet, he said, and invited me to come by his current place, Coco Pazzo, on the corner of Prince and Thompson, in SoHo, on either of two afternoons the following week. I could somehow sense there was at least a drink in it for me on top of anything I might learn (and I was right about that). But he also added, with seeming innocence, "It sounds strange, you calling him Tony. I never did and no one that I know did it."

When I read that, it made me laugh. From what I'd heard, this was classic Pino Luongo: three short sentences, one that promises warmth and generosity followed by a second and third meant to inform me that I hadn't done my homework and that I was woefully ignorant of my own subject, at least compared to him. I thought I had already set, or rather acknowledged, the terms of our relationship in my request for an audience, saying how grateful I'd be for a bit of his time. But he had nevertheless instinctively shot out a straight left, the way prizefighters will in the opening round, not so much to inflict pain but to establish status. Had this been the beginning of an actual relationship with Luongo, say as his employee, I'm sure it would have been the start of something bigger; and before I knew it I'd be like many of the other people who'd been part of his once potent empire: afraid to answer the phone because it might be him, the man Tony called the "Prince of New York Restaurant Darkness." In *KC*, he tells a story about an old Vassar friend who, when he learned Tony had just begun working for Luongo, said, "I guess this means that in a few months you'll either own your own restaurant . . . or be ground to dust." Ultimately, Luongo was a boss, not a dictator, and all he could do was fire you, right? Yet, as Tony wrote, "Fear, treachery, speculation, supposition, and anticipation permeated the air" wherever Luongo went.

It took me several passes through *KC* to realize how much Luongo has in common with Andy Menschel, another flavor of bully who, as we've seen, Tony also came to regard very highly. That may be because the differences that do exist between the two men are so stark. Menschel was a brash New Yorker who, as Sam Goldman once told me, was "not a food-smart guy—the only thing he knew about food was that if you were running a restaurant you had to have it." Luongo, on the other hand, exuded Tuscan charm even when he was being intimidating; and he loved fresh pasta, tomatoes, olive oil, and little pinches of sea salt as if they were members of his family. After emigrating at the age of twenty-seven, he had risen from dishwasher to owner of high-end Manhattan places like Le Madri, Sapore di Mare, and Coco Pazzo Teatro by understanding the soul and celebrating the transportive simplicity of Italian "mama" cooking. With four or five ingredients, he could make you a feast and a fan forever. Quite a few people cook like this now, but he was one of the first to do simple grandly.

As for their similarities, oddly enough, the two men, if viewed from the correct angle, kind of looked alike. Menschel, Tony said, resembled "an elongated Bruce Willis," while Luongo could be plausibly described as an Italian one. They also both took abundant pride in their every pronouncement being 100 percent bankable. And they were both hands-on types if they had to be, on top of every aspect of their business; in an emergency, they could fix the grease traps in their kitchens, the compressors in their freezers, or the delivery boy's bike. But most important, they both operated like autocrats and devoted a lot of thought and energy, as autocrats will, to keeping those around them constantly off-balance—even if they had to resort to utter bullshit to do it. Menschel, for example, got a lot of mileage out of that myth that he had killed in man in a bar fight.

As for Luongo, well, I can tell you with certainty that Tony Bourdain was called Tony by virtually everyone who knew him except for Menschel, who called him Flaco; Asia Argento, who called him Anthony (and insisted I do as well); and his second wife, Ottavia, who called him Mici, which started out as Micio, which in Italian means "kitty." Luongo himself called Tony Tony and nothing but Tony in his 2009 memoir, *Dirty Dishes: A Restaurateur's Story of Passion, Pain, and Pasta.* So as for his amazement that *I* was calling Tony Bourdain Tony? I'm guessing that was improvised on the spot, simply because as a person who was demonstrably not Giuseppe "Pino" Luongo, I needed to learn a lesson.

Whatever one thinks of him—and we'll get back to the Dark Prince in a moment—Luongo's restaurants were an obvious step up from where Tony had been just previously, which was on his crumb-flecked couch watching Court TV with Nancy, at least until *The Match Game* came on. Most weekday evenings in those days, the future world traveler and his wife could manage to make their way only from the *Simpsons* rerun that came on at 7:00 to the one that came on at 11:00. Usually they would order dinner in—Chinese eaten straight from the containers; pizza; or if they were in the mood for deli, Barney Greengrass, a longish walk from their place. When they did go out for drinks with friends, Tony fumbled for his wallet or just happened to be in the men's room while someone else picked up the check. "I didn't mind that he never paid," his longtime frenemy John Tesar (who is called Jimmy Sears in *KC*) told me. "He wasn't cheap, he just didn't have it, and he probably felt bad about that." But the worst part of going out was coming back. Their ashtrays overflowed with cigarette butts. Paint peeled from the ceiling. A Christmas tree lay sideways in their dark and never-used dining room for nine months. Although the sight of the tree saddened them, for a long time they could not figure out how to get rid of it without looking to their neighbors like the lost souls they did not yet believe they were.

Hope may not have sprung eternal but it still flickered intermittently in that cavernous sixth-floor flat. As often happens in life, Tony seems to have gradually come around to the opinion that the guy who had criticized him so viciously in a public setting,

Gordon Lish, was quite the asshole and that he, Tony, was allowed in a free country to think of himself as a literary man if it pleased him to do that. Perhaps it also helped that Tony as a writer had always been able to take a certain amount of criticism in the form of suggestions and editing, assuming such things came from the right person. Who knows—his innate contrariness may have also kicked in, guiding him toward the conclusion that if Lish was indeed the nation's most esteemed writing teacher, his pronouncements must then by definition be worthless. If he could focus on Lish as an authority figure, it would be a quick trip back to the laptop.

When he did start writing again, he wrote, as he always did, very quickly. "Tony was a tortured soul but not a tortured writer," Joel Rose told me. "He would sit down and there would suddenly be this *whoosh*—just pages and pages being produced." In a 2003 interview, Tony said there was "an element of shame" to his success as a writer, "because it's so easy. I can't believe that people give me money for this shit." Christopher Hitchens wrote just as easily and with that same whoosh effect, but for him that was more or less the end of the process. In Tony's case it was just the start. It was good that he tolerated editing so well because he often needed a good bit of it. He would write in a spasm of creativity and then move on to other things, as he always felt compelled to do, letting others—the people who do for a living what his mother did—tidy up after him. Ruth Reichl, when she was the editor of *Gourmet* magazine in the early 2000s, remembers him turning in what's known in the business as a "vomit draft" of an assigned article that her subordinates had then to sort out and shape into a finished piece with his good-natured but sporadic assistance.

Bourdain knew himself well enough to understand that if he just hung around, waiting for an editor to get back to him about a piece or do the slow, heavy lifting or the hunched-over watchmaker work necessary to make the writing sing, he might get to thinking and drinking more than usual, and he was already thinking and drinking far too much. Sometimes his editors had to go beyond their job descriptions in the service of his fire-hose prose. Rose told me he wound up writing large swatches of the so-called urban historical—a fancy term for a biography—*Typhoid Mary* that Tony published in 2010 (his only book in which a real or fictionalized version of Anthony Bourdain is not the center of the action). As a reader, Tony had relatively refined taste. He often said his favorite American novel was *Lolita* and marveled as many have at Vladimir Nabokov's ravishing mastery of what was his third language ("the language of my first governess in St. Petersburg, circa 1903, a Miss Rachel Home"). But when composing fiction Tony aimed at a wider, less discriminating audience, if only because, he said, he was getting up to work in the predawn hours and "I never had the time to sit there in my garret, you know, writing unpublished novels. . . . I just did not have the luxury or the burden of a lot of time to sit around and contemplate the mysteries of the universe." He was, after all, the son and grandson of men who together had lived a not-so-grand total of eighty-three years.

The clock in Tony's head ticked louder after he began cooking at Formerly Joe's in 1987. The place was indeed beneath him, or should have been at that point in his career, yet in retrospect it seems inevitable that he would work his way back into Andy Menschel's orbit. In *KC*, Tony says, without ever mentioning the name of the restaurant, that Bigfoot called to offer him a job as the lunch chef when he first opened the place. This is a case of Tony misremembering or, more likely, neatening things up for sake of the narrative. In reality he was the second chef at Formerly Joe's following a man named Alex who, according to ex-waitress Debbie Praver, was "short, heavyset, and good-natured—so exactly the opposite of Tony in every way."

Eggshells were frequently mentioned when I asked his old Formerly Joe's colleagues how approachable Tony was in those days. Praver, now a stand-up comic, said, "I always got the distinct feeling that I should not speak to him until he spoke to me." When he first showed up for work there, the initial impression he gave was of someone who was emaciated, jumpy, and hard used by life, a somewhat sad figure but a not uncommon sight in the restaurant business. At what amounted to his job interview, he'd asked to borrow $25 from his once and future boss and Menschel had responded by peeling off $200 from his wad—an act that made Tony think that he now couldn't spend the money on crack, as he'd originally intended, and so made him grouchy. Menschel, a master of mind games as well as the placement of salted snacks, no doubt delighted in messing with Tony by giving him the extra cash and thought he'd be interesting to have around again after a ten-year hiatus.

Tony was exceedingly easy to mess with in those days, when his mind roiled with a combination of creativity and resentment, and he seemed to suffer from at least a mild case of graphomania, a compulsion to write. In this latter sense—and in a few others, too, his drinking, his carelessness about his health—he had come to resemble an elongated version of perhaps the ultimate New York character, Joe Gould. Gould, who was made famous by the journalist Joseph Mitchell in the *New Yorker*, spent his life scribbling what he called *The Oral History of Our Time* in a series of dime-store composition books. Tony also always had a notebook which "he was always furiously writing and drawing in while standing in the kitchen or at the bar," Praver said. "The sheer amount of words, the density of the *ink* in those books told you something about the state of his brain." He had more ideas than the notebooks could handle. In his frequent downtime, Tony would grab a bouquet of markers and fill the kitchen whiteboard—where the daily specials would normally be listed—with the kind of gory comic-book images he'd been producing since high school: elaborate scenes of violent car wrecks and execution-style beheadings that would ingeniously incorporate a slab of bloody meat that he'd placed on a shelf at the bottom of the board. "It was never clear if his whiteboard art was supposed to be funny or scary," another waitress from that era, Lisa Wheeler, now a fitness instructor, told me, "but it did upset some people." On the one occasion when a coworker summoned the courage to erase his tableau du jour he got quite angry—and almost certainly not for the first time that day.

There were always two sides to Tony when he worked at Formerly Joe's. Praver told me that she remembers saying to someone, "Years from now we're going to open the *New York Times* and see something about Tony—either that he's become very successful or that he's a serial killer." His warm, witty, and enthusiastic aspect—

At Formerly Joe's.

the Tony that so many people described to me when they argued against the assumption that he was depressed—was often in evidence. On most days, after his hangover had subsided sufficiently, he had a ready and mesmerizing line of book or movie chat for the all-female waitstaff, with whom he had the ability to engage in intense discussion without ever seeming the least bit flirtatious. "I was struck by the fact that he would frequently mention his wife," Praver told me. "That made me feel like he was a good guy; but, to be honest, at the same time it also made me wonder who in the world would marry this man because, honestly, he was *a lot*."

It didn't take much to bring out the Mr. Hyde in him: a customer sending back a steak for being a bit too rare would do the trick. "Table five would like you to put just a *teeny-weeny* bit more heat on this," a waitress would say with disingenuous nonchalance—and then backpedal furiously out of the kitchen. Tony was as predictable as a tread-upon mine. "These morons, they don't know how to eat!" he would scream, then storm out the side door onto West 10th Street, where he'd pace the sidewalk, sucking furiously on that day's fiftieth or sixtieth cigarette. In the kitchen, the Chinese line cooks would stare blankly into the middle distance, sipping their Heinekens.

The other thing he hated passionately was being interrupted when he was scribbling in his notebooks. Formerly Joe's could get very quiet in the afternoons—one waitress, one drunk at the raw bar eating unshelled shrimp—which would allow Tony to get a certain momentum going with his writing. "I remember tiptoeing in and asking apologetically for a turkey sandwich and watching him go crazy because he was writing a short story or something" Praver said. "I wanted to say to him, 'Gee, this *is* a restaurant, it *does* seem to be lunchtime, and you *are* the chef'—but of course I didn't dare." Another ex-FJ waitress, the actress Claudine Ohayon, told me that if you broke his train of thought with any food-related business "he would actually scream, 'I'm better than this! I'm a writer!' while he threw pots and pans around." Ohayon and others did stress that even when Tony, in the midst of an "impassioned outburst," ordered a coworker to leave his kitchen immediately it was clear he wasn't angry at *them.* "It was more like he was mad at the universe, shaking his fist at the sky," Praver said. "He had these romantic ideas about how things ought to be, and when life disappointed him he'd erupt."

The résumé of an active drug user or drunkard can make for dull reading, even if there is an excess of drama in the day-to-day life. "I think the most boring thing about my life is that I was a junkie," Tony said in a 2003 interview with Bennett, explaining why he never got too granular about these years. The problem is that controlled substances sap your energy, leaving you marooned in situations that you would have long since moved on from had you been in your right mind. Tony should have left FJ's long before he did, in 1992, but—as someone who shook his fist at the sky would know all too well—he needed to be rescued by a deus ex machina. For him that would be John Tesar, a chef whom he came to like and not like and who liked and didn't like him. "I'll never forget the night I met Tony," Tesar said to me. "He had on cowboy boots and a leather jacket and was smoking a Lucky. And I thought, Very cool!"

Tony had a different kind of first impression after tasting a forkful or two of Tesar's food. In *Medium Raw* he called Tesar, "probably the single most talented cook I ever worked with—and the most inspiring. . . . His food—even the simplest of things—made me care about cooking again." The series of events that preceded their fraught relationship began when Tony took a few weeks off to vacation with Nancy in the Caribbean. Upon returning he was introduced by Menschel to a new chef whom the boss had hired to work the dinner shift. Tony probably noticed immediately that Tesar was about ten years younger than him, and he may also have had at least a vague sense of who he was. Tesar had grown up and started cooking in the Hamptons, where he developed a following that spread his reputation to the big city. After a brief moment of buzz in mid-eighties Manhattan at Arizona 206, he sank from sight via the usual excesses. Formerly Joe's, with its limited menu, was a big comedown for him, but then it was for Tony, too. The difference was that Tesar promised to have more of an upside. He would likely bounce back and then some. Tony grasped all this quickly and, to his credit, just as readily accepted it as fact. At Tony's suggestion they worked out an arrangement at FJ's where they cooked side by side. A friendship of sorts ensued—one involving weed and drinking and ski trips to the Catskills—and when Tesar moved along to a place called Black Sheep, he brought Tony with him. When later in 1992 he became the executive chef at the Supper Club, a big and booming nightclub/restaurant/dance hall on West 47th Street, Tony's was the first number he called. Tony now was in a clearly subservient position to Tesar—plating salads and squirting whipped cream on desserts for $120 a night, he said—but he was happier than he'd been in a long time on account of being "back in the bigs." Things would sort themselves out, he felt.

It certainly seemed like karma kicking in when a year or so after he started at the Supper Club his old Vassar dorm mate Gordon Howard called to talk to him about writing a book. They hadn't spoken in decades, but Howard had said many times back in the day—when he'd regularly hired Tony to write his term papers in exchange for drugs—that his oft-truant buddy was destined for literary success. Now he told a story of having found himself the night before at a party attended by a publisher at Random House's

Villard imprint named David Rosenthal and how in a drunken moment he had said to Rosenthal, "Argh, I know better writers than you do!" To which Rosenthal had supposedly responded, "Oh, yeah, smart guy, let's see some." Now eager to make good on his embarrassing boast, Howard, who ran a licensing management company and knew no other writer, asked Tony if he might have a book-length manuscript lying around that Howard could "submit" to Rosenthal as his literary agent. How did a fifty-fifty split sound? It sounded fine to Tony, even though the author usually keeps 85 percent. At least this time he wouldn't be paid in quaaludes.

For Tony this felt like the perfect excuse to finish the novel that he'd been fooling around with for several years. Not surprisingly, it was set in the world of organized crime—which Tony had long felt naturally drawn toward. "As a red-blooded American child," he wrote in in his 2006 essay collection, *The Nasty Bits*, he'd grown up idolizing "back-shooters like Billy the Kid, bank robbers like John Dillinger, racketeers like Legs Diamond, capitalist visionaries like Bugsy Siegel, and innovators like Lucky Luciano." The mobsters he liked best, though, were the ordinary soldiers who did the unglamorous, mundane work of putting the squeeze on hapless civilians via loan-sharking or protection rackets. "Guys who get up every morning, brush their teeth, shower, shave, then go to work at the serious business of committing felonies, these are the characters who continue to dominate my reverie," he went on to say. *Bone in the Throat*, as his novel would be called, afforded him the chance to marinate in that demimonde while recycling some autobiographical sketches of a certain drug-addicted chef and even working in a recipe for the Portuguese stew he'd learned to make in Provincetown. ("He seeded some red and green peppers, cut them into a medium dice. . . . He poured a healthy hit of ground cumin in after. . . . He added the cut squid, chasing it around with a large steel paddle.") Rosenthal liked the result well enough to publish it but not so much that he was willing to advance more than about $10,000 against royalties in a deal that earmarked only pocket change for promotion. Like most books by unfamous authors, it would pretty much have to sell itself and, like most books by unfamous authors, it didn't.

While, as has been already noted, it got its share of hard knocks, reviews overall were mixed. *Booklist* called it "Irresistible." The *New York Times* treated it briefly but enthusiastically ("beyond original . . . deliciously depraved") and—perhaps overly impressed with the author's backstory, or overly conscious of his being the child of an employee—named it one of the best mystery books of the year. But *Bone* still had all the flaws you're likely to find in a novel whose author did not worry much about plot and who in *The Nasty Bits* wrote, "I don't care 'who dunnit' . . . or even 'why he dunnit,' and my tastes in crime fiction reflect that attitude." In the first version of the book Tony turned in to Random House, every single good and bad guy came out alive in the end. When his editor pointed out that so much survival wasn't healthy in a murder mystery and tended to render it pointless, Tony shrugged, returned to his keyboard, and arranged to have one of his main characters die a slow death by deli meat slicer. It's a wonder he didn't ask, "Would you like a quarter pound of anyone else?" It was all the same to him, a writer who instead of spinning a taut yarn preferred to conjure a milieu. Audiences were sparse on the promotional tour that he paid for himself, and there would be no paperback version of *Bone* until he became a TV star. In the end the most surprising thing about the book was how little effect it had on his life. After threatening to become a professional writer since grade school, he had, at the age of thirty-nine, finally published a novel—and all it had led to was the realization that the next morning he needed to go back to work.

Not that work was such a terrible prospect just then. He'd made a connection with Random House that would lead to the publication of another book, *Gone Bamboo*, and he was having more fun at the Supper Club than he'd had at any job since the early days of W.P.A. It was his kind of over-the-top, only-in-New-York pleasure palace, a place not unlike the fetishistic nightspots that the flamboyant Stefon character once breathlessly described on *Saturday Night Live.* Each week saw a series of parties sponsored by promoters who catered to very specific tastes: old-school hip-hoppers, Latin funksters, Eurotrash, fusion jazz freaks, and of course cross-dressers, whose weekly hoedown, Chicks with Dicks Night, featured, said Tony, "towering transvestites and pre-ops tottering around on high heels to house and techno." And all this didn't start until the swing dancing stopped at around 11:00.

Surprisingly—and significantly, in terms of Tony's job satisfaction—the food was not an afterthought in this cavernous former theater, where the main dining room sat two hundred and the mezzanine accommodated one hundred fifty and there always seemed to be twice that number "lined up down the street and around the corner onto Eighth Avenue," awaiting admittance. From the start, a few years earlier, the owners of the Supper Club, inveterate lily gilders that they were, had hired top-drawer chefs who processed the size of the place not as permission to be mediocre but as a culinary challenge. That is why, as Rainbow Roomish as the enterprise may have seemed on the surface, Tesar and Tony never felt like they had traded the stifling simplicity of Formerly Joe's for jobs in a food factory. It was thrilling, Tony said, to buy $10,000 worth of meat every day, to push icy mountains of fish around the kitchen, and to issue orders by walkie-talkie to his far-flung line cooks. It was also cool to have his own carpeted clubhouse on the otherwise quiet third floor, where he and a bunch of

Dominican bros from the kitchen and custodial crew could repair for a few moments on an otherwise busy evening to smoke pot and watch chorus girls change costumes at the theater just across the way.

I got that last detail from Tesar, who appeared to be still ticked off with Tony for "getting the whole Supper Club crew on his side and turning them against me" so that he could eventually "steal" his job. "I'd go in the kitchen at, like, seven o'clock and say, 'Where'd everyone go?' And they'd all be up in that room with him," he told me. It's probably important to know that Tesar has a reputation for being prickly (*D Magazine* once called him "the most hated chef in Dallas"), but he and Tony had very different memories of that era. The way Tesar tells it, he took time away from the Supper Club to plan a "dream restaurant" in the Hamptons and to work as a personal chef for Mariah Carey and that Tony took advantage of these occasional absences to ingratiate himself with both the help and management for purposes of pushing Tesar out. "It was a classic example of how Tony could be two-faced," Tesar said. "I desperately needed that Supper Club job." Tony, meanwhile, saw the situation—and not just saw it but wrote about it in *KC*—as yet another example of how the perennially promising young chef could sabotage his own success. He says that while Tesar was off working in the Hamptons, roller-blading around the city, and "of course poking everything in a skirt," he, Tony, was forced to do double and triple duty at the Super Club—until one day management realized what was happening and officially made him the head chef. After he became famous, Tony tried to patch things up; when he got an offer to appear on a show called *Ready . . . Set . . . Cook* but found himself overcommitted, he passed the opportunity along to Tesar, who wound up doing six episodes. Trying his best to be gracious, Tony wrote in *Medium Raw* that "in a very direct way"

Tesar was "responsible for any success I had as a chef" after they'd met. Tesar is still mad at him, though. The last thing he said to me was, "Don't fall for that whole punk-rock-chef thing. That was just an act that Tony always hid behind."

And the man performing the act was . . . what? Not really a cool badass? Isn't his being no less earthbound than the rest of us a point in his favor? Several people I encountered in my travels asked me if I realized how physically awkward Tony was. "The real Tony was shy as fuck and awkward as fuck," Robert Ruiz of Formerly Joe's told me. "He walked awkward, he put his hands on the bar awkward." This does indeed need to be pointed out because Tony was tall and slender and spoke so eloquently and wore clothes so well that many regarded him as an especially graceful example of humanity. But it's true that he was no athlete and certainly no dancer, having probably turned down invitations to do the hokey pokey or its local equivalent at weddings on several continents. It's impossible to imagine Anthony Bourdain dancing. But his awkwardness spoke of his humanity and in doing so only underscored the metaphorical distance he'd traveled in his life. When we see him on TV, his success seems inevitable, but in reality it wasn't; things could have gone a very different way.

Things did go a very different way at Pino Luongo's restaurant company, Toscorp, which is what makes Tony's version of events there so telling. Tony came to Luongo on the suggestion of Ruiz. The Supper Club had shut down suddenly (and rather mysteriously) in 1995 after new management decided it didn't need its nightclub operations, and Tony, who'd already started checking out the help-wanted ads in the *Times*, had moved along, with his new friend Steven Tempel in tow, to One Fifth Avenue—which promptly closed out from under him. When Ruiz, who was working in Luongo's purchasing department, called to tell him about a sous-chef job that had opened at Le Madri, on West 18th Street, Tony had been hanging around at home for a several weeks doing not much, a state of existence that always worried his friends. "He wasn't actively calling people we know to pick up a shift here and there and I was concerned about him maybe turning into a bit of a bum," Ruiz told me. "I knew Tony needed something to occupy his mind."

Tony cleaned up well and could always change gears quickly. He had a good interview with the head chef at Le Madri, Gianni Scappin, at which he was awarded the sous-chef job and, to his surprise, asked about his interest in being the head chef at a place Luongo was opening just a few weeks later in the theater district to be called Coco Pazzo Teatro. He didn't know much about Italian cooking at that point, but Tony did what most men do when they are asked about an assignment they are in no way prepared to handle—he said it sounded right up his alley. In short order he was scheduled for a meeting with Pino himself.

Because he was Tony, he prepared by reading Luongo's books. And it went well—he had Luongo not at hello exactly, but at his first "fuck," "fuck" being one of Luongo's own favorite words, or so he told me in the course of our chat. "From the start Tony could make me laugh," Luongo said. "He had a routine about clearing the grease traps in the kitchen that was worthy of George Carlin. We spoke about the industry, about life, literature. I knew that if the chef's job didn't work out I would at least have someone I could talk to." In the cook-off Luongo staged for the final candidates, Tony in *KC* says he sealed the deal for his promotion by making grilled bluefish, never a popular New York menu item but a staple of Tuscan home cooking and a fish that Luongo mentioned often in his books. The way Luongo remembers it, though, Tony won the day with raviolini of brandade, a Provençal dish made of pureed salt cod, potatoes, and olive oil. He assured me he would never be impressed by "a piece of fucking bluefish."

In the end, Tony lasted only two or three weeks. "I was in way over my head—and we're not even talking about my relative ignorance of the cuisine," Tony said. What did him in, he noted, was the toxic politics—the constant maneuvering, occasional backstabbing, and self-abasement performed in the service of a man who, as he said in *Kitchen Confidential*, scared everyone by making "punishment for failure so sudden and final." Luongo, when I talked with him, dismissed that idea and said Tony's one and only problem in the end was that he was not equipped to be the head chef. "I came in one night at the dinner rush and, well, it had been bad before, but this night there was no food on any table," Luongo told me. "I went into the kitchen and Tony was back there with a cigarette dangling out of his mouth, cursing at the cooks. A little while later I took him for a walk around the block and told him that it wasn't working out, though we both knew that already. I brought him back in and we split a bottle of wine and parted as friends." By then everyone on the staff sensed what was coming. Tony says he lost eleven pounds while working seventeen hours a day, seven days a week at Coco Pazzo Teatro and by the end hated the director of human resources so intensely (for pretending that the business was not built on the backs of underpaid and undocumented Ecuadorians) that he dreamed of "smacking her stupid face with a pepper-mill." He said in *KC* that he was fired not by Luongo but by the general manager, who had tried, unsuccessfully, to ease him into a job as chef de cuisine. Whatever happened, Tony absorbed a severe blow to his self-image. He had always thought of himself as a strong second-tier chef who made up for what he lacked in culinary creativity by keeping any kitchen you put him in running smoothly. Here his skills as an organizer and expediter seemed to have deserted him—and Ruiz says he knows why: because he was psyched out by Luongo before he began. "That was the first and last time I saw Tony intimidated."

He had learned something, at least, about the power of fear.

PART THREE

What scratches others tears me to pieces.

—GUSTAVE FLAUBERT

As far back as 2003 Bourdain said "I harbor impure thoughts" about the Italian actress Asia Argento (at the 2017 Creative Arts Emmy Awards), but they didn't meet and begin their troubled relationship until 2016, on the set of *Parts Unknown*.

Chapter 11

For José de Meirelles, the co-owner of Brasserie Les Halles, Monday, April 12, 1999, began with a 6:00 a.m. phone call, always an unsettling thing. It was his night porter saying excitedly in rough English that there was a truck (or maybe trucks) parked in front of the restaurant on Park Avenue South. "What do you mean?" Meirelles asked. "What kind of truck?" When he hung up he was sure that the place he'd owned since 1990 with his partner Philippe Lajaunie was on fire. Since he lived only a few blocks away, he was able to hurry over on foot, sniffing the air as he trotted. The truck turned out to be not red but blue and white and festooned with the logo of WABC *Eyewitness News*. Its crew was mostly on the sidewalk by then, mingling with other media sorts, some of whom had arrived truckless but with plenty of gear and crew. "I'm the owner of the restaurant—what's going on?" Meirelles asked them. "Is something wrong?" Suddenly a strobe light went on and a microphone was thrust in his face. "Is it true that you recycle the bread and butter?" a reporter asked. "Why is it that when someone orders their steak well-done," said another, "you give him a piece of gristle or sometimes meat that has fallen on the floor?" And of course: "Is it really so dangerous to order fish on a Monday?"

April 12, 1999, was the day that the issue of the *New Yorker* that contained Tony's article "Don't Eat Before Reading This: A New York Chef Spills Some Trade Secrets" hit the newsstands—and based on the response to the advance copies distributed by the Condé Nast publicists over the preceding weekend, it was already promising to be the most talked about food piece in the magazine in twenty years. In those days before social media, when a magazine or even a newspaper article struck a chord, it could quickly become topic A. The New York media on that April 12 seemed to have no business more important than the bread, butter, and fish at Brasserie Les Halles. As morning turned to afternoon the ABC truck would be joined by vehicles and camera crews from at least ten other New York TV and radio stations. Virtually every inbound Les Halles employee would be pounced upon and interrogated about the restaurant's sanitary and ethical standards. Dozens of men and women on the street were asked if they would ever dine out again, knowing what the reporter had just told them about modern restaurant practices. Then at about 4:00 p.m., the author himself arrived—looking decidedly telegenic, thank goodness—and the frenzy kicked into a higher gear.

For the owners of Les Halles it was at first a puzzling moment. Meirelles and Lajaunie spent the day worrying that one cold-hearted New York City commission or another would close their place down and maybe their satellite branches in DC, Miami, and Tokyo, as well. Business had been pretty good of late—was this a sudden reversal of fortune? They had known that Tony Bourdain had an article of some sort coming out and that it concerned the restaurant business, but beyond that they hadn't discussed it much. They had found out about the piece two weeks earlier, at the same time everyone else who worked at Les Halles, when, about a half hour before the dinner shift, Tony said he had an announcement to make. Then, with that original smile of his stretched wide, he took from his wallet and held aloft a $10,000 check from the *New Yorker*, turning this way and that like the Wimbledon winner showing off his trophy. It was the most money he'd ever gotten for a piece of writing, he'd said, and in fact the most ever he'd ever had at one time in his life. And then he said, in response to the applause, "I'm gonna buy everybody a drink!"

The whole thing was kind of ridiculous, he felt. Tony had knocked out the piece almost as an afterthought after finishing his second novel, *Gone Bamboo*, and finding himself, as writers sometimes say, still "in the zone." And since he was Tony, it didn't take him long to complete. He'd been jotting notes for an Orwellian insider's account of the restaurant business since his days at the W.P.A. in the early 1980s, and so he'd had it organized in his head and didn't have to do any original research. He'd never thought it would amount to much, and when he finished it, he still didn't. He saw the potential audience as cooks, dishwashers, busboys, waiters, and the like, not regular restaurant customers who might be interested in what happens to the food they eat before it reaches their plates. He thought so little of the article, in fact, that he sent it first to the *New York Press*, which gave itself away in street corner boxes and paid its freelancers next to nothing. The little alternative weekly seems to have received it warmly, promised to send him $100 upon publication, but then sat on it for months. Tony apparently forgot about the article for a while himself, but then one night while sitting at home and stewing about life in general, as he was wont to do in those days, he suddenly felt underappreciated by the *Press*. "In a moment of drunken, late-night hubris, I said, you know, 'Fuck it—I'm taking the piece back—and I stuffed it in an envelope and sent it to the *New Yorker*," he said later. That was his story, anyway, and he stuck with it even though it wasn't exactly the truth.

What he didn't want to say publicly was that it was his mother,

Gladys, who had gotten the piece published in the much classier magazine. We don't know all the details, but she had seen the article and thought it good enough to put into the hands of Esther B. Fein, a *New York Times* colleague and the wife of the *New Yorker*'s editor, David Remnick. "My son has written something," she said, "and maybe you could pass it along to your husband." (Her tone, Remnick later said, was "apologetic.") When you're the editor of the *New Yorker*, or even his wife, people press manuscripts into your hands, or your email stream, all the time; but in this case Fein accepted it with a smile and that very night passed it along to her husband, saying, "Just be polite to Ms. Bourdain."

After Tony became famous Remnick was often asked to tell the story and he seemed to enjoy remembering it. "I opened the envelope with no expectations whatever and I immediately found myself entertained and riveted by [the piece]," he said, noting "you never know, good writing, where it's going to come from." He said he found Tony's stories about restaurant life "funny, a little gross," especially when it came to accounts of workers having sex in the kitchen, but that was okay "because the picture he painted of life inside a restaurant was so electrifying." He couldn't wait to let Tony know how he felt. "Any editor will tell you that the best thing about the job is saying 'yes'—it's calling someone up who's not used to it and saying, 'I want to publish your piece," Remnick would eventually reach Tony during the dinner hour at Les Halles, perhaps because his home phone had been turned off for lack of payment. Later when Tony was asked what he remembered best about the call he said, "I was . . . fileting a salmon."

Tony didn't have room in "Don't Eat Before Reading This" to sketch the colorful behind-the-scenes characters, like Bigfoot, Luongo, Steven Tempel, Adam Real-Last-Name-Unknown, and Jimmy Sears, who would help make *Kitchen Confidential* such a success, but in the space of about 2,700 words he managed to convey a good deal about his attitude toward professional cooking and hit all the tetchy talking points that would make him first a bestselling author and then a sought-after talk show guest. He decried sanctimonious vegetarians, incurable brunchers, and the indescribably annoying "can I have that well-done?" crowd; he waxed empathetic about the kitchen being "the last refuge of the misfit" and argued for the objective superiority of pork over chicken, all while giving the tantalizing impression that he was spilling more beans about the business than—if you look closely and subtract the revelations that he would eventually have to walk back, like the don't order fish on Monday thing—he actually was.

While he doesn't provide all that many biographical details in the article, he does let us know, via references to things like "royal navies of Napoleonic times," Orwell, Balanchine, and Hezbollah that he is the perfect docent for a *New Yorker* reader curious about what happens on the other side of the swinging doors. But was Tony really capable of producing *New Yorker*–quality prose? He said that the editors there barely touched his manuscript. That of course is what all writers will tell you, and Tony was already known in some quarters for his fast-and-dirty composition style. It certainly seems that Remnick, or someone beneath him, excised the business about chefs having sex on their cutting boards, or whatever it was that he had referenced as gross, because nothing like that appears in the published piece. And yet . . . how could an essay so redolent of Tony ("I wanted it all: the cuts and burns on hands and wrists, the ghoulish kitchen humor, the free food, the pilfered booze, the camaraderie that flourished within rigid order and nerve-shattering chaos") have endured much editorial intrusion? It most likely didn't. Tony was not a great writer; he was a very good one. But when you've found your subject, you don't even have to *be* a writer to make magic happen—and now at last Tony had found his.

Meirelles told me that within a day or so of the story's publication he realized it was anything but bad news for his restaurant. "I saw the reservations coming in," he said, "and I relaxed." A new category of New Yorkers, soon to be known as foodies, wanted to experience the earthy French comfort cuisine Tony had described in the piece—and maybe catch a glimpse of, or even have a word with, the tall, handsome chef who was suddenly all over the nightly news. And he was usually happy to accommodate them. The Formerly Joe's crowd would likely have startled at the sight of the Les Halles–era Tony, who was very laid-back and approachable, the sort of chef who mostly walked around the kitchen, nodded, and made suggestions to the harried line cooks.

"His easy take on life and food was very evident right from the job interview he had with me," Meirelles said. "He wasn't the strongest candidate I had because he had never worked in a traditional French restaurant, but he had the best attitude—unconventional, irreverent, confident within himself. He seemed in that sense to reflect our kind of restaurant—and also he made a very good onion soup!" Tony was conscious of how he'd changed. In the last paragraph of his *New Yorker* piece he wrote, "I used to be a terror toward my floor staff, particularly in the final months of my last restaurant. But not anymore. . . . these days, I'm the chef de cuisine of a much loved, old school French brasserie/bistro where the customers eat their meat rare, vegetarians are scarce, and every part of the animal—hooves, snout, cheeks, skin, and organs—is avidly and appreciatively prepared and consumed. Cassoulet, pigs' feet, tripe, and charcuterie sell like crazy."

The odd claim that Tony seems to be making here is that it was cholesterol and/or proximity to fellow carnivores that calmed him down and made him a more humane leader. More likely, though, he had aged and stumbled his way into the kind of life—no credit cards, no health insurance, behind on the rent, delinquent on his taxes despite having a satisfying and secure job and a sincere desire to be a solid citizen—that brought with it a feeling of resignation that led in turn to a professional mellowing. That "last restaurant" he referred to was Sullivan's, where he worked for a year as head chef between the Pino Luongo debacle and the happy marriage with Les Halles. The place, located in the venerable Ed Sullivan Theater (by then the home of *Late Night with David Letterman*), had an obvious theme but a confusing mission (Was it supposed to be the kind of place that Ed would hang out in? Was it meant to evoke his "really big shew"?) that had kept customers at bay from the start. As business dwindled steadily, Tony had briefly gone back to screaming and tossing the occasional pot. But in the end he'd decided that he wasn't in a bullying frame of mind. He didn't want to make his employees anxious for eight hours each day, like Luongo and Menschel and other dickish bosses, just because he could. It felt quite good to be as well-liked as he was as Les Halles, by both management and underlings. Of course, anything resembling happiness and serenity always seemed to make Tony a little nervous and usually became a way station en route to an entirely different feeling. In time his management style would change again.

The request from Meirelles and Lajaunie that Tony visit their Tokyo offshoot in order to make the food there more like the Les Halles in New York felt like a pat on the back and a gift from the heavens. He had never been to Japan, or anywhere outside the United States besides France and the Caribbean, and at age forty-three and broke as a joke, he had abandoned, he tells us in *KC*, all hope of having any further great adventures. For budgetary reasons—both his and the restaurant's—Nancy would not be going with him and that meant that in his off-hours he'd have complete freedom to wander around flaneur style, get in trouble, learn a thing or two—and, with Lajaunie one night, head down "a dimly lit stairwell in a deserted courtyard" for "the most incredible meal of my life." His description of the ensuing orgy of sushi and sake is as brilliantly paced as the meal itself no doubt was, as well as an early example of quintessential Tony. We feel his pain/pleasure as ten courses become fifteen and fifteen become twenty-something and the rice wine doesn't stop flowing until—with a bow and a polite scream of "*Arigato gozaima-shiTAAA*"—they leave and, after dropping off Lajaunie, he stops at a faux-Irish pub to have a couple of nightcaps. William Blake wrote in "Proverbs of Hell" that "The road of excess leads to the palace of wisdom," but for Tony on this occasion it led to the Tsukiji fish market, where he had to be in just a few hours to shop for the restaurant. Like Ernest Shackleton, Edmund Hillary, and Roger Bannister, Tony taught us much about the limits of human endurance, the difference being his focus on the liver.

The Japan trip started right after Tony had cashed Remnick's check and perhaps because he was feeling affirmed as a writer he began sending neatly crafted reports of the things he was seeing and doing to his old friend Joel Rose via email. "I couldn't stop reading them," Rose told me. "They were so funny and insightful." Rose by then was married to then Bloomsbury editor Karen Rinaldi and they had an infant son named Rocco. When Tony sent him a description of his trip to Tsukiji—he said he'd arrived at 4:30 a.m. to find "scallops in snowshoe-sized black shells laying atop crushed ice; fish still slopping, twitching, and struggling in pans of water, spitting at me as I walked down the first of many narrow corridors between the vendors' stands"—Rose felt compelled to show the piece to his wife, who was sitting on the floor in the next room breastfeeding their baby.

"Read this!" he said.

"I've got my hands full—read it to me," she responded, and when he did, and then ran through a couple of previous emails for good measure, Rinaldi expressed amazement. She knew Tony slightly at that point and was aware of his mystery novels, but this work seemed fundamentally different—and better. "Has he got any more stories like this?" Rinaldi asked.

"He's got a zillion."

In fact it was more like a handful, but one example of his nonfiction was about to be published by David Remnick. Rose asked Tony to send his wife the restaurant piece, and when she read it, Rinaldi sensed immediately that there was a book in the idea. Knowing that he'd be in a better bargaining position once the story came out, she quickly called Tony's agent, Kim Witherspoon, who'd brokered the tiny deal for his second novel, and made an offer of $50,000 for an expanded version of the article. It was a lot less than he might have gotten a couple of weeks later, but Rinaldi knew it would sound like a life-changing amount of money to him—too tempting to turn down—and so she not only came in relatively low but she added that if Tony didn't agree to her terms as soon as he returned from Japan, the deal was off the table. Rinaldi was only doing what she was supposed to do as an editor whose responsibilities included acquisition, and in any case this was only an advance against future royalties. If the book took off, as she guessed it might, his earnings would multiply.

Rinaldi and Tony were scheduled to have drinks to discuss the matter later that week, but before that could happen he had the experience of walking to work from jury duty, turning the corner onto Park Avenue South, and, much to his surprise (no cell phones yet), seeing the news trucks gathered in front of Les Halles and the reporters roaming the sidewalks with their microphones. He instantly sensed what the commotion was all about and for not the first time in his forty-three years he felt like he was living inside a movie—this one called something like *The Very Different Rest of My Life.* All he had to do was cross the street and make his entrance—and without the slightest hesitation he did.

Kitchen Confidential wasn't one of those books that wrote itself. Tony's whoosh technique wouldn't work unless he had a grip on what he wanted to whoosh about. Simply stringing together the events of his life in chronological order didn't seem like a promising plan because, for one thing, he was not yet famous enough for readers to care about anything not directly related to his (rather mediocre) career as a chef—and for another the "and then, and then" approach to storytelling can quickly become stultifying. Meanwhile, and maddeningly enough, it is an axiom of the publishing business that memoirists (and biographers) stray from the chronological approach at their peril, so natural does that method almost always feel when one is attempting to construct the kind of tale that keeps the pages turning. Beyond that, where would the drama and conflict in Tony's life come from? True, he had taken a lot of drugs in his day, but as we've previously seen, he understood that other people's addictions are boring; so unless it was handled with extraordinary deftness, that aspect of his life probably shouldn't be afforded much space. And then of course there was the slight problem that Tony actually didn't have all that many bombshells to drop about the things you ought to think twice about before ordering. How much can you pad out a section on the worms that sometimes infest swordfish without arousing suspicions that you ought to have stuck with a magazine piece?

Since this was his first nonfiction book, Tony on his own was not likely to solve many of these problems, and so the shaping of *KC* became from the start a team effort including Rinaldi, Rose, Bloomsbury editor Panio Gianopoulos, and Daniel Halpern, publisher of HarperCollins's Ecco imprint, who said, "He would turn in chapters and we would talk about how to structure the book. What should come out, what was repetitive." It is to the credit of all who participated in its construction that we take for granted how consistently engaging *KC* is, from the opening "Note from the Chef," in which he tells us how in love with and committed to the restaurant business he still is, to the chapter called "Kitchen's Closed," in which he tells us how in love and committed to his then-wife Nancy he still is. The fact that he turned out to be such a poor predictor of future events is hardly as important as his willingness to lay bare his emotions, to put himself out there and take the risk, in the manner of Montaigne, of being real.

If *Kitchen Confidential* had been a commercial failure, there'd be a lot of places to point a finger of blame. The book does follow Orwell's *Down and Out in Paris and London*, as Tony originally intended, but not terribly closely and not very far. For the most part it is sui generis, a miscellany going it alone in a genre where writers and editors all too often aim to find a winning formula. It has stretches of chronological narrative interlarded with chapters of advice about the purchase of kitchen equipment. It has moments when Tony invites us to cheer him as a hero of hedonism and stories that depict him as a hapless dope. It has a mock commencement address to the graduates of a culinary academy, a chapter about the pitfalls of restaurant ownership, and another about how people communicate in the kitchen—after which the narrative line, you notice only upon the second or third reading, is effectively abandoned. Fairly lengthy character sketches loom up and here and there and threaten to confuse the chronology, since the people he is writing about sometimes came and went from his life over the course of decades. If it hadn't sold, some people would surely have called it a mess. But it didn't just sell, it exploded.

"Utterly riveting, swaggering with stylish machismo and a precise ear for kitchen patois," said *New York* magazine. "The kind of book you read in one sitting, then rush about annoying your co-workers by declaiming whole passages," said *USA Today.* "Bourdain gleefully rips through the scenery to describe private backstage horrors never dreamed of by the trusting public," raved the *New York Times.* Eighteen years later, when Tony died, a spokesperson for his publisher said, "We actually keep quite a bit of stock of this title on hand because it's been a constant seller for us, week in and week out."

Tony quickly earned back the book advance and the money just kept coming. "He used to talk about how back in the day he and Nancy would lie in bed in their apartment and call up their bank to get the automated update on their balance," chef David McMillan told me. "They'd hold the receiver between them, each with one ear on it, and when the robotic voice told them the number they'd hoot and holler and laugh uproariously. Then they'd hang up and do it all again, time after time. Tony said to me, 'It never got old.'"

Except that for Nancy, who didn't care much about the money and didn't want all the attention that came with it, it got old very quickly.

Chapter 12

They landed in Saint Petersburg and Nancy immediately disappeared—at first into herself ("I don't remember her saying a single thing the entire trip," Zamir Gotta, the Russian "fixer" hired to help produce an episode of *A Cook's Tour*, told me) and then into the Hermitage, where she lingered for hours while Tony and crew attempted to get beyond the ruts worn by the tourist traffic in order to see the real city. "No museums for those guys," Gotta said. It was February 2001, the start of Tony's TV journey, the first season of his first show; but both he and Nancy had already fallen into certain patterns in regard to the medium, patterns that would never change.

Yes, he was more than a head taller, big, and gangly, while she was on the physically delicate side; he was on TV while she preferred to watch it—but Tony and Nancy were in many fundamental ways much more alike than different. Though now past forty they both remained strikingly naive about the world—still in need of parenting it sometimes seemed—people who, despite his job and her family money, couldn't for many years mange to stay solvent. "Can you imagine, they came to Saint Petersburg in the middle of winter without hats?" Gotta said. "My first job as a fixer was getting them some fur hats on the black market." He had to do virtually everything for them—rent an apartment, pick the restaurants they would visit, find them the home of a "real" Russian who would cook them dinner while the camera rolled, point them toward historical sites (like the Summer Palace of Catherine the Great) they might want to consider as backdrops if not destinations—even give Tony tips on how to feel comfortable speaking to Russians in front of the camera (especially when the Russians in question were screaming at the top of their lungs, pulling fish through a hole in the ice, and gulping from gallon bottles of vodka). In this sense, the *Cook's Tour* team had very different needs from the Western media hotshots who were Gotta's usual clients, and he says that the prospect of "working with a whole other kind of American" (which he defined for me as "the kind who doesn't call you up at 3:00 a.m. and say, 'My hotel can't get me a fucking cappuccino!'") sounded intriguing enough for him to say yes to a job that—as the show's producer, Chris Collins, described it to him on the phone from New York—apparently had no limits.

In Tony and Nancy Gotta got precisely what he'd bargained for. Neither of them would ever be mistaken for a network suit. When he picked them up at the airport Tony was wearing his signature earring and his signature thumb ring, which combined with their well-worn clothing led Gotta to conclude that they were "down-to-earth" types. "They basically presented like hippies," he said. Still, when, upon arriving at the apartment he'd procured for them, Gotta discovered that the hot water wasn't working, he braced himself for a blowup. "Shitty situations like that are common in Russia, but in my experience Americans are not used to shitty situations and they don't deal with them easily," he said. Instead of complaining, though, Tony said, "No big deal—we'll survive," and suggested they drop their unpacked bags in the apartment and all go out to dinner. This c'est la vie approach to accommodations was definitely *not* the start of a pattern for Tony, who became progressively pickier about creature comforts as the seasons wore on. For putting him a room where he couldn't shower after an eleven-hour flight, a fixer in the *Parts Unknown* days would have been immediately fired. Back then, though, Tony seemed happy just to have a roof over his head.

Gotta took them to a favorite haunt of his, which happened to be just a few snowdrifts down the street. As the vodka "started flying and flowing," he said, Tony, aware that he had no reputation to precede him, eagerly told his beloved origin story—mentioning the descent into hard drugs, the still-dunkin'-fries-at-forty part, the meteoric success of his book, and now the television gig that had happened long after he'd given up on being anything special. All the while, Nancy sat quietly, seeming like she was trying to efface herself from the scene. What looked like a mismatched couple was actually two extremely shy people, dealing with their condition in their own separate ways. As Tony's fame grew, he would have ever greater opportunities to perform away his anxieties, as he was doing that night, and that would drive a wedge between them—but at the beginning of Tony's ascent he and Nancy were, Gotta said, "more like best buddies than a fiery romantic couple," respectful of each other's coping mechanisms and still basically living life from cigarette to drink to cigarette.

But what about the TV show they had come to Russia to make? Gotta wondered. Wasn't there some kind of, you know, *plan* for that? As he and Tony talked deep into the night, Gotta could see that the star had a lot more to say about what he *didn't* want to do—"travelogue stuff," TV clichés—than what he would like to see happen on camera. "There was really no script, no outline," Gotta said. Which is not to say that Tony wasn't well prepared in his way. "He had obviously done his homework," Gotta said. "He wasn't the type who'd take a course to learn anything, but he was very self-educated on Russian history and culture. He knew all about, for example, the *Aurora* cruiser that fired the first shot during the 1918 October Revolution, he was a big fan of Sergei Eisenstein and his movie *Battleship Potemkin.*" It was on the question of exactly how Tony and the crew intended to use this vast store of knowledge that everyone became a bit vague. Gotta thought their approach to making television—which was basically to go where the day took them and rely on Tony or (in this case) Chris to have last minute brainstorms—was "scary and amateurish, but in a good way."

Once the ideas started flowing, they never stopped. At the end of the meal, a slightly tipsy Tony surprised everyone—including, most likely, himself—by asking Gotta to appear on camera as his interlocutor and foil. The fixer—sad eyed, overweight, perpetually unshaven, and utterly inexperienced at being "the talent"—hesitated at first, but Tony assured him he'd be fine. "I feel like I can relate to you," he said. "And besides this way I can speak to you in English and not just approach strangers who have no clue what I'm talking about." The spur-of-the-moment decision turned out to be an early and vivid example of Tony's golden TV gut: Gotta proved a natural ham and a font of valuable info—but it was also a pretty significant adjustment to be making well past midnight on the day you're scheduled to start shooting. On the other hand, why the hell *not* fly by the seat of your pants? Anything a normal professional TV person absolutely wouldn't do was, in Tony's contrarian view, automatically and without a doubt better.

The next morning he and Gotta improvised a corny little skit in which they met like a couple of Cold War–era spies exchanging code words on the public square (clichés were permissible if you were spoofing them), and they were off to the races—not just in regard to the Saint Petersburg shoot but also in terms of an extended working relationship. Gotta would eventually appear in ten other episodes of Tony's shows and occasionally introduce him on his speaking tours before he was pushed away in the end like almost everyone else.

Tony may have seemed like the ultimate antiauthoritarian, take-this-job-and-shove-it sort, but he didn't leave Les Halles immediately after *Kitchen Confidential* made him at least semi-rich. He'd been around the restaurant business long enough to know that success can go south quickly. It really wasn't all that weird for the guy who sometimes came to work, he said, "slathered in TV makeup" to still be cooking steak frites and osso buco because all those one-shot guest appearances he was making to promote *KC* didn't add up to true celebrity. It's always amazing how many people *didn't* see *Letterman* last night. And besides, he had hired a former line cook of his, Beth Aretsky, to be his personal assistant; and with her handling his bookings and all the other details, he could shuttle between his chef's job and the talk show circuit with a minimum of fuss. The real burdens of success hadn't arrived yet. He was still only author famous.

He wouldn't become a household name or face until he got a regular TV gig. Fame, like heroin addiction, takes persistence. But in early 2001 Tony wasn't dreaming of upping his Q Score or of anything long-term concerning television. Why should he be? *KC* by its nature did not lend itself to adaptation (as a short-lived sitcom based on the book would prove beyond a doubt). Of course, success always smokes out the people who want to help you capitalize and are willing to torture your original concept beyond recognition to do it. One afternoon he got a visit in the restaurant from two "important looking" men eager to talk to him about transforming his memoir into a reality series. This opportunity he wisely declined without even passing it by his agent. His way of capitalizing would be the traditional and relatively dignified one: he would write another book that would be marketed as "by the author of *Kitchen Confidential*." It just made sense. He now had carte blanche—or anyway carte ecru—at Bloomsbury; he was a writer and writers wrote books, so why *not* do that? What the book would be about, though, he didn't immediately know. Book ideas had never been Tony's strong suit. He once confessed as much to an old high school friend who had a drink with him circa 2005; but anyone can see the problem by perusing his oeuvre—which, on the nonfiction side, is mostly cookbooks and compilations of shorter pieces—or by considering the idea that he came up with in this case. Essentially it was that he would "travel the world in search of the perfect meal."

Although it may at first seem otherwise, traveling the world in search of a perfect meal is in its own subtle way a truly terrible idea for a book; it's too on the nose, too obvious to ever blossom into something worth reading. Indeed, I would go so far as to call it an unprofessional idea, in the sense that it feels like the kind of idea that someone not in the book business would come up with (and think rather brilliant). If I had to assign it a letter grade I would give it a gentleman's C. But books are one thing, TV another. If you call it a *TV* idea it improves significantly—especially if you consider what Tony looked and sounded like, his status as a veteran chef, how prone to interesting first impressions of places and things he always was, and the fact that he was still for all practical purposes a travel virgin. As a television idea it's a solid A- if not an outright A. But don't take my word for it.

Consider how a seasoned TV pro like Lydia Tenaglia reacted when she saw an item in a newspaper saying that Bloomsbury had signed Anthony Bourdain for a travel book called *Cook's Tour*, which would be about his traveling the globe in search of the perfect meal: she snapped to attention and showed the story to her boyfriend/colleague, Chris Collins, sitting at the next desk. And when they read on together and learned that Tony would be heading out soon for Japan and from there moving on to Vietnam and then to Cambodia and so forth in search of a meal that any fool would instantly know he was never going to actually discover, Tenaglia said aloud, "That's our shooting schedule!"—and cold-called him at Les Halles.

Tony was initially annoyed by their interest in him. The thirty-something Tenaglia and Collins were not exactly major players in the television industry at the time. They were, rather, freelance shooter-producers whose claim to fame was a blood-soaked reality show called *Trauma: Life in the E.R.* that ran on the TLC Network. The idea behind *Trauma* was to tell the true stories of the medical professionals whose lives were then being dramatized and glamorized on the hit NBC series *ER* that starred George Clooney. It was not junk TV. *Trauma* was produced by the TV arm of the *New York Times* and had earned four Emmy nominations, but it wasn't the kind of show Tony watched; and when Tenaglia floated the idea of pitching a *Cook's Tour* TV show to the Food Network he decided they had "problems far beyond the usual lack of imagination." Didn't they know that Tony had been publicly knocking Food Network stars like Emeril and Rachael Ray, that his disgust with the channel and all the cheesy, second-rate reality and awards shows it stood for "was already shtick, part of a stand-up bit that would live on long after I stopped performing it"? When they called back a week later to say they had set up a meeting with him through his agent, Kim Witherspoon, in order to discuss their TV idea further, Tony said he was "actively pissed off. This, I was certain, was a waste of fucking time. I bothered to neither shave nor shower for the meeting."

Tenaglia remembers that when they arrived, in the lull between the lunch and dinner rushes, he was sitting at the bar with his chef's whites unbuttoned, having a drink. Apparently he found it hard to maintain his anger in the face of their flattering enthusiasm, because he heard them out graciously when they described very broadly the series they had in mind and said yes to their request to just watch him for a while, moving around in the kitchen and issuing orders. Tenaglia worried about his height and the need to keep that from being a distraction for viewers, but she liked that he seemed clearly "in control" of his environment. She also liked that he was obviously warming to the idea of having them come with him as he made his trip around the world. In an interview they filmed a few days later in the restaurant's basement, Tony made what she called a romantic little speech about the possibility of traveling the world at his age and expressed his gratitude for finally getting to wander. The Food Network took one look at the heartfelt, ten-minute soliloquy and agreed to two seasons, an initial order of twenty-three episodes, of the barely sketched out series.

And so began a journey full of joy and money and sex and love that he would never come home from. Watching him go, over the course of twenty-three seasons, from *A Cook's Tour* to *No Reservations* to *Parts Unknown*, would be like watching the Beatles evolve from a quartet of jangly mop tops to a fraught little artists' commune that could no longer cohere; pretty much everything about Tony's TV work would get richer, more nuanced, and also sadder as time passed. *A Cook's Tour* was "that earlier, less good show on that other, crummier network" he would write in later years, but at least no one could ever accuse it of being too slick. Not so long as Tony strutted about in a goombah-ish black leather jacket that his buddy Steve Tempel had picked up for him in a thrift store—or wrote lunkheaded voice-over lines like, "If you don't want to go to Saint Martin, you're too dumb to live!"

In the first episode they shot, in Japan, he still seemed to have one foot in and one foot out of the venture. The raw romanticism of his Les Halles interview abandoned him and he could barely acknowledge the camera. He was so bad that he actually seemed to be bad on purpose. "There was almost a deep reticence and a slightly adversarial relationship between what we were trying to capture and what he was trying to capture," Tenaglia said. "Because in his mind he was a writer and he was gonna go into that Edo-style sushi place and he was gonna have this experience and then he was gonna go back to his hotel room and write about it. That's a very different exercise than taking your experience and then translating that for an audience in a visual medium." Tenaglia and Collins had gotten married just before setting out on the five-week trip, in December of 2000, and they had arrived in Tokyo with a feeling of elation: new project, new friend, new life. But when they retired to their hotel room to watch the dailies of Tony failing to be a TV presence; they felt sick. Collins saw a man who "did not engage with us, who would not acknowledge our presence and that we were working together." They both surmised that Tony was using the show as a way to cover his book's travel expenses but that otherwise he resented their presence on his world tour. "It was a ruse, it was him thinking, 'I'm going to double-dip here,'" Collins said. Then, while they were tearing their hair out, Tony announced that he was going back to New York for a while.

"You gotta fly home?" Collins said.

"I always cook dinner for my wife's family, Christmas dinner."

He'd been away from Nancy nine days at that point but he missed her badly, even though things between them lately had been tense. She hated the idea of him having a TV career that would keep him on the road constantly and would eventually, if it was any kind of success at all, bring them the attention and social obligations that she abhorred. It may have been at least partly out of loyalty to her that he was being so weirdly resistant to the efforts of Tenagalia and Collins. The book version of *A Cook's Tour* would be dedicated to his wife of seventeen years and start with an open letter to her: "Dear Nancy, I'm about as far away from you as I've ever been—a hotel (*the* hotel, actually) in Pailin, a miserable one-horse dunghole in northwest Cambodia, home to those not-so-adorable scamps, the Khmer Rouge." He would close the letter with "I miss you. I miss the cat. I miss my own bed, *The Simpsons* at 7:00 and 11:00. I could really go for a cold beer. A pizza. Some chopped liver from Barney Greengrass. Toilets that don't double as showers. I'll call you when I get back to Phnom Penh or Battambang. Love you. Tony."

Those homely sentiments, though they may have pleased the groundlings, were, by the time the book was published in November 2001, an artifact of a lost world. The trip home for Christmas a year earlier seems to have jolted Tony onto a different course. The real Nancy may have been sterner or more distant than the one he'd yearned for in Tokyo—or he may have realized he was vainly chasing a pre-*KC* memory and that he couldn't have both his partner in crime and his new life. The holidays are often a time of dashed expectations and corresponding adjustments. For whatever reason, though, when he returned to Japan, less than a week after he'd left (and somewhat to the surprise of Tenaglia and Collins, who'd thought it was fifty-fifty they'd ever see him again), he seemed willing to treat the TV camera as something other than an enemy, to put aside his them-against-me feelings, and start to settle in with the members of what would soon become his new family:

Tenaglia, Collins, and their associate producer Diane Schutz. For a TV neophyte, he had (and would always have) remarkably strong opinions about the medium and the ways the show should and shouldn't present him to the public; but now at least he was able to maintain a sense of humor about it all, even when the standing around and waiting that comes inevitably with documentary television cut into his daily writing time. In a matter of days he'd earned himself a silly nickname: Vic Chanko, which he said was a reference to "an enormous meal of chanko-nabe, a less-than-light hot pot dish favored by sumo wrestlers" that they'd bonded over one especially drunken night. Now when he balked at doing something that a crewmember requested, they'd say something like, "Vic Chanko says it's a no-go," and everyone would laugh and move on.

By the time they got to Vietnam, the second stop on their tour, Tony was already starting to enjoy, as he tells us in *Medium Raw*, "the new-to-me process of telling stories with the help of an all-new chest of toys: cameras, editing boards, sound editing." As he walked the streets of Ho Chi Minh City, and chatted with Philippe Lajaunie, the co-owner of Les Halles who'd been flown in to be his cohost because of his knowledge of the French colonial culture in Vietnam (and because the team had already discovered that everything worked better when Tony had a buddy to play off of), his research kicked in and "suddenly he was firing on all cylinders with all of these frames of reference. Books and films and things he had seen," Tenaglia said in a 2018 interview with The Ringer. "He had his well. And he could dip into the well. We were all kind of playing with the idea of film references and book references and going to the Continental Hotel where Graham Greene was and trying to capture that."

It didn't take Tony long to discover that the TV approach sometimes trumped his prose descriptions, especially when it came to food. For example, in the book *A Cook's Tour* he speaks of the high-end *Edomae* sushi he experienced on the trip thusly: "Perfect. *Perfect.* The best sushi ever. The best. Far and away. Let me repeat: the best, finest, freshest, best-prepared sushi meal I've ever had." On TV, rather than strain and sputter like that, he could at least show you the food as it was presented, and, at the moment of consumption, let you see the pleasure on his face. But his most critical choice wasn't between print and television just then, it was between the familiar and the unknown, between Nancy and . . . whatever it was that was just around the bend. "She identified television early on as an existential threat to our marriage," he said. "I felt like the whole world was opening up to me. I'd seen things. I'd smelled things. I desperately wanted more. And she saw the whole thing as a cancer."

Technically that's correct but what really hurt her was that he was breaking their pact. They had an understanding, those two, going back to the days when they were fledgling banditos, the real-life version of the kids in *Drugstore Cowboy*, the latter-day Bonnie and Clyde. And it was something like this: the couple that steals horses together stays courses together. Neither of them, under this probably never spoken about but nevertheless very real accord, was allowed to suddenly find religion, become a nine-to-fiver, join the army, or make any other kind of lurch toward so-called respectability that would result in the other suddenly being at loose ends. For the most part this arrangement favored Nancy, who wasn't inclined to work or even leave the apartment very often. Tony seemed cool with it for quite a few years—until he wrote a bestselling book, then got an offer to travel the world with a camera crew in tow. Now, the way she saw it—actually, the way they both saw it—the only remaining questions were how flat would he leave her and when would he go.

He hung in for a while, mostly because the idea of leaving her felt so shitty. Drinking buddies like Robert Ruiz would remind him that he and Nancy had had "a beautiful and rare thing" going for many years and tell him not to act like a "typical asshole," tossing aside a first wife after he'd become successful. Echoing others, Ruiz told me Tony always lit up when he spoke about Nancy and was always true to her, "even when he had the opportunity not to be, like when Formerly Joe's closed for good and we all went to Brooklyn and partied for three days straight and there were a lot of chances he let pass because he was married to Nancy." That was in 1992; I'm not sure he remained husband of the year material in the latter stages of the marriage. Steven Tempel told me about a fling Tony allegedly had with a cute young pastry chef at Les Halles "that he couldn't stop talking about, it was so exciting to him"; and Beth Aretsky recalled that when she accompanied Tony on his *Kitchen Confidential* book tour, it was her job as his PA to "intercept and divert the less attractive women who swarmed around him during the autograph sessions so he could hold court with the beauties," one of whom would likely find herself invited out for drinks. He also used Aretsky's credit card to buy gifts for women he was seeing on the side, she believed. Still he never wanted to hurt Nancy.

After he'd finished shooting the first season of *A Cook's Tour* he had their Riverside Drive apartment completely remodeled in the hope that even if it didn't save their marriage a revitalized living space would make her feel more optimistic and secure about the future, whatever it might turn out to be. But then of course he went right back on the road again, as his contract and by now his heart and mind, too, said he must. He could feel the gears shifting inside of him, new priorities coming to the fore; it was like puberty redux. A novice traveler not long before, he now felt proprietary about the world. "When I'd set out," he wrote in *Medium Raw*, "I'd see a sunset or a temple and want, instinctively, to turn to my right or to my left and say to somebody, anybody, 'Isn't that a magnificent sunset?'" And now? "I became selfish. That sunset was mine." He hated to admit it but he was starting to suspect, God help him, that his show might be *important*.

Beth Aretsky told me that when Nancy noticed him taking himself too seriously—when he started talking about "my legacy" and his show's "mission"—she would mock him for his pretentiousness, and not always in a lighthearted way. Aretsky also said that late at night when the cocktails kicked in, the same woman who could just sit silently smoking for hours would occasionally go on long talking jags that sometimes seemed to embarrass Tony. It would be wrong to think of her simply as "poor Nancy," Aretsky said; she was highly intelligent and very capable of defending herself or even striking the first blow. Capable, too, of being a person in her own right with her own pluses and minuses. The general consensus among Tony's friends was that she had been there for Tony, financially and otherwise, when he needed her but that all she got in the way of thanks was a broken heart. I don't think Tony would disagree with that, even though he was the one who broke it. "There were things that I wanted, and I was willing to really hurt somebody to have them," he said in the *New Yorker*'s Patrick Radden Keefe profile. Leaving Nancy was "the great betrayal of his life."

After two seasons, "important" was probably not the word the Food Network would have chosen to describe *A Cook's Tour*. They would have more likely said "expensive," especially considering that their audience much preferred a series called *Unwrapped*, which showed how things like movie candy and frozen French fries were fabricated in mass quantities, a series that cost a fraction of what *A Cook's Tour* cost to produce. For Tony and his TV compadres, taking meetings with network executives became tantamount to taking one on the chin. That episode he wanted to do with master chef Ferran Adrià, who had agreed to let Tony peek behind the scenes at El Bulli, the avant-garde Spanish restaurant that many called the best in the world? *"Yeah, I don't know about that . . . our viewers don't have passports."* But as for that episode he'd already done, "The Barbecue Triangle"—Kansas City, Houston, North Carolina? *"We sure could use a lot more like that."* And so it came to pass that by mutual agreement *A Cook's Tour* would come to a conclusion at the end of its second season.

It turned out that Tony cared more about not being on television than he liked to admit. Although he was mentally prepared to go back to being a chef if he had to—or perhaps become a full-time book writer—it worried him that Tenaglia and Collins weren't getting a positive response when they pitched a similar series to other networks. At one point, when the people who'd wanted to produce a *Kitchen Confidential* reality series reemerged to express their continuing interest, Tony considered saying yes—until his TV partners talked him out of it. Their argument was that if that show flopped, as it likely would, he would be forever tainted as someone who had sold out and lost; he might even wash out of the TV business permanently. It was good that he waited. In October 2004, after they had been turned down by twelve networks, the Travel Channel, which had been the first to say no, changed its mind and agreed to greenlight three episodes of a series to be named later.

He had clawed out only the most meager of commitments after making, with his first show, something considerably short of a splash. He felt himself becoming the kind of person he always made fun of: the TV "personality" whose primary goal is to remain on television. But in spite of all that, Tony's confidence had not eroded. Indeed, after two years of trying and learning on *A Cook's Tour* he was surer than ever that he'd gone a long way toward locating the pitfalls that lay between him and a very ballsy, funny, engaging travel series. When you talk about celebrities, the subject of imposter syndrome often comes up; and when I asked Tony's old friend Sam Goldman if he thought Tony had suffered from it, he said, "Yes, definitely." Well, then, I responded, so why was he always so confident in his ability to make TV shows? Goldman had a ready answer. "If you read up on imposter syndrome like I did when I was trying to understand Tony," he said, "you'll find it's a two-part thing. Tony certainly had the 'I'm going to be found out at any moment' part, but he didn't have the 'I'm not good enough' part, at least as far as being on TV. He felt from the start that there was no one who knew more about this kind of TV than he did."

Showing their panache, Tony, Tenaglia, and Collins delivered a pilot episode called "France: Why the French Don't Suck." It still needed some shaping, but it was clearly not your grandfather's travel series or even just another episode of *A Cook's Tour*. On the day they turned it in to Patrick Younge, the Travel Channel's brand-new president, the top-rated show on the network was the *World Poker Tour*; and because the Travel Channel really had nothing else that was working—and because, as noted earlier, worthwhile travel shows are a rare and precious thing—they seemed to be running it every other half hour round the clock. The Travel Channel was addicted to the *World Poker Tour* the way the Food Network was addicted to barbecue. It's to Tony's credit that he knew that and nevertheless gave them "France: Why the French Don't Suck." After Younge watched it, he didn't say no but he did use the word "fuck." What he said exactly, he told me, was "Well, it's black and white. He's smoking, which means we'll have to go to standards and practices. Where the fuck are we going with this?"

Really, who *was* this Bourdain guy? Yes, everyone knew about *Kitchen Confidential*, but that had been a couple of years earlier—and so, in light of "France: Why the French Don't Suck," it was a more than fair question. All Younge, who is British, knew was that Tony's previous employer had wanted to turn *A Cook's Tour* into "what we call in the business a chat-and-chew show," and Bourdain didn't want any part of that. So Younge did what network presidents do and assigned executives to help Tony "develop" his project, or at least he tried to do that. As it turned out, the first few people he asked to work with Tony all had too many commitments already, or dental appointments or some other reason they couldn't oblige him, as much as they might have wanted to. The job finally fell to a striking thirty-something woman named Myleeta Aga, who had come to the Travel Channel from the BBC and who knew little more about Tony than Younge did but who found herself intrigued by the fact that "so many of my colleagues were saying Anthony Bourdain was so troublesome," and that the show he was proposing "didn't fall squarely in the channel's brief," being as it was not even slightly about poker. "We were really servicing a very middle-American audience," she told me, "a sit back, sip a margarita, and don't give me too much to think about crowd—and Tony's show was clearly something else."

Looking through the file the Travel Channel had already compiled on him, Aga quickly got a sense of why her fellow executives were running in the other direction. The notes she read indicated that "you really had to lean into a conversation with Tony sometimes because he was so opinionated." Another thing she thought she could see, reading between the lines, was that Tony, however good he actually was at making TV, was getting a bit carried away with himself and could stand a little reining in. For example, he wanted—or rather was insisting on—calling the new show *The Bourdain Experience.* She greatly preferred—"for its multiple layers of meanings and the curiosity it would pique," as well as for its lack of cheesiness—another title that had been proposed by the network's marketing department: *No Reservations.*

A heated debate was in the offing, Aga suspected, when she got on her very first call with Tony—who may or may not have said hello before he started insisting that his name be in the title. Whether or not a star would be born, a dick would definitely need to be dealt with.

Chapter 13

Tony and Ottavia Busia were married without fanfare but not without joy at city hall in New York on April 20, 2007. He was fifty, she was twenty-eight, and their daughter, Ariane, about ten days old. A few months before, Ottavia had been lying on the couch in the apartment they shared on the Upper East Side of Manhattan, watching *Dancing with the Stars*, when Tony suddenly popped the question. "We were scheduled to fly to Miami in a few days to spend the Christmas holidays there, and he'd been planning to ask me then, but he couldn't wait," Ottavia told a friend. "So he just went to the closet and came out with a jewelry box and proposed. I was shocked."

But of course very pleasantly so. "I had never been married or even engaged before. I never thought I'd get married—I loved my independence, but now. . . ." Tony had done a good job picking out the ring, she said. "I hate jewelry, so it was a perfectly understated piece." They were both "extremely enthusiastic" about getting married. "Sure, I had seen glimpses of darkness here and there in Tony, but I wasn't really worried," Ottavia said. "He had been very open about his past, and, if anything, I thought that beating an addiction spoke volumes about his strength and resiliency." Her parents still hadn't met her husband-to-be—that wouldn't happen until they appeared on the Sardinia episode of *No Reservations* a year and a half later—but "they trusted my judgment and of course they were thrilled to become grandparents." As he'd demonstrated with Nancy—and in contrast to the kind of situation he would find himself drawn to later—Tony seemed to love the idea of marrying into a family of solid citizens with traditional values.

Tony and Ottavia's first impulse, after she'd composed herself and said yes, was to think in terms of a small ceremony, barefoot on the beach, in front of their favorite hotel, the Raleigh, in Miami. But the more they thought about it, the more they realized they'd be too busy in the coming months to plan even a modest event, so instead they went the city hall route, as Matt Damon and his girlfriend had done, as Joe DiMaggio and Marilyn Monroe had done long ago in San Francisco. Tony's former PA, Beth Aretsky, the Grill Bitch, told me she was their sole witness. About a week later Tony had to leave for Tuscany to shoot an episode of *No Reservations*, and Ottavia went along to make it a honeymoon of sorts—"the closest thing to a honeymoon we would ever have," she said. They had as much fun as possible under the circumstances but she also got a sobering taste of the future, by virtue of Tony's long daily absences. One day while he was off shooting, the episode's fixer said to her, "I don't know how you make it work with that guy, what with all the women who are always trying to get with him."

Tony was addicted to being overbooked, as he had once been to hard drugs, but Ottavia also knew well what it felt like to have an overcrowded schedule. She had studied dentistry in her native Lombardy, but when she met Tony, she was managing and also serving as the hostess at a popular restaurant called Geisha on East 61st Street, where his good friend Eric Ripert was the consulting chef. She'd gotten to know Ripert and his wife, Sandra, in 2002, when, fresh off the plane from Italy and speaking almost no English, she'd landed a job as a hostess at Ripert's main place of business, Le Bernadin. Ottavia was beautiful, smart, and feisty. She was basically happy at Geisha, but because of the brutal hours her position demanded she had no time to cultivate romantic relationships. Tony, who had by now settled into a schedule that kept him away from New York for 250 days a year, was basically in the same boat. Thinking that they should meet, if only to have a little commitment-free fun on the fly, Sandra Ripert obtained Ottavia's permission to pass along her contact info to Tony. "Like everyone else in the restaurant business, I'd read his book, and I'd seen at least a few of his shows," Ottavia said. "I thought, why not?"

Tony emailed her on Thanksgiving Day 2005 and they arranged to meet the next evening, which turned out to be anything but a Black Friday. "The date was great—we went to a cigar bar because we both smoked cigarettes then and that was the only place you could sit and smoke and talk." They talked mostly about the restaurant business and "he told me about the wild last couple of years of his life," a period when he'd ended his first marriage and, as *No Reservations* become more and more successful, had started to be recognized on the street. They ended up at his apartment—"a small one-bedroom in Hell's Kitchen," Ottavia said. "He still didn't have much, but his place had lots of character and was filled with mementos from all his travels. He texted me the following morning, asking if I wanted to go out again that night. He wanted to get sushi. I turned him down. I was terribly hungover. But then I emailed him a few days later, asking if he wanted to hang out again and he said yes."

After they'd been seeing each other for about three months, Tony invited her to go with him to the South Beach Wine and Food Festival in Miami. They stayed, naturally, at the Raleigh. "On day two we were by the pool," Ottavia said, "and I told him I wanted to get a tattoo at the shop where the show *Miami Ink* was filmed. He said he wanted one, too, and suggested we get the same one. I didn't think that was such a good idea—I mean, we had only been casually dating, but then he sketched a beautiful knife on a legal pad, and I love knives, so we ended up getting it together." A short while later, Tony and Ottavia were out with the Riperts in New York, and when Ottavia raised a glass to toast Tony for something, Eric Ripert noticed that Tony had a tear running down his cheek as he listened. "Oh, my God," he thought. "This guy is in love."

It was good to see the SS *Bourdain* finally steaming into a snug harbor. The previous few years had brought some stormy seas. After he and Ottavia got their tattoos and became a couple, Tony confessed to having had suicidal feelings following his breakup with Nancy in early 2005, saying that while trying to obliterate his guilt in the bars and whorehouses of Saint Martin, he'd repeatedly driven drunk in hopes of having a fatal crash. In *Medium Raw*, written several years later, he told a similar story to the wider world, describing how he'd followed a dark island road "until it began to twist along the cliffs' edges approaching the French side. Here, I'd really step on the gas . . . depending entirely on what song came on the radio next. I'd decide to either jerk the wheel at the appropriate moment, continuing, however recklessly to careen homeward—or simply straighten the fucker out and shoot over the edge and into the sea." It was an odd, complicated, and, by at least one measure, curiously feminine way to approach self-destruction. Men, the experts tell us, tend to go for the simpler, irreversible methods of suicide like a bullet to the brain (or a noose around the neck), while women in their wisdom tend to prefer an approach that's less reliable.

Did Tony want to kill himself or not? It's a good question, but it's also fair to wonder if this flirtation with disaster really happened. As the writer Maria Bustillos has pointed out, the chief male protagonist of Tony's 1997 novel *Gone Bamboo*—the "six foot four, thin, and deeply tanned" Henry Denard—considers a strikingly similar scenario when motor-scootering around Saint Martin in a state of deep frustration about his wife (who happens to bear a strong resemblance to Nancy). If Tony was imitating his own fiction, written eight years earlier, why didn't he mention that in his later book? Surely he couldn't have forgotten. Did he think no one would notice?

Tony's feelings about Nancy were of course tangled with his feelings about himself, but they don't seem to be quite the same feelings that he described to the world. For all the remorse he showed about divorcing Nancy, he never for even one weak moment seemed to be pulled by sentiment back toward the life she represented. "When you have too much painful history with a person," he once told Josh Cogan, an on-set photographer for the Travel Channel, "it's not wise to look in the rearview mirror." His break with Nancy was clean and permanent, their main form of communication going forward being his monthly alimony check. His intense sadness over the split seems to have been mostly a matter of his mourning his own self-image—as someone who would never do the classic, coldhearted, assholic husband thing to a hapless "starter wife."

Paula Froelich, a journalist who dated Tony for about a year before he met Ottavia, told me she believes that "Nancy was the only person he ever really left"—that is, until the last couple of years, when he abandoned almost everyone as a prelude to checking out completely. I hadn't looked at it that way, but it's true that he did have great difficulty ending things (like his TV show), that he'd begged Ottavia to stay married to him long after they'd stopped living as man and wife, and that he rarely if ever cut off former girlfriends completely. Tony, Froelich said, would always keep her apprised of the most personal matters, even though she was a reporter for the *New York Post*'s Page Six. The last time he saw her, in 2016, he took her off to a quiet corner of a restaurant and said, "I met this Italian actress. She's a little crazy." Not being able to end that relationship may have cost him his life.

Froelich was with Tony during a time when he himself was starting to get a bit . . . eccentric. Most of their dates were the normal things: movies, dinners, parties, drinks at Siberia, the dive bar in a subway tunnel at 50th and Broadway. And some of his unpredictability was entirely benign, mere Bourdain quirkiness. For example, while he would have been instantly seated at the best restaurants in town, Tony sometimes preferred a particular Ruth's Chris Steakhouse located in midtown that seemed indistinguishable from any other outlet in the national chain. "He was very excited about going there," a drinking buddy of Tony's, Chris Wilson, told me. "He'd wag his finger and say, 'Always order the rib eye!'" One night when Wilson and a girlfriend double-dated with Tony and Froelich at this Steakhouse, Chris watched his pal holding court in hilarious fashion and thought, "Wow, here is this famous guy just winging it for us and the waiters, but he's every bit as well-spoken and witty as the Anthony Bourdain you see on TV." Every bit as acerbic, too. When Wilson's date went to the ladies' room, Tony leaned across the table and said, "You *do* know your girlfriend is retarded, right?"

But the Tony whom Froelich saw in more private moments was "getting ever stranger," she said, and not always in a cute or funny way. "He reached a point where he didn't want to answer the phone or get the door," she told me. "It didn't seem like a 'star' thing. I'd ask him why he felt that way and he'd just say, 'I'm not good at that, I just don't do that, I don't know,' and try to wave it off." One of Tony's longtime TV directors, Tom Vitale, in his 2021 book, *In the Weeds:*

Around the World and Behind the Scenes with Anthony Bourdain, says that Tony stopped ordering room service because of his phone and door issues, and so, at those increasingly frequent times when he also felt unable to leave his room to face the world, he sometimes went hungry until one or another of his crewmates could order something for him. But what Vitale diagnoses as agoraphobia (and in turn sees as a symptom of imposter syndrome) came on relatively late in Tony's life and was not always present (Tony was out and about in Kaysersberg shooting his show on the day he killed himself). When he was dating Froelich he seems to have been going through something more like a weird Greta Garbo phase. On a trip back from India, where they'd gone to attend the wedding of one of Froelich's friends, the airline counter person offered Tony

Except for it being on a Tuesday, Tony and Nancy had a very traditional church wedding in 1985, with a reception at the Vanderbilt Mansion and cake by Sylvia Weinstock.

an upgrade to first class for the eleven-hour flight, and he took it without explanation or apology, leaving Froelich in business class. It was a strange ending to what had seemed like a fun time, and his obliviousness, or whatever it was, worried and angered her, Froelich said. After they landed in New York, he called a car and dropped her off at home, but the next day she told him she didn't want to see him anymore. "It was the third time I'd broken up with him. I was running out of patience. He was getting too . . . odd." The memory of this seemed to upset her slightly. "But you know what," she said, after a pause, "that was just the way he was. If you told him he'd done something wrong, he wouldn't do it again. What can I tell you? That was Tony."

Ottavia, in contrast, was more like the women Sky Masterson, the lovable lothario from *Guys and Dolls*, references when he says that dames treat men like suits and always want to take them in for alterations. As soon as they started to get serious, she adopted a different and more active approach to the project that Tony always was. She tried to be gentle, because she understood from the start, she said, that "Tony was a fragile person," but the makeover she wound up effecting was fairly extensive. With her encouragement, Tony in 2006 all but stopped drinking and gave up smoking cold turkey, as she did herself. By exercising more, he lost the little potbelly he'd developed as well as the facial puffiness that some colleagues at the Travel Channel had started to notice. In the process he also seemed to become less paranoid and therefore less socially hesitant. His first visit with a doctor in many years happily resulted in a clean bill of health. Ottavia also brought order to Tony's finances. Although his income was steeply on the rise, she'd had more money than he did when they met, and a much better credit rating. By adding him to her American Express account, she got him his first credit card in roughly a decade. To make sure nothing went amiss, she took on the tasks of balancing his checkbook and paying his bills.

No doubt the strictest rule Ottavia laid down concerned prostitutes. Tony had told her that for the last few years before he met her he'd been paying for sex on a regular basis while on the road and between trips in New York. After he left Nancy, prostitutes became part of a life that also included conventional longer-term relationships (such as the one with Froelich), brief flings he might have with some of the more attractive women he interviewed on his show, and the somewhat ambiguous arrangements he maintained with one or two female staffers at Zero Point Zero Production, the company that Lydia Tenaglia and Chris Collins had started when Tony's show moved to the Travel Channel. When he was traveling for *No Reservations* Tony would sometimes ask the show's fixer where he might "meet some girls" that evening. In New York he got referrals from a few of his chef friends who also used prostitutes or he would ask a colleague at ZPZ to order up a woman for him from a particular website or from some other source. Usually, for the sake of privacy and efficiency, the prostitutes came to his apartment on 49th Street between Eighth and Ninth Avenues. Ottavia told a friend that Tony did not have unusual bedroom preferences or an extraordinary need for sex, but she supposed that he used the prostitutes to "take care of normal urges in a no strings way." While she wasn't judgmental about his past, she made him promise, once they became a couple, that he would stop using prostitutes under any circumstances. Based on what his friends and colleagues told me, while Tony did regularly binge on cigarettes and alcohol when he was out of her sight, he apparently for a good while steered clear of any type of extramarital sex.

It's interesting to see the effect on Tony of the Ottavia way. We tend to equate freedom with happiness, but he was clearly much worse off emotionally and physically in the period before he met her, when he was doing and not doing whatever he pleased. As Geoff Dyer says in his insightful memoir *Out of Sheer Rage: Wrestling with D. H. Lawrence*, "It's easy to make choices when you have things hampering you—a job, kids' schools—but when all you have to go on is your own desires, then life becomes considerably more difficult, not to say intolerable." Tony loved his new guardrail-equipped personal life and loved especially coming back to Ottavia and the peaceful, orderly home she provided.

She was still only his girlfriend at that point, but missing her made getting stuck in Beirut for ten days in the summer of 2006 almost unbearable. Tony and his crew had gone to Lebanon "looking to make a happy food and travel show," he later said, but when Israeli bombs suddenly started falling on the capital city, and the airport closed, he found himself speaking directly to the camera about the absurdity of coddled media elites like himself and his colleagues sitting by the hotel pool while "the people and the neighborhoods I had just been getting to know" were "hammered back twenty years." Watching it again in 2021, I found it a curiously unriveting episode that captures all too well the tense tedium of a certain kind of sporadic modern warfare—but there's no denying that it turned out to be a critical forty-three minutes of television. At first Tony hadn't wanted to assemble the footage they'd shot into a show, feeling, correctly, that it would look at least a little self-pitying and not at all like an installment of *No Reservations.* But the larger truth he and the network would stumble upon was that his rapidly growing audience was eager to see him push away from the table and go out and grapple with the world as it was. Even before his Beirut adventure aired, expectations for the show shifted and Tony ditched his tacky leather jacket and started morphing from touring cook to knight errant—the perfect mix of action and reflection. The Anthony Bourdain who would become a household name, dine with a president, and stun the world with his suicide was gradually coming into focus. At the time, though—before the U.S. State Department literally called in the marines to finally get him and the others out of Lebanon—all he cared about was being back in the arms of his beloved Ottavia. Ariane was conceived on the night he came home. When Ottavia told him she was pregnant, and asked if he wanted to discuss a plan B, he didn't hesitate. "No, let's spin the wheel again," he said. At fifty, he wasn't exactly a Pollyanna, but he'd stopped scoffing at the idea that happiness was possible. Weird as it seemed to an aspiring misanthrope like him, everything was coming up roses.

In the scheme of things, Tony didn't really need the blizzard of publicity he got by being stuck in Beirut. *No Reservations*, in its second season, had already replaced the *World Poker Tour* as the Travel Channel's tentpole show and it was still gathering momentum. The Beirut episode may have been an important moment in terms of public perception, but the real turning point, Myleeta Aga, the executive in charge of the show, told me, had come a year earlier, in the first season, with the production of episodes five through eight—Vietnam, Malaysia, Sicily, Las Vegas, Uzbekistan, and New Zealand. That was when Tony finally relaxed and found the voice that he used on the Beirut episode to wonder if "the good and the bad don't wind up getting ground under the same wheel" of political oppression.

Before that he'd been wasting energy trying to prove, to viewers and Travel Channel executives alike, how much of a maverick he was when all anyone wanted out of him was a good story, told from his point of view. As soon as Aga settled the question of what the title of the show would be, Tony started griping about the opening title *sequence.* Patrick Younge, the former network president, told me: "We got this message from him that said, 'The sequence that is supposed to be hip, edgy, and cool is in fact trite and dated and would have been cool in 1962.' And he went on: 'I don't know what ninth circle of hell the creator of this abomination inhabits, but I feel my enthusiasm for this project straining.'" When Younge looked for the inciting offense behind these obnoxious threats and insults, he discovered that what Tony was upset about was the specific shade of blue in the background of the titles and the decision to use digital images rather than the nostalgic Polaroid-type pictures that he'd said he preferred. Tony ultimately won that battle, but in the process everyone at the network got a glimpse of a man whose temperament had to be managed with care.

It just so happened that Aga, the only person at the Travel Channel willing to take on the challenge of turning *No Reservations* into something more than a cable TV curiosity, also understood the correct balance of acquiescence and limit setting necessary to get the best out of Anthony Bourdain. In this sense, she was like Tenaglia and Collins, who were sometimes Tony's friends and sometimes his parents, pulling him aside, giving him stern talking-tos, saying, "We know you're tired but simmer down." Aga actually liked the fact that even in his first few months at the network, when Tony was still basically groping to find his groove, he displayed absolutely no humility. He was someone who, like a book, lent himself to extended study, a man whose measure couldn't be taken in a single meeting. "He didn't talk a lot in our first in-person interactions," she told me. "Mostly he sat there listening, but I could sense that he was not just hearing my words but picking up everything in the environment around him, the objects, the other people in the room, the vibrations that were happening in that moment, and, you know, storing it all someplace for possible future use. He might seem reserved or even a tiny bit distracted, but really he was taking everything in, a stationary but very *active* presence."

You know you're charismatic when people talk about the way you sit. Tony couldn't help but project an aura of specialness. He wasn't just another big ego who needed nervous young people with Ivy League educations to remove the brown jelly beans from his dressing room bowl. He would move in that general direction as time went on, his energy waned, and he collapsed back into the management techniques of Andy Menschel and Pino Luongo, but at this point he was, rather, a man with a clear and specific vision for a TV show—a show that, in his first few months at the channel, suffered from only one problem: it didn't quite exist yet. What still needed birthing at that late date was the fully fledged Bourdain persona, the all-important lens through which his audience viewed the world. Watching him do the final construction on his future self was, Aga said, an abiding privilege. He made the transformation very consciously, with a Hawaiian shirt here, a certain splash of music there, an achingly personal allusion in the voice-over, and an occasional phone call informing Aga that those fuckers in the marketing department had no idea how to talk about his show. He worked both from the inside out and the outside in. He followed his gut instincts but also incorporated lessons he'd learned from movies and other TV shows, often negative lessons, things not to do. "Tony was very deliberately who he was. He wasn't accidentally who he was," Aga told me. When it all came together in the middle of the first season, somewhere between Vietnam (a country that for him always induced epiphanies) and New Zealand, she found herself working closely with "a guy who could honestly say, 'Yes, I know why I'm on this planet!' and she got swept up in the exhilaration of having an unambiguous hit, as virtually everyone involved with the show did.

People sometimes argue about the high point of Tony's career in much the same way that sports fans disagree over which iteration of LeBron James—the one from the Cavaliers, the Heat, or the Lakers—was the greatest. If you polled a bunch of Bourdain aficionados, probably no one would say Tony topped out on *A Cook's Tour*, and many would vote for *Parts Unknown*, but most people will tell you his golden age occurred on *No Reservations*. This was the era—144 episodes, made between 2005 and 2012—in which his social consciousness seemed most satisfyingly countervailed by his hunger for food and fun. "His heart still had a lightness then," Aga said. "He was difficult at times but everything wasn't life and death yet. He could tease me about my willingness to work with a certain other Travel Channel host who he felt didn't meet his intellectual standards, but it was only teasing—and then he'd turn up making a guest appearance on that same host's show." In this first rush of success Tony publicly apologized to Rachael Ray and Emeril for having once suggested that they represented everything that was wrong in the universe. And he was looser on the show, willing to reveal his vulnerable side for the sake of something other than laughs. On the Malaysian episode, being afforded the honor of slaughtering a pig by a tribal community in Borneo leaves him obviously shaken. "I'm trying very hard to keep my cool here," he says, sucking hard on a cigarette after he has driven a spear though the animal's heart. "I'd like to burst into tears and start shaking uncontrollably, but that wouldn't do, would it?" By simply being honest about his feelings, he connected to a broad range of demographic groups—which the industry will reward one for doing. A few years into the *No Reservations* run, when his chef-pal Scott Bryan observed, over a drink, "You must be making pretty good money now," Tony nodded and said, "About four million a year."

For Ottavia, the Sardinia show, shot in 2008, was the best of the good times. The theme of the episode is a family vacation during which she, Tony, and one-year-old Ariane meet up with her parents and other relatives and basically eat their way around the Italian-but-not-Italian island where her father was raised and where she took vacations as a child. It's Tony and Ottavia's kind of place, "a place where everyone has to carry a knife" to hack away at the cured meats and cheeses that the locals keep putting in front of you. Ottavia, who gets a good deal of screen time and uses it well, told friends that she can no longer watch the episode because it makes her too sad to see her parents falling in love with Tony. "We traveled together as a family for those first few years and we were all so happy back then," she said. "Sometimes it was hard to spend hours in hotel rooms with a small child, in a foreign country, waiting for Tony to come back from his shoot. But at least we were together every night." Tony seemed to feel the same. He says on the voice-over that it feels like "I'm getting a bonus round in life, probably undeserved, from some insane pinball machine and the bonus points just kicking in regardless of how I've played it. I'm a sickeningly happy guy these days." The tables they sit at are as long as the sunsets, and filled with people who have become his family. Ariane toddles into and out of the frame. The Cannonau and Vermentino flow. And Tony thinks of death, but in a happy way, as something distant and distinctly Sardinian: "I imagine myself keeling over among the tomato vines in a backyard someplace with a slice of orange in my mouth." As Montaigne knew, the end needn't be awful. Get out your knife, the prosciutto is coming round again. "What do you do," Tony says just before the credits roll, "when all of your dreams come true?"

Chapter 14

In the early spring of 2017, Tony's friend and occasional TV sidekick, the food writer Michael Ruhlman, emailed him to say that he was planning on getting married, and on April 7 Tony responded in this way:

"Congratulations! Love flourishes everywhere. I, too, am happily in love. Ottavia and I are very, very amicably separated while I am deliriously deep in a relationship with an even more badass woman, the Italian director and actress Asia Argento. Google that shit."

Not that Ruhlman could have known at the time, but Tony's brief message fairly bristled with red flags. His relationship with Argento was nowhere nearly as healthy as he, probably in all sincerity, insisted it was. The word "happily" for example was a whiff of wishful thinking that was contradicted by their increasingly frequent fights about how their lives might or might not fit together; disappointment and anxiety were much more common feelings for him (and perhaps for her, too) than serene contentment. They were already at, or getting close to, the point where Tony would tell Ottavia that Argento was "a cancer that has taken over my whole body and which I can't get rid of."

"Director and actress" is technically correct but also at least a little misleading. Argento was a former "Horror Princess," to quote the cover of the March 26, 1999, issue of *Femme Fatales* magazine—her father is director Dario Argento, the king of Italian horror, and she appeared in his *Demons 2*, *Trauma*, and *Dracula 3D*—and her career had not exactly organized itself around a robust demand for her services. Italian reality shows and increasingly low-budget movies seem to have been her means of survival since she hit a professional peak of sorts with a costarring role in a mediocre mainstream thriller, the Vin Diesel vehicle *xXx*, in 2002. She complained, "They always give me the same role. I interpreted every possible variation of the prostitute, the lesbian one, the go-go dancer." The arts of course are not a meritocracy. The fact that Argento, a single woman of forty-one with two children, was struggling to pay the rent in her working-class Roman neighborhood does not necessarily mean she was an inferior actress (or director, though her forays into that area were infrequent and not associated with success). Yet Argento had had her shot at the big time; she just didn't stick as a movie star. Notice that even as Tony fluffed up her credentials he had to admit that Ruhlman would need to google her to get a true sense of where she fit in the film business. Eight months earlier, when Tony had first told her about his love affair, Ottavia, though a fellow Italian, had also needed to google Argento. And when she did, "One of the very first things that came up," she told a friend, "was a picture of a woman making out with a dog."

Argento was basically a B-list actor who trafficked in early twenty-first-century outrageousness. Although some of her provocations seem tame now, she always had a good sense of where the taboos were at any given time and how to (sort of) push past them. Before Tony met her, she had openly bragged about her one-night stands, given the finger to paparazzi, dyed her hair various colors that do not occur in nature, suggested that she was having real sex in certain movie scenes, called former lovers deadbeats and drug addicts, criticized her parents for ruining her childhood, and appeared on the cover of *Rolling Stone* with a large tattoo of an angel emerging from the front of her unbuttoned pants ("my flying pussy tattoo" she called it in interviews). Like the producers and directors that she accused of typecasting her, she leaned heavily on her inherent sultriness to get publicity or just to get people upset. It is not a crime to be a disrupter or to have adolescent instincts in middle age, as Tony himself knew from firsthand experience. But while she also wrote a novel and magazine pieces and released a record album in addition to her work as an actor and a director, Argento had become, by the time of Tony's email to Ruhlman, a textbook example of a gossip girl, someone more present in the scandal sheets and tabloid TV shows than on the stage or screen, a person of no discernible seriousness. As the American novelist Andrea Lee, who has spent decades in Italy, told me, "I think of her as an extreme example of a standard type of woman I have encountered here—magnetic, demonstratively wild, and theatrically troubled; deep into sex and perhaps drugs but somehow tolerated with a shrug as a basically nice young woman gone astray."

But all that changed—if not in Italy, then pretty much every place else—when a piece about the producer Harvey Weinstein, written by Ronan Farrow, appeared in the *New Yorker* in October 2017. Coming on the heels of a similar story in the *New York Times* published a few days earlier, Farrow's article accused Weinstein of sexually assaulting certain female stars of his movies as well as women who worked in the offices of his company, Miramax. Farrow's reporting effectively built on the *Times*' by providing additional names and case histories that he'd assembled after interviewing some of Weinstein's alleged victims. One of those injured parties was Argento, who had starred in a movie called *B. Monkey* that Miramax distributed in 1999. She told Farrow that Weinstein forced oral sex on her in 1997. She was twenty-one at the time of the rape and an aspiring starlet for whom Weinstein's help could make a life-changing amount of difference. Even now, in 2017, he could still "crush" her, she said, which is why she had hesitated so long before coming forward. Argento's statements, read in combination with the others', seemed to confirm everything the public had long suspected about Hollywood's casting couch culture. But hers, even more than the others', was not a simple story, as Farrow cautioned near the top of his piece. The assault she described was, she'd said, the beginning of a five-year relationship with Weinstein during which they periodically had consensual sex and he paid for her childcare (he even once took her to meet his mother). In the interviews she did in the wake of the *New Yorker* piece, the second, somewhat confusing part of her story sometimes didn't come up, but when it did Argento played down her post-rape connection with Weinstein by suggesting that that relationship was purely transactional—one of those deeply unpleasant but necessary things an actress must do from time to time to have a career. She said she never enjoyed the sex with Weinstein, calling it "onanistic." At other times she said that Farrow, on account of space considerations, had overcompressed the true facts of the matter—but that the distortion would take too much time and energy to unravel. The more important point, she insisted, was that she had been raped.

Her explanations were a tough sell in the Italian press, which had been cocking an eyebrow at the claims she made against various lovers and relatives for years—and which at times had shown itself to be smugly misogynistic. One publication in her home country said she had no right to make accusations about things that happened twenty years ago; another said she should be grateful to Weinstein for treating her to oral sex. But initially at least the overall worldwide reaction was more sympathetic. As Argento continued to step up and into the role of feminist champion—she made a stunning speech at Cannes in May 2018, saying that Weinstein had raped her at that very festival twenty-one years earlier, and "even tonight, sitting among you, there are those who still have to be held accountable for their conduct against women"—she was increasingly seen as the face and voice of the burgeoning #MeToo movement. Some thought that she had at last found a worthy outlet for her fierce energy, and perhaps her true calling.

It wasn't her feminist principles that first attracted Tony's attention. On January 10, 2003, he had sent an email to Laura Albert, the author (under the name of J. T. LeRoy) of *The Heart Is Deceitful Above All Things*, praising the bestselling story collection as "an inspiring piece of work that left me gnawing my own liver with envy," and expressing interest in the forthcoming movie version, which Argento was scheduled to star in and direct. "I harbor impure thoughts on the subject of Miss Argento," he told Albert. Tony had probably seen the actress in one of her father's films, which sometimes caused a minor sensation in Italy, especially when she appeared nude. But the film adaptation of *The Heart* would be a box office and critical failure. ("Unwatchable," said the *San Francisco Chronicle*; "Well-nigh unwatchable," said the *New York Times*.) After it came out, Albert would be unmasked as the female novelist behind the nonexistent young male memoirist named J. T. LeRoy; Argento would admit that she had slept with the young woman who had been posing as J. T. LeRoy in TV interviews (thinking until the last minute that she was a man); and Tony seemed to forget about the whole impossibly complicated scandal. He would not communicate with the object of his impure thoughts until early 2016. So although Argento would come to be seen by many of Tony's supporters as the femme fatale responsible for his suicide, she cannot be cast as the *malafemmena* who ruined his marriage.

There was no *malafemmena*. The union that had seemed so solid in Sardinia started to fall apart soon afterward and for the most ordinary and predictable of reasons: time and distance. "Things always change after you have a child," Ottavia told a friend. "We gradually went from the usual great honeymoon sex to not much action going on. We were both tired all the time and also increasingly apart. As Ariane got older, it got harder and harder to take her out of school, and so she and I stopped traveling with Tony. And that was really the beginning of the end of it all. We just were never together anymore."

Separation for them had all the usual consequences, including infidelity. As Tony became increasingly famous, she said, "I started to hear rumors of him hooking up with colleagues and guests on the show—Nigella Lawson and Padma Lakshmi or any other particularly attractive guest he might have on that week. [There is no evidence that he had an affair with either Lawson or Lakshmi.] I also suspected that he was starting up with prostitutes again. It was torture. But I knew he'd left his first wife because she didn't tolerate his new career, so I tried to be supportive." Ultimately, Ottavia said, she and Tony got used to the long separations and gradually fell out of love. "We never said, 'We've drifted apart,' but the feeling was mutual. There was no finger-pointing, no fights, no blaming. As time passed I was happy to discover we had a much better relationship as friends."

It wasn't that easy to be Tony's friend. Although he'd acquired a wife and child, he had little time for other people. As his celebrity grew and the opportunities multiplied, all his relationships and other pursuits became secondary to the exhilarating business of being Anthony Bourdain. Money was coming in, but with Tony it was never the money—it was the ride itself that he found so fascinating. Who else got hoisted on the shoulders of millions and carried off to some exotic locale?—or at least that's how it felt sometimes when he traveled for his TV show. After all, he was in Chile or Montana or Provence only because of the widespread demand for his personal take on the world. He often derided TV personalities whose first and foremost objective in life was to continue being on TV, but this was heady stuff with which no cozy hearth could possibly compete. He could see the love for him in his burgeoning ratings and, now more than ever, on the faces of people he passed on the street. At book signings, female fans pushed behind his table to fondle him. On those increasingly rare occasions when Ottavia was present, women sometimes mistook her for his assistant and gave her messages, suggesting drinks or sex, to deliver to him. Crazy people surfaced—stalkers who couldn't handle their hopeless devotion; at least one carried a gun. Most of the time, though, he was off doing the job that, as Myleeta Aga said, he by then knew he was put on the planet to do: "I mean," she said, "the man was just *soaring*." In its sixth season, the one after they went to Sardinia, Tony and company shot in Paris, Panama, Istanbul, Prague, Ecuador, various spots in the midwestern United States, China, Maine, the Caribbean, Madrid, Liberia, India, Dubai, Rome, and Beirut again.

By now he and his ZPZ buddies had taught themselves a thing or two about how to make superior travel television, and they relished the chance to practice their arcane art. Getting people from various cultures to act naturally in the presence of a New York–based film crew, brandishing all the latest equipment, was a point of pride with them. If they were shooting a restaurant scene or found themselves at a party, they always partook of the food, drink, and conversation as if they belonged there. "The idea," said Tony, "was that everyone should think of these guys as, at worst, a bunch of annoying relatives with a camera, not as an invading army from outside." The ZPZ team also always held their cameras low, below shoulder level if possible, so it wouldn't feel like they were lording it over the people they were shooting. Simple common sense and little tricks of the trade made a big difference—and when you feel like you're the best at what you do, it's fun to do it.

Tony was especially pleased with a procedure he'd developed for reducing his time at each shooting location. Instead of hanging around for hours, waiting for equipment to be set up, he would stay in his hotel room until the last minute, when an air-conditioned car would deliver him to the set. After he'd done his interviews and other business, he'd give the order to "go wide," signaling the end of the shoot, and then, often without so much as a nod or wave, climb back in the car and return to the hotel. This was diva behavior but by design. By swanning in for circumscribed periods he could, he knew, keep everyone nervous and on their toes. Beyond that he could use the extra time he had in his hotel room to write books, articles, and scripts and to communicate with networks, publishers, business-people, and his agent about taking on even more projects. Essentially he was gorging himself on the demand for his services just because he could—and because he always harbored the suspicion that tomorrow all the attention could go away. At the end of the sixth season of *No Reservations*, when a more reasonable person would have taken a break, he instead struck an agreement with the Travel Channel to do twenty episodes of a show they'd call *The Layover*, which was pitched to him as a servicey guide to places he was scheduled to be anyway.

Of course the adrenaline could only carry him so far. Looking back, Tony's great ride through the popular culture seems more Ferris wheel than roller coaster, the apex being indistinguishable from the start of the descent. Shooting *The Layover* turned out to be a dreaded chore; because the episodes had virtually no narrative line, there was no setup time that he could spend in his hotel room and the camera was always right in front of his nose, begging for a Bourdain-worthy line or facial expression. "He absolutely hated making that show," said Ottavia, who despite their separations spoke to him by phone almost daily. "He had to eat so many meals in one day. He was feeling physically ill from it. He gained the most weight he ever gained then. He was so glad when it was done."

But also, because he was addicted to being busy, he was disappointed that it was over as well. Tony's solution to any work-related problem was always to work his way through it, and if the sun had risen in the east that morning, he would drink his way through it as well. He had been a teetotaler only in the presence of Ottavia, and once they started living separate lives, not even then. As far back as 2008, in the midst of a shoot in the Philippines, he was knocking back beers at nine in the morning and talking between takes about how exhausted he was from the relentless travel. "He said all the flights and scheduling was wearing him down," Joel Binamira, a Manila businessman who appeared in the episode, told me. "He said he was thinking of moving to Vietnam where the food was good and life was easier. He was playing with the idea of giving it all up." Binamira said he was struck not just by Tony's talk of retirement at the age of fifty-one but also "by the sheer amount of beer he could consume in a single day."

Tony may have been the most talented travel show host ever to appear on TV, but in some ways he was not cut out for the job. The one thing that is always certain about travel is that it will wear you out; and Tony, as a very active alcoholic, was constantly ingesting a substance that is certain to exacerbate fatigue. It was not just Binamira who noticed how much Tony drank before, after, and while the camera rolled. The English writer Geoff Dyer, who appeared in a sponsored spinoff called *Explore Parts Unknown* that was filmed in Ireland, told me that "apart from having the feeling that I could have been friends with him—something I imagine a lot of people felt—the only remarkable thing about our encounter was that he drank three pints of Guinness, and it was just lunch!" At the exquisite twelve-seat Rakuichi noodle restaurant in Niseko, Japan, the head chef and proprietor, Tatsuru Rai, shared with me his fond memories of Tony downing "sake, sake, sake for five hours." David McMillian, co-owner of the Joe Beef restaurant group in Montreal, told me, "An hour before shooting it would always be, 'Okay, let's crack bottles, let's get in the mood, let's start the party. He had a theory—a correct theory—that drinking made for great TV because there's a feeling of uncontrolled generosity that goes with it, a feeling of all or nothing that the audience picks up on. And so it was that the star always needed to have a certain cascade of cocktails to be in the mood." The mood never lasted, because at some point in the processing of whatever poison one has picked, the body turns the lubricant into a depressant. "I'm so hungover, I

With his second wife, Ottavia.

just want to crawl in the bushes and die," Tony said to Eric Ripert on an 2018 episode of *Parts Unknown* set in the glorious French Alps—but he might have rasped something similar on any morning shoot over the course of his sixteen-year TV career.

The other extra burden Tony carried with him everywhere he wandered was his intense shyness. It took a lot out of him to encounter new people, so sensitive was he to their likely inclination, as well to his own corresponding disinclination, to engage. The renowned sushi chef Naomichi Yasuda told me one night in his Tokyo restaurant that when he and Tony met during a shoot of *No Reservations* in 2013 they instantly recognized each other as the sort of person who understood that they "already had enough relationships," and that "because most relationships are basically one-way," they had no desire to take on any more. "I am a person who has no interest in being part of a community—I do things my own way," Yasuda said as he made me exquisite sushi from tuna and mackerel that he had, in defiance of conventional wisdom, purchased at past-peak-freshness prices at the Tsukiji fish market and then flash frozen. "I am the first and the last at what I do in the way that I do it—and Tony was the same way."

During the last few years of *No Reservations*, keeping people at a distance from Tony became an increasingly important task for his ZPZ travel mates. The local freelancers they hired were always reminded that the seemingly easygoing TV presenter was not, in real life, their friend, and that he and he alone would initiate whatever conversations might occur. "If you ever found yourself riding in car or van with him, you quickly figured out what the deal was," one of those part-time crew members told me. "If anyone is going to be telling stories, it was going to be Tony. He was a great storyteller so that was fine—but you had to understand that Anthony Bourdain was never going to be listening to *your* stories."

Tony was always adjusting the distance between himself and even those he'd already accepted into his circle, attempting to find a comfort level he could live with. "By informal agreement you went with Tony's direction when it came to friendship," David McMillan told me. "His relationships changed over the years and to stay friends with him you had to be aware of what the current mood was. In the earlier times you could say, 'Fuck you!' and throw him in a snowbank and he'd handle that just fine. But as time went on there were rules and you had to play by them or you could easily fall out of favor. For example, you didn't sit down with Tony and ask about new girlfriends or any intimate questions. You had to let him take the lead on stuff like that." On the marathon car rides they sometimes took from airports to shooting locations, McMillan said that Tony could be "a flat-out musical bully. You could spend nine hours straight with him and there was no way he was going to play your music even for one song. I'd be, like, 'You should check this out,' and he'd be, 'Yeah, whatever.' If I did get a song played in the car, it wasn't worth it because he would just rip me apart for my selection." McMillan's business partner Fred Morin told me that after he became a TV star Tony "had to be right about everything. He was relentless. Dave and I are sober now, but back in the days when we were still drinking if we got into an in-depth conversation with Tony about French cooking and we'd school him, that meant we had to let him school us on something else."

Tony didn't apologize for his lack of charm behind the scenes, but he did at least once try to explain it. "I change location every two weeks," he told Patrick Radden Keefe of the *New Yorker*: the "care and feeding required of friends, I'm frankly incapable of. I'm not *there.* I'm not going to remember your birthday. I'm not going to be there for the important moments in your life. We are not going to reliably hang out, no matter how I feel about you. For fifteen years, more or less, I've been traveling two hundred days a year. I make very good friends a week at a time."

His plan sounded reasonable, but in the real world it didn't seem to work. Chef Yasuda believes that, despite Tony's attempt to set boundaries, being Anthony Bourdain wore him down. "For Tony each new episode was in the end like a new job with new people," Yasuda said. "The stress that causes, I believe, led to his heavy drinking. And the heavy drinking led to suicidal thoughts. And the thoughts led to his . . . bon voyage."

Tony had by 2012 very obviously outgrown the Travel Channel. His two rabbis there, Myleeta Aga and Patrick Younge, had moved on to other jobs years before, and the bean counters that succeeded them had started making the same noises—about the inherent beauty of barbecue-centric shows set in the good ole U.S.A., about their audience not owning passports—that the Food Network had made eight years earlier. The real deal breaker, though, was when the Travel Channel recut a finished episode of *No Reservations* to include a shot of Tony getting into a Jeep angled in a way that made its Chrysler logo plainly visible. Tony, as he said in the chapter of *Medium Raw* called "Selling Out," wasn't as fixated on the idea of moral purity as he'd once been. He'd come to realize that like Emeril and other celebrity chefs he'd criticized for their product-placement and endorsement deals, he'd reached a point where he had a fair number of people depending on him for support or employment and needed to think in terms of their, as well as his own, security. (He loved to tell the joke about the man who asks a woman if she'd sleep with him for a million dollars. When she says yes, he says, "What about for one dollar?" When she takes offense, he says, "So, we've established you're a whore. Now we're just haggling over the price.") Tony would be a whore—but only when the price *and* the product were right. He routinely turned down the most lucrative offers, which always seemed to be connected to the cheesiest, chanciest things—the diarrhea treatments and the eponymous restaurant chains. Always he wanted agency in his own abasement. He never got it at the Travel Channel in the matter of the purloined Chrysler plug, but he did get the chance to rail against his employer and to tweet obscenities about the car company—which for him at that time was a thing perhaps almost as good. Anger was in those days becoming his default state of being. He ranted upward as well as downward, at the bosses and at the crew, and always for the same basic reason: no one was capable of meeting his standards.

The offer to switch from the Travel Channel to CNN came at precisely the right time or precisely the wrong time, depending on whether or not you put the life before the career. In retrospect, it's clear that Tony desperately needed a respite, a chance to step back, recuperate, and consider the price he was paying for his success in terms of the person he was turning out to be. Instead he got—deservedly, in some ways—the break of a lifetime, a windfall of money and moral support that triggered another adrenaline rush and affirmed his belief that he understood better than anyone else in the world how to do whatever you would call what he was doing. Mark Whitaker, then the managing editor of CNN, was the first at the network to suggest calling Tony in for a meeting and was delighted to discover that his contract with the Travel Channel was coming up for renewal. "He came with his agent, Kim Witherspoon, and he seemed flattered by our interest," Whitaker told me. "He listened politely to what we had to say, which was that CNN would be a higher-profile platform for him and that we could provide journalistic cover—security cover—that he couldn't get at a smaller cable outlet. We didn't talk money at the first meeting, but before he left I asked him to sign my copy of *Kitchen Confidential*, which he did and also added his drawing of a kitchen knife. I thought we were in a good place with him." They were; a deal for an initial sixteen episodes a year was soon struck. In his book *In the Weeds*, Tony's longtime director Tom Vitale recounts the moment that Tony told him about the channel change: "You can kiss those fuck-tards at Travel Channel goodbye. . . . *No Reservations* is OVER! Congratu-FUCKING-lations, Tom, we're moving the FUCKING show to FUCKING CNN! Can you FUCKING believe it?!?!"

His excitement was justified. *Parts Unknown* quickly became the deluxe version of his previous TV projects, one of the best-looking and most-engaging shows on television and before long the highest-rated hour on CNN. He had more cameras, more crew, a bigger travel budget—and it was all very visible on the screen. Said Vitale: "CNN gave us the creative freedom to experiment as well as the platform and tools that allowed the show to become what it always wanted to be." Having started, in the *Cook's Tour* days, with a half-case of equipment, they were now hauling around thirty cases. Beyond that, said producer Chris Collins, CNN gave them "the confidence to go do that which you know how to do, and to grow it." In time Tony would get to fulfill various lifelong dreams, like going to the Congo to retrace the journey of the mad ivory hunter Kurtz from Joseph Conrad's *Heart of Darkness.* He got to work alongside idols like the director Darren Aronofsky, the writer Jim Harrison, and the cinematographer Christopher Doyle.

It was wonderful and it was never enough. Tony was becoming ever more like Emerson, who said, "I seek the Vatican, and the palaces. I affect to be intoxicated with sights and suggestions, but I am not intoxicated. My giant goes with me wherever I go." Being only one place at a time made Tony anxious. In brief moments of downtime during the shooting of his meal of bun cha with Barack

"Low plastic stool, cheap but delicious noodles, cold Hanoi beer—this is how I'll remember Tony," said Barack Obama (with Bourdain in Vietnam in 2016).

Obama in Vietnam in 2016, he was on the phone with Harley Flanagan, leader of the Cro-Mags, arranging an episode that would be set on the Lower East Side. Does it redeem Tony any to say that he pushed himself as hard as he pushed everyone else? He was certainly getting more hard-hearted. The second time he and the crew shot an episode in Borneo, ten years after the first, he was able to kill the pig without hesitation. The people who traveled with him, the people like producer Helen Cho and director Tom Vitale, who talked about experiencing his "dagger eyes" and called him "duplicitous, unforgivable, probably criminal, and usually extremely effective," were not surprised that he now leaned on the spear so blithely. "You never said 'action' to him, you never said 'cut,' you probably didn't look at him," one veteran crew member said. If you did he might respond by saying, "You're off the show." And he might really mean it.

"It's very rarely a good career move to have a conscience," Tony said. That beleaguered inner voice, though, was not quite dead.

Chapter 15

No one fully understands Tony's relationship with Asia Argento. Some say, "Oh, it was just a lot of teenage boy crap." (I was amazed by how often that exact phrase cropped up), but Tony was nearly sixty when he met her, and no naïf. Ottavia has said that when she tries to explain the affair, which she watched unfold from a front-row seat, to herself or a friend, she finds herself falling back on a cliché. "Asia's power is hard to figure," she said. "I can't get beyond her having some kind of evil spell on him, as ridiculous as that sounds." One thing that complicates matters is that it felt more like two different relationships were happening simultaneously. If you charted Argento's fervor level over the last two years of Tony's life it would take the (familiar, in these cases) shape of an arc. Tony's line would be straight and steep and ever upward. What we may never know is what was hauling him so relentlessly toward the sun.

It was August 2016, Tony, Ottavia, and Ariane were out in the Hamptons having a fine beachy week with some friends and family members when he suddenly said they needed to talk and asked Ottavia to find a good time. From the look in his eye it didn't seem like bad news so she didn't worry. They weren't living as man and wife anymore, but they were relaxed about their current circumstances, as their shared vacation suggested. To hear Ottavia tell it, their new way of living had quickly come to feel natural, perhaps (as ironic as it may sound) because Tony's absences were so long and frequent, and he had such an eventful life away from home, that the impossibility of the marriage became all the more obvious and inevitable seeming.

If there was anything close to a specific moment when Ottavia felt that they'd reached the end of the marriage, it had come a few months before, back in the spring, when the apartment next door to theirs became available and Tony told her he wanted to rent it and transform it into his man cave. Ottavia couldn't help but notice that "it wasn't a small studio, it was a full-size one-bedroom apartment." As it turned out, she said, "he wasn't thinking in terms of a man cave with a billiard table and a large-screen TV but something like a regular long-term space with his own bedroom and living room. He had someone cut an opening between our apartments, so it wouldn't feel like we were completely separated. But I think that was when I stopped thinking of us as a couple and instead something more like co-parents or friends. Tony always said we were a family of weirdos and I can't deny that the new arrangement worked well for me. Eventually we ended up buying a different condo that was a combination of two apartments, so he could still have his own wing."

What Tony wanted to say to Ottavia that day in the Hamptons was that he'd been involved with Asia Argento for the three or four months since they'd shot an episode of *Parts Unknown* together in Rome. It's unclear why she had resurfaced in his consciousness after so many years, but we do know that he followed Argento on Twitter sometime early in 2016, and after she followed him back he DM'ed her and they started chatting. Before long he invited her to be a guest on his show and she agreed—though it appears from their emails that she turned down his offer of a $13,000 appearance fee. They met for the first time on the set—at a restaurant in her Vigna Clara neighborhood—in May of that year, in front of the crew and, in a manner of speaking, in front of the whole world. His fresh haircut and, yes, teenage boy nervousness can be seen in season six, episode nine. So can her beauty, intelligence, and fierceness. She makes a good first impression. In an email to me in which she declined to be interviewed for this book, she quoted Oscar Wilde: "It is always Judas who writes the biography." Like Pino Luongo, she knows how to flick the jab, and in boxing as in life that is somehow always admirable.

Argento and Tony got very serious very fast. Almost from the start it seems that she was telling him about her most intimate problems—that she felt the fathers of her children did not spend much time with or provide financial support for them, that she herself was strapped for cash, and that she struggled with a craving for "Charlie," which was her nickname for cocaine. But instead of buying her a copy of *Dating for Dummies* and then running in the other direction, Tony plunged ahead heedlessly. His emails from this period show him scurrying between the roles of drug counselor, fitness coach, and rich uncle or some might say sugar daddy. When he told her that she needed to get more exercise to occupy her mind and elevate her mood (Argento's mother, the actress Daria Nicolodi, said on Twitter in 2016 that Asia is bipolar), and she said in response that her boxing trainer only came once a week because she couldn't afford to pay him, Tony said, "Say the word and I will put the guy on retainer. I'll pay him to come kick you out of bed and chase you around the gym no matter how you feel. You need a scheduled training (or a scheduled something) that's pretty punishing every morning as early as possible—something you HAVE to do. A routine. Helps me. Don't give the Bad Brain a chance—or the time—to start rationalizing. Maybe that's why I fill my schedule so pathologically. To not give my lazy, junkie side any opportunities to fuck up—sorry, I'm starting to sound like one of the Moonies."

When she asked him in a text for "a good reason not to do Charlie," he said, "Because you will feel really horrible and neurotic and then have to drink a boatload to knock yourself out and will then wake up hating yourself feeling sick and ashamed. And you got responsibilities beyond tonight that will be impacted. Also because I love you and it makes me frantic with worry and concern when you harm yourself or are unhappy. And coke = unhappy. Every time." He also told her to hire a nanny and that he would take care of all childcare expenses (as Weinstein had for a while). His basic message was that it was wonderful that they had found each other and together they could alleviate each other's problems: "We are junkies. Remember? And however improbably, incredibly, living (believe it or not) in hope."

But she does not seem interested in hope—or in listening to his problems. When he says this: "Wrote all morning (which is probably what's making me so restless, morbid, bad brain). Sitting at the bar downstairs. This urge, this need to make shit, to create, to write, to make shit . . . to be good at something. Is this a blessing or a curse? Writin' books. It's a drop down a deep chasm of doubt."

She says this: "You have work. I have nothing."

Tony and Argento had their share of blowups early on as they tried to hammer out the rules of their relationship. Two months after they'd met, in July 2016, Tony rented a villa in southern France where they planned a weeklong getaway, but Argento canceled at the last minute, after Tony had already arrived, saying she was tired of being a weekend wife and would be breaking up with him permanently unless he told Ottavia about her and moved out of their apartment immediately. Tony was very angry and disappointed, and after they finished fighting on the phone he went out to a restaurant and drank so much that he blacked out. This had rarely if ever happened to him (he was known for being able to hold his liquor), and it scared him. When he woke up hours later in his villa, not knowing how he'd gotten there, he was panicky and called several people including Nancy to make amends for any harm he'd ever done them. "He thought the blackout was a sign that he was reaching the end," Ottavia said. "He told me that he'd always felt he was going to die prematurely, like his father had, and now that time was getting close."

Tony didn't say anything to Ottavia about Argento when he made his amends to her, but a month later he was standing in their Hamptons kitchen describing how excited he was to finally be in a healthy relationship. Ottavia took him at his word and said she felt happy and excited for him. There were tears and hugs. In the interim he had of course capitulated to Argento's demands. He would be moving out of their apartment, he told Ottavia, to a two-bedroom place in what was then the Time Warner Center (now the Deutsche Bank Center) in Manhattan. Tony reported back to Argento that he had done as she asked and delivered the news of their involvement; but a few days later she complained to him that she was still seeing pictures on Instagram of him, Ottavia, and Ariane having fun in the Hamptons. Tony asked Ottavia to stop posting family photos, even pictures of just him and Ariane, since being with his daughter would suggest that he had at least briefly been in his wife's company. He said the situation would only be temporary to "make Asia feel comfortable" and that in reality nothing in their routine was going to change. "He told me he would still come to our apartment every morning to see Ariane waking up, he would make a point to cook her breakfast and take her to school and pick her up. He said we would still have dinner together and sleepovers."

Tony's intentions were good. "He kept his bedroom and his office the way they were. His closet was full of clothes. He barely took anything with him to the new place," Ottavia said. But none of his predictions about how life would be going forward came to pass. It was an unrealistic plan from the start, given that he was on the road for two-thirds of the year and that when he was in New York, he spent time on side projects like the food-centric game show *The Taste*, which ran for three seasons on ABC, and the Bourdain Market, an Eataly-spired conglomeration of street-food stalls that was supposed to occupy the 57th Street pier on the Hudson River but which collapsed under the weight of its own ambition. But Tony was more than just an increasingly absent father; he was increasingly like a frightened hostage victim putting on a performance that was difficult for Ottavia and nine-year-old Ariane to watch. When asked by interviewers about the recent changes in his personal life, he would express great excitement about Argento, "the Italian director and actress," while dismissing the last ten years of his life with a shrug—or an oft-repeated joke about how he had "gone to bed with Sophia Loren but woken up with Jean-Claude Van Damme" (a reference to Ottavia's interest in the martial arts).

In September 2016, with the assistance of his ex-girlfriend Paula Froelich, Tony planted a story in the *New York Post*'s Page Six, saying that he and Ottavia had split and were living entirely separate lives. It was never enough, though, because his audience of one needed constant reassurance, and he was always worried about her getting tired of the whole complicated situation and breaking up with him. "When he did come over for dinner and Asia called, he always felt he had to speak to her immediately," Ottavia told a friend. To get private time "he would tell Ariane that he had to run out to the ATM or give her some other excuse and then he wouldn't come back for two hours, or maybe not at all. Or he would tell me to have dinner ready by the time he arrived, because he didn't have time to hang around with us, but then after he left he would post Instagram stories of himself sitting alone in a bar. It was all done for Asia's sake, but the problem was that Ariane had Instagram. She was seeing it, too, and it confused her and broke her heart."

From the start of the relationship with Argento, Tony pushed for them to see each other as much as possible. His repeated offers to pay for a live-in nanny seemed motivated to a great extent by his desire for her to come visit him, either in New York or, in one early instance, Los Angeles, where, in September 2016, he would be filming an episode of his show. "I'm delighted you will accept help," he said in an email on September 5, 2016. "Give me a routing number and I can have my assistant wire transfer directly to your account. This is a huge relief for me—and the knowledge that you can then count on someone to watch your kids while you work or when you fly off to be with me makes me happy." Speaking of the Los Angeles shoot, he says, "BY ALL MEANS come see me. The show will be interesting and . . . you can always hang by the pool and work on your tan if you don't feel like joining me on location (where you are more than welcome). The director [Tom Vitale] is very nice and VERY sparing of my time. I'm usually in and out with him, no waste, no waiting around. I should have tons of time before, after, and in between scenes."

Soon after she traveled to LA, they made a plan for Tony to visit her immediately after Christmas at her home in Rome. He had been there before and enjoyed cooking for her and her family and posting pictures of their happy times on social media—pictures that Ariane also saw and was hurt by because Tony was by then coming to see her so infrequently. Argento was scheduled to be shooting a movie with her ex-husband, the director Michele

Civetta, in December, but the plan was for her and Tony to get together during a holiday work break. As the time of the visit drew nearer, though, she told Tony not to come after all because she'd be too busy. When he kept pressing and insisting, though, she admitted that Civetta was staying at her apartment and that they had slept together.

Tony flew into a rage and broke up with her on the spot. Not only had she ordered him to avoid being photographed with his ex-wife, Argento had in past years criticized Civetta for allegedly spying on her and trying to portray her in the media as an unfit mother. Now all that didn't seem to matter; Argento made up her own rules as she went along. Tony's first call was to Ottavia. He told her he was heartbroken and planned to hire "two Ukrainian hookers" to help ease the pain. Over the next few days, "he told everyone the relationship with Asia was over and everyone was relieved to hear it," Ottavia said. Tony's friends rallied around him. Witherspoon, who was headed to Paris on a business trip, suggested he come with her, to play the flaneur for a few days and clear his head. Tony was in an agitated state, though. At first he agreed, then canceled on her. Then he went to Saint Martin but came back a day later, saying he was too miserable to sit on the beach. His next move was to go see an old girlfriend in San Francisco. She had suggested that he come and he saw it as an invitation to rekindle the romance—but when it turned out that she wanted only to console him as a friend, he flew back to New York the next day. He wound up spending New Year's Eve in his old apartment with Ottavia and Ariane. A short time later, though, he was back with Argento.

Tony would gratefully accept any shard or promise of time with Argento that he could get, but what he really wanted was for them to share their lives. That was, for many reasons, a truly daunting problem and one they probably shouldn't have been facing so early in their relationship. She was put off by what she quickly began to see as his neediness and his suffocating attention; and while she occasionally professed her love for him, she also reminded him that they had made no promise to each other, about sexual fidelity or anything else. Tony, while often acknowledging that was the case, nevertheless persisted, proposing his crazy idea of both families sharing a mountaintop in Italy and other less than thoroughly worked out notions. What if she moved to New York City? Tony wrote excitedly to Argento, saying he had decorated his new apartment with her in mind. Argento from the start refused to consider cohabitation, although for a while she thought that living in New York might be good for her career as a #MeToo activist. Perhaps taking some encouragement from that, Tony tried to enlist Ottavia in making it easier for Argento to make the transatlantic crossing. In the past he had often relied on Ottavia to do what might be called his dirty work. "Once when a picture of him looking particularly ripped came out, and people started to speculate about him taking steroids, he asked me to log in under a false name and dispel the rumors," she said—though the rumors were actually true. "There was always this double standard with him that if someone was saying something nasty online about my appearance I was supposed to let them talk and not be bothered by it. But if someone said anything negative about *him*, then it was the end of the world." In this case he asked Ottavia to see what she could do about getting Argento's then eight-year-old daughter Nicola into Ariane's private school and to promise to make sure Ariane would be friendly toward Nicola if and when Argento ever made the move.

In addition to pressing himself on Argento, Tony was pressing Argento on everyone else. "He would frequently inject her into the conversation and talk about how great she was and insist that he was so happy," the filmmaker Amos Poe, who appeared on the 2018

Lower East Side episode of *Parts Unknown*, told me. His infatuation seemed so intense, said Poe, "that I took it as a warning sign and told him, as a fellow recovering addict, 'Tony, it's great to be romantic, but never be romantic about romance because it will take you down.'" Chef David McMillian told me he came away from shooting an episode in Newfoundland with Tony in 2017 thinking "Wow, he is strange. He's like a child who has met his first girlfriend. It seemed like the puppy dog love that most men experience in their teens—the kind where you want to sit outside her window to see if she is with another man. Everybody has a relationship like that, but you almost always have it before you turn twenty." Tony heaped praise on Argento publicly and privately for her intelligence, bravery, acting and directing skills, and for somehow saving his life. In a text to Ottavia he called her "the only woman who can love me the way I need to be loved"—and on another occasion when he was rhapsodizing about Argento noted rather cluelessly, "I used to feel that way about you." On Mother's Day 2017 he tweeted and posted Instagram stories praising Argento's maternal instincts and talents but never mentioned Ottavia or his own mother, who was still alive. In the 2021 documentary *Roadrunner: A Film About Anthony Bourdain*, director Morgan Neville includes a telling clip of Tony going on and on about Argento's amazing ability to parallel park.

Apart from the damage it was doing to him, and to the relationship itself (there was never a sign that she enjoyed his excessive advocacy), Tony's apparent obsession with Argento started to put a strain on his professional life. By the time he'd met her, burnout and success had already turned him into a very particular kind of creature: the boss from hell whom the wider world reveres as a saint and whom his own superiors have more or less given up on managing. Whereas once he had sought wisdom from Hunter

Thompson, Stanley Kubrick, and Frank Zappa, his most obvious influences now were Andy Menschel, Pino Luongo, and his own mother. "Proper planning and preparation prevents piss-poor performance" had long since been replaced by "You're off the show" as Tony's favorite phrase—and even when he didn't mean it literally or permanently, those words naturally stung. In his book, Vitale tells us that Tony "recruited informants, disseminated fake information, and stoked interteam rivalries, pitting director against director, camera against camera, to motivate everyone to do our best work. In a weird way," he goes on, "making the show felt like going to war, without the guns. . . . Is there such a thing as *vacation-of-a-lifetime* PTSD where your main tormentor is also your hero, mentor, and boss?" Working with Tony had become, he said, "some Gordian knot of irreconcilable contradictions, basically a giant mindfuck."

The advent of Argento only made the atmosphere at ZPZ Production worse. The fights and anxieties that defined the relationship put an additional strain on their star. His constant promotion of her for guest starring spots and directorial assignments also weighed on the minds and hearts of the colleagues who'd been flying around the world with him for years, putting up with a lot but, as corny as it may sound, always being buoyed in the end by the belief that they were being led by an extraordinary man on a quest for television excellence. Now it seemed like Daddy had gone round the bend. Argento had been charming in the Rome episode and her personal connection to Tony had added to the hour's intrigue. But from the start the secret of Bourdain TV was that it showed you the world through the eyes of one trenchant traveler; the idea of them gradually turning into a team seemed antithetical to good storytelling. Moreover Argento's résumé gave no reason to consider her a particularly good director (nor was she, as they soon discovered, especially pleasant to work with). The resistance to her on the part of the producers and crew was mostly silent and passive, but Tony didn't fail to pick up on it. Still, that didn't stop him from continuing to put Argento forward for jobs on *Parts Unknown* that he felt would bolster her career and bank account—and thus possibly shore up what he always suspected were her less than rock-solid feelings for him.

The behind-the-scenes maneuvering on the 2018 Hong Kong episode demonstrated how life had changed for everyone involved with *Parts Unknown*. The original director was Michael Steed, a ZPZ mainstay who had worked on about sixty episodes of Tony's various shows. When Steed was hospitalized for emergency gallbladder surgery in late 2017, Tony immediately saw it as an opportunity to wedge Argento into the schedule and insisted that she direct the episode—the Hong Kong–based cinematographer Christopher Doyle, famous for his collaborations with the director Wong Kar-Wai (*In the Mood for Love*, *Chungking Express*), had already been hired to shoot. Argento, perhaps knowing that she would not be warmly received by the crew, seems to have proceeded with some reluctance. The end result was a beautiful looking episode that begins with a quite worried looking Tony thinking out loud (via voice-over) on the Star ferry that connects Hong Kong with Kowloon: "Chapter One. To fall in love with Asia is one thing. To fall in love *in* Asia is another. Both have happened to me." His life, he goes on to say, is "a gift, a dream, a curse. The best thing, the happiest thing, but also the loneliest thing in the world."

Clearly, he's got it bad and that ain't good, but how much of that strikingly lit shot—and the rest of the (more conventional but decidedly even better than usual) hour—can be credited to Argento's talents as a director? Someone in a position to know told me that from the start of the shoot everyone sensed she was not up to the task and that Tony and Doyle constantly rushed in to help her with diplomatically put suggestions and corrections. She was involved enough in the production, however, to have a tiff—or some kind of tense moment—with Tony's longtime cinematographer Zach Zamboni, an extraordinarily talented member of the crew with whom Tony had over the years been especially friendly. At 9:45 the morning after the incident, Tony came to Zamboni's hotel room in Hong Kong and, according to what Zamboni later told a friend, "fired me like I was a stranger," with virtually no explanation beyond the fact that anyone who could not get along with Argento was "off the show." Zamboni tried to appeal. The precipitating matter was so slight that he wasn't sure what had happened, but if there had been a "miscommunication," he told Tony he'd be happy to discuss it and, if it seemed appropriate, offer an apology. He had found so many other ways to solve problems involving Tony's show over the years, he said, why not this? Tony "coldly" declined the offer, he said, and left the room.

Tony's urge to protect and defend Argento reached new levels of intensity when the *New Yorker* published its story about Harvey Weinstein in October 2017. It's not clear if Tony knew of her involvement with Weinstein, but when the news broke he did something similar to what he did in Hong Kong—he rushed to her aid before she asked for any assistance, not worrying if he might be providing more help than she wanted. He demonstrated his support for her by extolling her bravery and by publicly apologizing for glorifying the bro culture of the restaurant business in *Kitchen Confidential.* He also scrambled to get her a book deal by finding a ghostwriter he felt they could trust and then connecting with his agent (the book never appeared). Farrow's article of course precipitated an avalanche of similar accusations. When, about six weeks later, women started to come forward to accuse Mario Batali of sexual harassment and abuse, Tony denounced the old friend who had appeared on several episodes of his show. He also leaked additional information about Batali to the media and pressured his assistant Laurie Woolever, who had once worked for the chef, to come forward with stories of her own. When she hesitated and offered only to say "no comment" if asked about Batali, Tony said that wasn't enough. "No comment ain't gonna work," he said to her in a text. "You will need something ready, specifically saying if you saw anything untoward. We have seen this with Weinstein and the people who worked with him. If you are fast and firm and decisive you will be fine." (She ultimately declined to speak about Batali.)

"Tony was always on the right side of the issue, but it was kind of scary how obsessed with Mario he was," Ottavia said. When his friend Michael Ruhlman said something neutral about Batali to the press at around this time, Tony cut off all communication with him. When Batali himself emailed Tony to ask if the leaks were coming from him, because he couldn't believe they would be, Tony responded tersely and noncommittally. In a text to his friend the Toronto restaurateur Jen Agg, Tony said, "I've been helpful putting some of the women together with other persons who are willing to go on the record. When you shoot a predator this big, you HAVE to shoot him in the head, first shot. You wound him, it's very dangerous." Ottavia said, "Tony's reaction seemed unhealthy to me. If a friend of mine had been accused of a criminal act, I would be angry, sad, disappointed, not giddy with excitement waiting for more news to drop, like he was. I don't think the old Tony would have done something like this."

In the aftermath of Ronan Farrow's *New Yorker* article, Argento seemed to focus most of her wrath on the author, and of course Tony was there to support her. She couldn't get over the fact that Farrow had in her opinion mangled the facts. Although she continued to be widely perceived as the legitimate face of the #MeToo movement, and would be invited to speak at Harvard and Cannes, she felt Farrow had hurt both the cause and her personal reputation and she wanted him to write, and the *New Yorker* to publish, a correction that would say . . . well, she was never clear about just what, but something that better captured the nuances of the situation and made her victimhood more clear. As they discussed over text how to handle the situation, she and Tony came up with a nickname for Farrow (who is openly gay): Lipgloss Traitor. When she told Tony that Farrow had responded positively to her invitation to discuss the matter further, Tony said, "Doesn't want to mess up his hero image. Or his lip gloss."

Tony was operating on autopilot by this time: Argento's enemies were his enemies, her friends were his friends. When Argento told him that she thought Annabella Sciorra, also a Weinstein accuser, desperately needed money to pay her rent, Tony immediately sent a check. And when Sciorra wrote back to thank him and say she had actually spent the money on a dress to wear to the Oscars, he shrugged it off. "I don't regret it," he told Argento. "She's a mess. But, yes, a slave to the machine." Then, lavishing the praise as he usually did, he added, "You are the only one who hasn't tried to monetize or try to turn this into a career opportunity or a photo spread. You should feel good about that, my A."

In April 2018, with Argento still fuming about Farrow, Tony wrote to David Remnick of the *New Yorker*:

> *Fairly or not, it was unavoidable that some of the women would feel some resentment at seeing Ronan in a tuxedo every night on IG with different famous people, accepting kudos, however well deserved—as they go on with their lives and their difficulties. And that is, unfortunately, the case. Nothing to be done about that. If I were Ronan, I sure as shit would be enjoying my moment. But*

in Asia's case, it's those three words that continue to bear down on her every day. "Five-year relationship." Every day. On social media and in the Italian press. There's a million graceful ways, by my way of thinking, that Ronan could address this. As a matter of human decency and mercy. This is not an argument over the merits of the case. Technically, yes, whatever twisted, awful, absurd, punishing situation she found herself in in the years following her initial assault could be construed as a "relationship." But that is, unfortunately, not common usage. She has suffered and continues to suffer in the cause of brevity. I understand that there was a time that she understood it. But with every passing day, as those words continue to be used to dismiss her or attack her, her feelings become more toxic.

It would be a small thing to look back in wistful reflection and express regret that that part of her life could have been more fleshed out, better explained, or otherwise described. But it would mean everything—the world—to her.

I love this woman. She paid a terrible price for her honesty. And I feel awful that I told her that if she went on record, she HAD to tell everything—no matter how awful or embarrassing—as it was entirely likely she would be sued, and to leave out anything would open her up to an evisceration on the stand and in the tabs.

Please help her. I ask as a friend and as an admirer. Of both yours and Ronan's. You guys are deservedly on top of the world right now. Reach down and help a broken soul.

Remnick's response was sympathetic and admiring of Tony and Argento. But Remnick pushed back against the idea that his magazine had injured her with three words, saying Farrow had tried, in the original piece and a follow-up that ran three weeks later, to put Argento's comments and actions in context. He suggested that their real problem was not the *New Yorker* but other media—"Twitter, the tabloid press and God knows what else . . . that attacked her in vile terms." He asked for some time to think about the matter, promised to discuss it with Farrow, and mused about the possibility of her giving an interview to the Italian press. But he also expressed dislike for Tony's suggestion, made in a follow-up email, for a dual interview with Argento and Farrow that would take place on CNN or PBS, saying he didn't want Tony to "engineer something, even with the best of intentions."

It's interesting that Remnick should put it that way, because Tony was squarely on the road to hell. "He seemed paranoid all the time after the Weinstein article came out," Ottavia told a friend. "He was drinking a lot and Ariane and I would rarely see him. I was checking on him constantly because I was so worried about him. He would call me in the middle of the night asking me to come over to his apartment when he knew I couldn't have possibly left Ariane alone." In the spring of 2018 he started seeing a therapist, something he'd done it seems only once before, briefly, after his breakup with Nancy. "He said he was afraid he would have drunk himself to death otherwise," Ottavia said. "I was very relieved, and because he told me things were much better, I started worrying less. Of course, now I think he was just trying to make me back off."

Tony found himself in a bind. He wanted more than anything to be Argento's supreme benefactor, but he could sense that his attempts to give her money and moral support were not being received warmly and in fact were having a negative effect on their love affair. She was willing to accept financial help, but because she didn't like feeling beholden to him, she resented the fact that he was to a great extent paying her bills. Meanwhile, she seemed increasingly opposed to receiving help in the form of employment on his show. Perhaps she just wasn't interested in travel television or she sensed the lack of professional respect and even the hostility on the part of Tony's colleagues. Nonetheless Tony was *always* there for her. "Oh, my A, I believe in you, more than I believe in myself," he said, but texts like that were exactly the problem. His devotion was getting even more ridiculously excessive and sometimes felt belittling in an old-fashioned patriarchal sort of way. Tony in texts to Ottavia acknowledged that he understood that the more he did for Argento, the more he drove her away—but his serenity was not the only thing that hung in the balance, especially when she started to make noises about pulling out of the Southern Italy episode of *Parts Unknown* that had been built around her appearance as guest star. Because the tightly scheduled series could not accommodate major last-minute changes, a huge mess would ensue if she flaked out and canceled on them, and Tony would bear the brunt of the blame and the embarrassment. That the I told you sos would all be unspoken only made the possibility of experiencing them that much worse.

After Tony, in advance of Father's Day, reminded Ottavia not to post any pictures of him and Ariane on Instagram, lest they upset Asia, he and Ottavia discussed the current state of affairs via text:

> **OB:** You didn't want me to put a pic that had you in it because Asia would freak out and I have the feeling that will not change anytime soon. I'm tired of pretending I don't know you. Or that we are never in the same place together.
>
> **AB:** I feel you. But I was being honest. The pap[arazzi] situation is horrendous. Since I left you guys, though, she's freaking out. The whole idea of being a Brangelina is abhorrent to her. Or even a "couple" with expectations. And I don't expect you to vouch for her. Particularly because I'm almost certainly going

to end up fucked over. I find myself being in the terrible position of being hopelessly in love with this woman. Right now I don't even know if Puglia is going to happen. This is what I live with every day. And I hate my fans, too. I hate being famous. I hate my job. I am lonely and living in constant uncertainty. And I'm sorry.

It is a terrible thing, love. It certainly hasn't worked out for me. Nothing but pain and humiliation between rare moments of incredible joy.

I loved you like that once.

OB: What do you mean you don't know if Puglia will happen? What's going on? You asked for good luck like you were going to Afghanistan.

AB: I feel her love fading.

And when that happens I behave like a hurt schoolboy and she hates that.

I don't know that either of us can ever love or be loved.

OB: I'm sorry. I was under the impression that you guys were basically honeymooning and everything was great.

AB: It's an attractive quality to me. To be impossible . . . sick. And, yeah, it was like a honeymoon a week ago. I never know.

I think all the press depicting us as great lovers sickens her. She is ferociously independent.

If she pulls out of Puglia last minute, I will cancel the episode. And big scandal humiliation at work. But I couldn't go forward if she bails. And I think she's gonna bail. I can feel it.

Fuck.

How the fuck did I find myself here?

OB: This is ridiculous, you have to go forward. Think about all the people who depend on you for the show and who've been working their asses off preproducing. I can't even imagine canceling the Sardinia show at the last minute after nearly creating WW3 to get all the scenes together. I don't know how central she is in this Puglia episode, but it would be highly unprofessional to pull out.

AB: I don't know if I have the strength.

She put it all together for us.

The humiliation alone would be awful. And the grief.

OB: She can't pull out three days before, it's ridiculous.

AB: I don't know. Maybe I'm being overly pessimistic.

It wouldn't be the first time, though.

OB: Were you guys okay while you were together a few days ago?

AB: Yes.

Great.

She's pulled out last minute before. France. New York . . . she gets scared. She gets crowded. She feels like I'm trying to own her or buy her or get too close and she freaks. And I understand. She's had some bad men in her life. She looks at me sometimes and expects a bad man to pop out.

Her last husband was a fucking monster, jealous, stole her diaries, tried to take her kids.

OB: I think when you are not together and you are not there to reassure her, she creates a thing in her head.

AB: Yep.

Chapter 16

"As long as you are here, perhaps you would like to have a conversation with the peyote plant. I can help you. I can take you into the desert. I can show you the medicine. You just tell me, would you like to chew the plant or make it into a tea? It is up to you. The only thing is, if you are going to have the conversation, we must spend the whole night by the river under the stars. Would you like to come?"

Sometimes it was still the best job in the world.

The off-camera invitation came from Sandro Canovas, an activist who helps people around Marfa, Texas, make houses out of adobe. This was in the spring of 2018, when Tony had just weeks to live and kind of looked it. He and the crew were working on a West Texas episode of *Parts Unknown* and Canovas was one of the people he'd met and interviewed, along with a leathery one-eyed saloonkeeper, who told them that gentrification had made it possible to get calamari in Marfa; a family of ranchers who still worked their cattle on horseback; the daughter of the late artist Donald Judd; and a small team of women who made "unbelievable" gas station tacos. In short, it was a glorious but typical edition of a show that, if you could get past the host's kind of moon-rock pallor, appeared to be still in full stride. During a break, Tony and Canovas were sitting around on the steps of a church with some others, drinking tequila and its crazy cousin, sotol, and Tony squinted out at the landscape and said, "I really like this place. I'd like to come back in the summer with my girlfriend Asia and drop some acid and just go into the desert." Canovas didn't say anything then. But later, when he was able to get Tony alone, he told him that he had an idea that might interest him.

"I don't take many people to do this," Canovas told me. "I have access to the medicine and I'm very protective of this tradition. When you achieve this higher state of consciousness, you're going to be able to send this energy in the form of messages and thoughts. You're going to show up in other people's dreams. It's powerful. I never take those hipsters who come from Austin and are trying to find the spiritual life without the proper respect. I knew Tony would understand because of all he had seen in his life."

Tony told him that the trip into the desert was impossible—their schedule was too tight. Just three days to shoot so many things, then off to the next place, etc. Canovas said he understood. Then a few hours later Tony texted him saying, "Okay, we're on."

It was just the kind of side adventure that his fans might imagine him having wherever he went, and it was also just the little bit of hooky playing he sorely needed. They met up after that day's shooting and headed south in Canovas's car. As they drove deeper into Mexico, Tony told him the story about trying to kill himself once by driving drunk in the Caribbean. He didn't tie that feeling in to anything that was going on in the present, but he said that he felt he now was at a crossroads in his life. "I have the best job in the world, but I'm sick of it, sick of all the travel, sick of paying my ex-wife's mortgage." They both laughed at that.

Twenty miles past the border they were pulled over by the *federales.* "Where are you going?" one asked.

"I'm taking my friend to see the scenery," Canovas said.

"Let me see his documents."

Tony didn't have a passport or a tourist visa with him, only his driver's license, which the *federales* weren't impressed by.

"I'm going to have to arrest your friend and take him to immigration. He'll probably be there till tomorrow morning."

"That's not going to happen, Officer, because if we do that my friend's friends will cut off my balls. We're going to fix it up right here, and me and my friend are going to be on our way."

Canovas gave the *federale* all he had, $40, and the *federale* said, "Boys, that's not going to cut it."

They both looked at Tony, who looked out the window and sighed, then went into his wallet and came up with $80, which Canovas combined with the forty and passed along to the officer.

"Just drive safe," said the *federale.* "Stay out of trouble."

Bourdain harvesting a peyote plant in 2018.

In the desert they sat for a while by the campfire, drinking mescal. "He told me that the only two people he loved in this world were his daughter and Asia."

After they'd made and drunk the peyote tea, Canovas left Tony alone for about an hour. "I always do that when I bring somebody, and sometimes when I come back the people are very emotional, even in tears, but Tony was very put together, smoking a cigarette and drinking sotol. He told me he'd had a dream, though, and we talked."

"Did he say what he'd dreamed about?" I asked.

"Yes," said Canovas. "Dinosaurs and Harvey Weinstein."

On the way back Tony mostly listened as Canovas talked to him about his own struggles with addiction and thoughts of suicide at a time when he'd lost his job and the woman he loved because of crack. "After all we've been through," he said, "after crawling through the valley of darkness after we'd lost everything and wanted to kill ourselves, don't you think life is worth living?" He said that Tony responded by shifting his weight around in the passenger seat and staring right at him and saying, "Absolutely, Sandro. Life is worth living."

Life was getting tougher all the time, though. In November 2017, a month after she'd told the world that she'd been raped by Weinstein, Argento received notice that she was being sued by Jimmy Bennett, the actor, who had played her son in the 2004 movie *The Heart Is Deceitful Above All Things* for sexual assault. Bennett was alleging that the incident occurred in a California hotel room in 2013, when he was two months past his seventeenth birthday and Argento was thirty-seven. She had given him alcohol and oral sex, then climbed on top of him, he said. The story would not break publicly until after Tony's death, in August 2018, when the *New York Times* would report that it had obtained documents and photographs supporting Bennett's claim, asking for $3.5 million in damages for emotional distress, lost wages, and assault and battery.

Tony and Argento spent the early months of 2018 discussing how to handle the matter from a legal and public relations perspective. Emails leaked to the gossip website TMZ later showed that she had initially denied the allegation to Tony and said that it was Bennett who had assaulted her. "I wasn't raped, but I was frozen," she told him. "He was on top of me. After he told me I had been his sexual fantasy since he was twelve." Tony believed her, or at least pretended to. He told her that paying the man they both ridiculed as "the donkey" was "no admission of anything, no attempt to buy a cover up, simply an offer to help an obviously tortured soul who is desperate and trying to jack you for money." Argento replied: "I will never buy his silence for something that isn't true, since I am also broke."

Tony paid her legal fees and hired a private detective who would try to dig up dirt on Bennett that could be used to blackmail him or sully his reputation. He ultimately gave the actor $380,000 in exchange for his promise not to pursue further legal action. It was the classic celebrity bombshell scandal, waiting to explode in the press, the sort of shitshow that Tony, just a few years earlier, could not have imagined himself involved in, the antithesis of all he had once hoped to stand for as a public man.

In general he was falling apart, but those last weeks were up and down. Just before he got on the plane to Kaysersberg, the CNN publicist Karen Reynolds called him to say that the Hong Kong episode had premiered to terrific reviews and ratings and he was "so happy—I mean giddy," she said. He texted her saying, "This is the high-water mark, this is the best thing I've ever done." But it was difficult for him to sustain good feelings. Between the lines, Argento's emails were telling a sad and, to him, frightening story. There were no more "I love yous," no more "I'm forever yourses" coming his way. "She just constantly asked him to do things for her, to fix her issues, help her with her 'activist career,'" Ottavia said. "And she wasn't even nice about it. She would tell him her life would be over if all of her issues weren't taken care of immediately and he of course would be terrified."

It seemed like all they did was fight. Mostly she complained about him being too possessive. Later Argento would say, "I always told him my kids came first, my work came second, and he came third." One of his main worries, though, was that he would someday come fourth or fifth, behind her man or men of the moment. It wasn't simple jealousy that was gnawing at him, he tried to explain in private exchanges with her; it was his fear that she would destroy their chances of sharing their lives by getting involved with outsiders. The distinction may seem subtle, but it was important to him.

Their relationship had by June 2018 evolved into something bizarrely complicated and decadent even by the standards of celebrities and others not bound by the usual societal—or logical—considerations. As far as he knew, she hadn't been with anyone else in their time together except her ex-husband, Civetta—though both agreed they theoretically had every right to have additional lovers (as long he steered clear of Ottavia). He apparently had maintained no side relationships since meeting her except for the prostitutes he continued to frequent, presumably telling himself they didn't count because there was no emotional involvement and because he and Argento were so frequently separated. Meanwhile he did his best to keep Argento loyal to him by giving her money and moral support as well as by ingesting large amounts of steroids, human growth hormone, and Viagra so that his age was less likely to come between them. It was this world-class mess of what had once been a love affair that Tony was desperately trying to keep going when—with him just settling in to begin the Kaysersberg shoot with Eric Ripert—Argento showed up on the paparazzi websites cavorting in the streets of Rome (and in the lobby of the Hotel de Russie, where she and Tony had enjoyed romantic interludes) with a handsome young French journalist named Hugo Clément. Sometimes, if rarely, the ZPZ crew had welcomed Tony and Asia's phone fights, thinking they might end in a permanent breakup. These phone fights were different.

A mysterious Twitter account called @justicefortony—it has since been taken down but it is thought to have belonged to a member of the ZPZ crew—put out the word that Tony and Argento "started fighting on Tuesday, June 5. Tony had to leave the set multiple times to talk to her on the phone. Things escalated on Wednesday when by all accounts she told him she no longer wanted to be with him. Everyone was keeping an eye on him all day and night because he was incredibly distraught. More screaming phone calls through the day. By Thursday he seemed to be better and kind of wanted everyone to back off."

One possible reason for his elevated mood was that he'd had a good time the night before when, with the cameras rolling, he and Ripert had visited a two Michelin star restaurant called JY's in the nearby town of Colmar. The proprietor and chef, Jean-Yves Schillinger, had met Tony fifteen years earlier when he'd had a place in New York City; and as Tony and Ripert experienced his high-toned take on Alsatian cooking, memories came rolling back on waves of crisp local whites. Toward the end of the meal, Schillinger, a handsome blond Frenchman of fifty-five, proposed that he, Tony, Ripert, and the crew make a beer run to Freiburg, Germany, thirty miles to the southeast, for a nightcap—and off they all went like a bunch of spring breakers. *Parts Unknown* was not regularly broadcast in Kaysersberg, which accounted for Tony's anonymity there, but it did air in Freiburg, and as soon as Tony entered the crowded beer garden he became Anthony Bourdain again, the recipient of *allos*, *prosts*, and hearty handshakes, all of which he returned with a wide smile. "He enjoyed every minute of it," Schillinger told me when I visited his restaurant. "He lit up like the Tony I once knew. Everything was normal."

That night before he went to bed, Ripert, who had the room next door to Tony's at their hotel, Le Chambard, and who had of course been worried about his friend, put his ear to the wall and heard peaceful snoring, and slept better himself as a result.

His whole adult life, drinking and eating with friends had been Tony's definition of joy. And he had a particular affection for the hearty cuisine in that sauerkraut-scented corner of the world. But the night out with friends, away from his phone, may well have

AWAY with tears and sighing,
And leaden-eyed despair :
Life is a flight for flying
Serene through sunlit air :
'Tis a ball if you 'll but fling it,
A sceptre if you 'll swing it,
A song if you 'll but sing it,
And singing, find it fair.

What of the darkness pending ?
The game may yet be won ;
Life showeth not the ending,
But somewhere is the sun.
'Tis a garden if you 'll tend it,
'Tis a bow if you 'll but bend it—
A fool is he who 'd end it
Before the game is done.

Asia Argento sent me this poem by the New England landscape painter Roy Elliott Bates (1882–1920).

triggered a moment of self-discovery. By briefly reliving his past with Schillinger and Ripert and his crew, he may have gotten a glimpse of how far he had come. By experiencing what he had been, he may have seen more clearly what he'd turned into—a character out of a sordid, slightly deranged James Ellroy novel, a doomed and desperate lover who hired a private detective to soil an obscure kid actor for the sake of a woman who respected him less for each effort he made on her behalf. The kind of man who had talented, loyal people living in constant fear of being banished from a show for which they'd worked hard and given up much to make great. It was an especially horrible thing for Tony to learn about himself, that he had lost his integrity in pursuit of a woman who seemed to spend her life performing for the paparazzi and clowning on Instagram, but perhaps there was some consolation and peace in finally seeing things for what they were.

The next day Tony was fighting with Argento again. She was pulling out of the India episode in which she'd been scheduled to appear, she said, because she couldn't stand him and his possessiveness. His browsing history showed that in the last three days of his life he googled "Asia Argento" several hundred times. On the night before he died he was involved in a text exchange with her:

AB: I am okay. I am not spiteful. I am not jealous that you have been with another man. I do not own you. You are free. As I said. As I promised. As I truly meant.

But you were careless. You were reckless with my heart. My life. De Russie . . . It's only that that hurts', my A.

Perhaps it's in both our characters. But you are always honest with me. I want to be honest with you.

I do not begrudge you this part of you.

As I hope you will not begrudge me.

But it's that that stings.
I meant and mean everything I have ever said to you.
But I hope you will have mercy on me for these feelings.

AA: I can't take this.

Argento goes on by saying that she can no longer stay in her relationship with Bourdain, who has shown that he is all too similar to the other men she has dated.

AB: It would have been so easy to have helped me out here.
I required so little. But "fuck you" is your answer.

As they continue their dialogue, she complains about his "idiot possessiveness," calls him a "ducking [sic] bourgeois," and tells him to "call the fucking doctor." "I am the victim here," she says.

AB: My A. I can't believe you have so little affection or respect for me that you would be without empathy for this.

After the next day's shoot, Tony turned down Ripert's suggestion of dinner and went out by himself. He ate a lot and drank a lot. Ripert got up in the middle of the night and again put his ear to the wall, but he heard nothing.

Epilogue

Tony often said that it would be great to go out in Spain with a big hunk of pork in his mouth or at the Chateau Marmont like John Belushi. And when things didn't go so well, he frequently threatened to hang himself from the shower curtain rod. In the event, though, he hanged himself in what has become, thanks to Robin Williams and Kate Spade and now him, the preferred celebrity style—from a doorknob, in a sitting position, leaning forward until

From his last hotel room, Bourdain could see a medieval tower and vineyards.

he blacked out and then was asphyxiated. Although the last website he visited, after a few more Asia Argento googles, was a prostitution service, the gendarmes declared that he died alone and—in case you've heard the rumors about autoerotic asphyxiation—with his zipper closed, if not with his boots on. He was wearing jeans, a polo shirt of unrecorded color, and socks. He'd had a lot to drink but was probably sobering up when he made the decision. In the hours after he died, Argento, not knowing what had happened, continued to text him, saying, as she had said many times in recent weeks, that she wanted to break up.

I spent the night of November 28, 2019, in the room where Tony died—I guess because I believed the great biographer Richard Holmes, author of *Shelley: The Pursuit* and *Coleridge: Darker Reflections*, when he said that the serious life writer should always "physically pursue his subject through the past." The Manon Suite, as it's called, after the innkeeper's daughter, is very nice and comfortable, though not at all rustic like the outside and most of the common areas of Le Chambard, decorated as it is in a rather modern-looking black and white and purple theme and containing all the latest amenities. If Tony had wanted a taste of the old France, though, all he had to do was open the shutters. The rugged stone "witches' tower," believed to have been a part of the town's fortifications in the Middle Ages, stands less than a city block away from the hotel and beyond it lie the fields where Riesling grapes have always grown. In fact, Tony did shoot some scenes from this window that he used for an Instagram story. He also posted pictures of the constellation of tiny, electrically lit stars in the canopy above the bed.

Which makes me think he must surely have noticed the several large pictures on the walls—black-and-white photographs of Manon and her female cousin, both of whom appear to be about the age Ariane was in 2018—and went ahead and took his own life anyway, by which I mean, even though these images might well have reminded him of his beloved daughter. I mention this because Dennis Mullally, the bartender at Formerly Joe's, and a lot of other people I talked to for this book told me they were angry at Tony for not thinking of Ariane when he killed himself. How could he have behaved so thoughtlessly? they said. Some called it child abandonment. But was that really the case? Since Tony left no suicide note in which Ariane's name might have appeared or from which it might have been omitted, it's impossible to say how she figured in his final thoughts. She may have been very much on his mind that fateful night and Tony's exit strategy at least in part an act of paternal love. More than one mental health professional has told me that people on the brink of suicide may believe they are doing their friends and family members a favor, since their loved ones will surely be better off without them.

The other thing I should tell you about the room is that while I was unpacking, the sliding closet door suddenly started moving of its own accord and with enough momentum to lurch off its track and stop just short of where I was standing. An act of aggression or the semblance of an embrace?

As of this writing Tony's brother, Christopher Bourdain, still has Tony's ashes. When Kim Witherspoon put him in charge of organizing the memorial service that Tony did eventually have—on September 27, 2018—Christopher briefly considered giving each of the guests a little vial containing a portion of the remains, an idea for which he almost lost his planning privileges. The event—which was heavy on Tony's business connections and quite light on the kind of old friends discussed in *Kitchen Confidential*—was held in

Chris's favorite Chinatown restaurant, the Golden Unicorn, just a few blocks from Tony's favorite Chinatown restaurant, the Oriental Garden. Most of the speeches were just fine, my sources told me, but Chris's seemed tinged with resentment, perhaps because he felt that in the last year or two Tony had ghosted him, or because he was still angry that ZPZ Productions had not asked him to take over as host of *The Layover* when Tony got tired of it. "His tone at the memorial was, like, 'You all think Tony's so great? Well, let me tell you a thing or two,'" Fred Morin, the Montreal restaurateur, told me. Other people made a clumsy attempt to turn what was supposed to be a tribute into a roast. As the speeches wore on, his daughter got increasingly upset and Ottavia took her home early.

Acknowledgments

This is a book that relied heavily on a fair-sized group of Anthony Bourdain intimates (and friends of intimates) who preferred not to be identified. I owe those sources tremendous thanks but I am no less indebted to the people who spoke to me over the course of the two and a half years I worked on this biography and did not mind being named. They include, in alphabetical order, Myleeta Aga, Laura Albert, Jessica Alger, Beth Aretsky, Asia Argento, Dae Bennett, Joel Binamira, Andrea Blickman, Nancy Bourdain, Chris Boyd, Scott Bryan, Paul Cabana, Sandro Canovas, Josh Cogan, Holly Critchlow, Ariane Daguin, Christopher Doyle, Wylie Dufresne, Geoff Dyer, Edie Falco, Esther B. Fein, Abel Ferrara, Harley Flanagan, Paula Froehlich, Maria Gardner, Sam Goldman, Zamir Gotta, Laurel Graeber, Bobby Gray, Daniel Gray, Joh Gwin, Chris Hanley, Roberta Hanley, Don Hecker, Richard Hell, Caroline Hirsch, Kai Eric Hyfelt, the Orange Janitor, Edu Kariuki, Patrick Radden Keefe, David Kinch, Emily Klotz, Philippe Lajaunie, Andrea Lee, Pascal Lohr, Pino Luongo, Adam Lupsha, Kimmarie Elle Lynch, Francis Mallmann, David Mansfield, Lark Mason, Bonnie McFarlane, David McMillan, José Meirelles, Jason Merder, Fred Morin, Mitch Moxley, Emily Mraz, Dennis Mullally, Nick Mullins, Enid Nemy, Diane Nottle, Carina Novarese,

Claudine Ohayon, Christopher Phillips, Amos Poe, Debbie Praver, Richard Price, Doug Quint, Midori Rai, Tatsuru Rai, Ian Rankin, Christian de Rocquigny du Fayel, Joel Rose, Robin Rosenblum, Michael Ruhlman, Robert Ruiz, Tim Ryan, Julie Scelfo, Jean-Yves Schillinger, Michael Schnatterly, K. F. Seetoh, Kim Severson, Elaine Sheldon, Vijayeta Sinh, Uday Sripathi, Steven Tempel, John Tesar, Nick Valhouli, Vellini Verso, Brendan Walsh, Toj Ward, Stephen Werther, Tracy Westmoreland, Lisa Wheeler, Mark Whitaker, Michael White, Chris Wilson, Richard Wolffe, Naomichi Yasuda, Patrick Younge, Diego Zakduondo, and Michiko Zentoh.

I also owe thanks to those who helped connect me to people in Bourdain's orbit, a group that includes Niklas Amundsson, Ethan Crenson, Doug Crowell, Cutler Durkee, Diana Eliazov, Emily Lobsinger, Elaine Louie, Robert Sherman, Lucy Rendler Kaplan, and, in a funny but as it turned out very important way, Kim Witherspoon.

I am grateful for the support and counsel I received from Kristine Dahl, my brilliant and always supportive agent at ICM, and from the quietly amazing Bob Bender, my editor at Simon & Schuster, who over the course of five books has never failed to save me from myself. Kris's colleague Tamara Kawar went above and beyond to help me track down a few persons of interest who happened to have ICM connections; and Bob's colleagues at S&S, editor Johanna Li and copy editor Martha Schwartz, made everything go smoother and read so much better.

My wife, the writer and psychotherapist Sarah Saffian Leerhsen, is the love of my life *and* a superb editor. I can only thank God for that.

Endnotes

Many sources are noted in the text. Those not so identified are listed below.

Prelude

The opening text exchange was provided by a person close to Tony and Ottavia Bourdain. The information in the opening section was obtained from James Kaplan's books *Frank: The Voice* and *Sinatra: The Chairman*. The quote that begins "Travel isn't always pretty" is from the soundtrack of *Roadrunner: A Film About Anthony Bourdain*. The information about the immediate reaction of Bourdain's inner circle and his relationship with his mother came from confidential sources. The statistic on Google searches for Bourdain's suicide came from Google Trends. Information on the immediate reaction of the crew to Bourdain's death and the police investigation in Kaysersberg came from confidential sources; Christian de Rocquigny du Fayel, deputy director of Criminal Justice, Criminal Affairs, and Pardons, who conducted the investigation of Bourdain's death; and interviews by the author conducted in Alsace, France. Bourdain drank Bombay Sapphire martinis in the presence of several journalists, including the food writer Helen Hollyman. Karen Rinaldi's essay "Why Anthony Bourdain Matters" appeared in the June 20, 2018, issue of *Publishers Weekly*. The quote that begins "There was chaos swirling around him at all times" comes from an episode of *Parts Unknown* called "Behind the Scenes" that first aired on October 28, 2018. The quote that beings "I travel around the world, eat a lot of shit" appears in the *New Yorker* profile "Anthony Bourdain's Movable

Feast," by Patrick Radden Keefe, February 13 and 20, 2017. Bourdain said "Not giving a shit is a great business model for TV" during an October 23, 2006, talk (with Michael Ruhlman, Eric Ripert, and Gabrielle Hamilton) called "How I Learned to Cook" at the 92nd Street Y in New York that was released by Audible on March 26, 2007. The quote that begins "a sort of gonzo-travelogue" comes from *Medium Raw: A Bloody Valentine to the World of Food and the People Who Cook* by Anthony Bourdain. Bourdain said "the strange and terrible powers of television, etc." in "Anthony Bourdain: The Upsell Interview," with Helen Rosner and Greg Morabito, Eater's Digest, October 24, 2016. The quote that begins "Any director with an idea for anything that is likely to cause fear and confusion at the network" comes from Bourdain's "Field Notes" for the Hong Kong episode of *Parts Unknown*, published on explorepartsunknown.com/destination/hong-kong/, May 30, 2018. "The single worst, most disgusting and terrible-tasting thing" comes from the *Wall Street Journal* article "You Eat That?" by Rachel Herz, January 28, 2012. Bourdain's quote about eating the still-beating heart of a cobra appears several places including *Anthony Bourdain: The Last Interview and Other Conversations.* The quote that begins "the world is filled with people doing the best they can" comes from a video interview Bourdain did with *Fast Company* magazine in 2013 called "Anthony Bourdain: Our Last Full Interview," which is available on YouTube (https://www.youtube.com/watch?v=vUEFdWAKpfo). Director Tom Vitale's quote about fun comes from the *Parts Unknown* episode titled "Behind the Scenes" (season 12, episode 6). The Bonnie McFarlane quote comes from my telephone interview with her. I interviewed Joel Rose at his home in Manhattan. I interviewed David McMillan in person in Montreal. Bourdain's comments to his wife, Ottavia, come from a confidential source. Lionel Trilling's quote is from his introduction to Orwell's *Homage to Catalonia* (New York: Harcourt, Brace, 1952).

Chapter 1

Bourdain said that "the great chefs understand human desire" in *Anthony Bourdain: The Kindle Singles Interview* by David Blum. Kimberly Witherspoon's quote about needing to protect the brand comes from a confidential source, as does Ripert's statement about controlling the narrative. Helen Rosner's quote comes from her introduction to the misleadingly titled book *Anthony Bourdain: The Last Interview and Other Conversations.* Daniel Halpern said that Bourdain knew "what he wanted to stand for" in an interview with Chris Crowley in *New York* magazine. ("He Always Understood That He Was Blessed: Writing Books, and Building a Legacy, with Anthony Bourdain," April 23, 2019). The description of life in Leonia comes largely from confidential interviews, interviews with Bourdain's childhood friends, and the Bergen *Record.* The *New York Times* article about Leonia, "Well-Read, Well-Shaded and Well Placed," by Jerry Cheslow, appeared in the real estate section on June 15, 1997. Bourdain's early unpublished writing was supplied by a confidential source.

Chapter 2

Bourdain spoke on several occasions—on his TV shows, in talks he gave, and in interviews—about his father and their trips to Hiram's. The quote that begins "He never saw me complete a book" is from "Anthony Bourdain: The 'Parts Unknown' Interview," with Kam Williams of *NewsBlaze*, January 9, 2015. Bourdain's memories of his father and the quote that begins "doodlings of goofy Nazis" come from *A Cook's Tour: In Search of the Perfect Meal.* Much of the information in this chapter come from the author's interviews with a dozen or so of Bourdain's high school friends. The story about Anthony Bourdain's grandfather Pierre being "adopted" by American troops appeared in the *New York Tribune*, July 31, 1919, and numerous other newspapers. Information about the elder Pierre's life in America came in part from US Census records. The quote that begins "My father was, to me, a man of mystery" appears in Bourdain's *A Cook's Tour.* Information about Bourdain's father's education came from Yale University. Some details of Pierre Bourdain's employment history came from his obituary in the *New York Times*, April 30, 1987. An account of the robbery of Martha Sacksman's apartment appears in the New York *Daily News*, April 29, 1949. Information on Milton Sacksman was obtained from US Census records and from numerous newspaper articles about his criminal activities, including the *Paterson (New Jersey) News* of December 8, 1948.

The account of the Bourdains' life in Leonia comes from remarks made in numerous interviews by Anthony Bourdain, confidential sources, and interviews with his childhood friends. Bourdain called his father "a man of simple needs" in a June 2012 *Bon Appétit* article that was republished by *Bon Appétit* online on June 8, 2018, as "How Anthony Bourdain Came to Be Anthony Bourdain." Some of the details and quotes in this chapter come from *Kitchen Confidential*. The quote about the "full build-out" comes from the *WeathSimple* interview mentioned in the main text. The Legal Notices ad concerning the auction of the Bourdains' house appeared in the Hackensack *Record* on October 15, 1962. The quotes about Tony and his brother, Christopher, come from a confidential source. Several of Gladys Bourdain's former colleagues at the *New York Times*, including Diane Nottle, told me the story about her misunderstanding what job she was interviewing for when she was first hired. The quote about the Bourdain family dynamic came from a confidential source. The quote about Bourdain's introduction to sushi comes from an article he wrote for *Bon Appétit* that ran in the June 2012 issue and was reposted on the magazine's website immediately after his death. Bourdain's eleventh grade English class essay came from his personal papers. Bourdain talked about his mother's cooking in *Behind Every Great Chef, There's a Mom: More than 125 Recipes from the Mothers of Our Top Chefs*, edited by Chris Styler. Anthony Bourdain's student evaluation at the Englewood School came from a confidential source.

Chapter 3

The information about Bourdain floating a plan to live on a mountaintop in Tuscany with Asia Argento, Ottavia Bourdain, and their children came from a confidential source. The information about Bourdain being taken to college by his parents came from a collection of his unpublished early writing, passed along to me through a confidential source. The quote that begins, "I spent most of my waking hours drinking" comes from *Kitchen Confidential*, as do the immediately subsequent quotes. Information about Bourdain's school ranking came from a confidential source. Bourdain frequently referred to himself as a "hotel slut." Julian Barnes wrote of "that rare and oxymoronic thing, the wise tourist" in *Something to Declare: Es-*

says on France and French Culture (New York: Vintage International, 2003), where he also quotes Edith Wharton. The quotes about Vassar from Elizabeth A. Daniels, William W. Gifford, and Lucinda Franks come from Franks's article "Whatever Happened to Vassar" in the *New York Times*, September 9, 1979.

Chapter 4

The Chris Bourdain quote that begins "No, no, no" came from a confidential source, though he said similar things publicly. Lydia Tenaglia's quote about the camera looking into Anthony Bourdain's nose came from "The Last Curious Man: The Enormous Life of Anthony Bourdain, According to Those Who Knew Him Best," by Drew Magary, *GQ*, December 4, 2018. David Simon wrote about Tony on his blog *The Audacity of Despair* on June 11, 2018. The information about Bourdain's growth spurt in high school came from Sam Goldman. The quotes about Bourdain's room at Vassar came from the file of unpublished juvenilia that I was allowed to see. The quotes about Provincetown and the kitchen crew he worked with come from *Kitchen Confidential.* Details about Joe DiMaggio and Marilyn Monroe come from *Joe DiMaggio: The Hero's Life* by Richard Ben Cramer. George Orwell's quote about autobiography comes from his essay "Benefits of Clergy: Some Notes on Salvador Dali," first published in 1944. The quote about Bourdain's use of hyperbole comes from "Cooking Up a Mystery: An Interview with Anthony Bourdain," by Jessica Bennett, *Rain Taxi Review*, Summer 2003, reprinted in *Anthony Bourdain: The Last Interview and Other Conversations.* Bourdain denied being a journalist on many occasions; this quote about not feeling qualified is from "Anthony Bourdain: The Upsell Interview" by Helen Rosner and Greg Morabito, October 24, 2016.

Chapter 5

The quote that begins "I like the regimentation" is from an article in the *Guardian* titled "Kitchen Devil," June 10, 2001. The quotes about the Culinary Institute of America come from *Kitchen Confidential.* Information about Tony's life at the CIA came from his CIA contemporaries Nick Valhouli and Tim Ryan. The quotes starting "That kind of love" come from "Anthony

Bourdain's Moveable Feast," by Patrick Radden Keefe, *New Yorker*, February 13 and 20, 2017. Bourdain said, "I do not need to be adored" on the Reserve Channel show *On the Table* with Eric Ripert, Episode One, July 19, 2012. Tony's Zero Point Zero crewmates talked about his habit of saying "Only pat the baby when it's sleeping" on the "Behind the Scenes" episodes of *Parts Unknown* in 2018. My impressions of Donald Trump come in part from personal experience; I co-wrote Trump's second book, *Surviving at the Top.*

Chapter 6

The quote that begins "an old-fashioned classic six" came from an interview I did with a Formerly Joe's coworker of Bourdain's who asked not to be identified. A friend of Nancy Bourdain's told me about her occasional interest in becoming a shoe designer. The Bourdain quote "No sports car was ever going to cure my ills" appeared in *Medium Raw*, as did his memory of "a filthy-looking office on the ground floor of a housing project" and his reference to "little-boy dreams of travel and adventure." The Michael Schnatterly quotes came from a phone interview I did with him. Robert Ruiz's quotes came from a series of telephone interviews I did with him. The Eric Ripert quote about cooking side by side with Bourdain came from the *New Yorker* profile "Anthony Bourdain's Moveable Feast," by Patrick Radden Keefe, February 13 and 20, 2017, as does his quote starting "I have a rampaging curiosity." The Scott Bryan quotes come from an interview I did with him. I spoke with David McMillan in person in Montreal. Bourdain talked about how he "went for the money" in *Kitchen Confidential*, among many other places. The A. J. Liebling quote comes from *Between Meals: An Appetite for Paris* (1959; reprint, New York: North Point Press, 2004). Gordon Ramsey's quote comes from *Roasting in Hell's Kitchen: Temper Tantrums, F Words, and the Pursuit of Perfection* (New York: HarperCollins, 2006).

Chapter 7

The quote about "eating garbage at the top of the world" is from *Kitchen Confidential*; the one about "cement-like bechamel" is from *Medium Raw.* The quote from Philip Roth comes from *Conversations with Philip Roth*, edited by George J. Searles (Jackson: University Press of Mississippi, 1992).

Andy Menschel's self-description comes from *Kitchen Confidential.* Information about Sam Goldman came from my interviews with him. Goldman was also one of about ten people I talked to about Menschel.

Chapter 8

The quote about the original W.P.A. being snooty and pretentious comes from the New York *Daily News*, August 24, 1981. The information about chefs Jan Birnbaum and Alain Sailhac comes from Andrew Friedman's book *Chefs, Drugs and Rock & Roll.*

Chapter 9

I interviewed chef Fred Morin in person in Montreal. Nancy Putkoski's quote about using heroin comes from "Anthony Bourdain's Moveable Feast," by Patrick Radden Keefe, *New Yorker*, February 13 and 20, 2017. The quote that begins "We behaved like a cult of maniacs" and the following quotes come from "Anthony Bourdain: My Favorite Mistake," *Newsweek*, June 26, 2011. Bourdain made his comments about cooks not being rock stars on "Anthony Bourdain: The Eater Upsell Interview" podcast with Helen Rosner and Greg Morabito, October 24, 2016. Harold Bloom wrote about his theory in *The Anxiety of Influence: A Theory of Poetry* (New York: Oxford University Press, 1973). Bourdain said he saw "someone worth saving" in the 2014 Massachusetts episode of *Parts Unknown.*

Chapter 10

Bourdain's quote about writing being shamefully easy came from Jessica Bennet, "Cooking Up a Mystery: An Interview with Anthony Bourdain," *Rain Taxi*, Summer 2003. Ruth Reichl talked about Bourdain's "vomit draft" in Alan Sytsma's " 'It Was Kind of Magical': Ruth Reichl on Anthony Bourdain's 'vomit draft,' and what her ideal magazine would look like in 2019," *New York* magazine, April 2, 2019. Vladimir Nabokov's quote, "The language of my first governess," is from *The Enchanter*, translated by Dimitri Nabokov (New York: Putnam's, 1986). Bourdain talked about not being able to sit in a garret writing unpublished novels in the October 2016 Dave Davies's *Fresh Air* interview, "In 'Appetites,' Bourdain Pleases the Toughest Critic (His 9-Year-Old)." The accounts of Bourdain's angry behavior at Formerly Joe's came from my interviews with the former staff. Bourdain said his junkie years comes from *Kitchen Confidential.* The quote about dreaming of "smacking her stupid face with a pepper-mill" was in an interview in the *Rain Taxi Review of Books*, Summer 2003.

Part Three

The Gustave Flaubert quote comes from his letter to George Sand of May 10, 1875, published in *The George Sand-Gustave Flaubert Letters*, translated by Aimee L. McKenzie (New York: Boni and Liveright, 1921).

Chapter 11

I interviewed José de Meirelles, co-owner of Brasserie Les Halles, at his restaurant Le Marais, in midtown Manhattan. Philippe Lajaunie spoke with me very sparingly over email. Bourdain told his version of how his article got to the *New Yorker* in the April 2013 issue of *Delta Sky* magazine. Esther B. Fein confirmed that Gladys Bourdain had given her a copy of Anthony's article to pass along to her husband, David Remnick. Remnick's quote that begins "I opened the envelope with no expectations whatever" comes from "New Yorker Editor David Remnick on Anthony Bourdain," by Matt Buchanan, *Eater*, June 8, 2018. The quote about how he found Bourdain's stories comes from the *New Yorker* podcast, Episode 69: "Bun Cha with Obama, and Trump's New World Disorder," February 10, 2017. Bourdain's quote about fileting the salmon when Remnick called is from his *Delta Sky* interview. Bourdain described his sushi meal with Lajaunie in *Kitchen Confidential.* David Halpern's quote about Bourdain's writing method came from the Grub Street interview, " 'He Always Understood That He Was Blessed': Writing books and building a legacy with Anthony Bourdain," in *New York* magazine, April 23, 2019.

Chapter 12

Bourdain's account of meeting Lydia Tenaglia and Chris Collins came in large part from *Medium Raw.* Lydia Tenaglia's quotes about first encountering Bourdain come from "Tony's Compass: How Anthony Bourdain

Became the Food TV Star of a Generation," by Alan Siegel, *The Ringer*, December 18, 2018; "The Last Curious Man," by Drew Magary, *GQ*, December 4, 2018; and "Meet the Woman Who Turned Anthony Bourdain into a TV Star," by Ivy Knight, *Vice*, May 12, 2017. The quote that begins "that earlier, less good show," comes from Bourdain's *No Reservations* Facebook blog Snarkology: The Sweet Science, January 24, 2009. The information about Vic Chanko came from that Snarkology blog post and from a confidential source. Bourdain's quotes that begin with "I felt like the whole world was opening up to me" come from "Anthony Bourdain's Moveable Feast," by Patrick Radden Keefe, *New Yorker*, February 13 and 20, 2017. Tenaglia's quotes about Bourdain's behavior in Japan come from "Tony's Compass." Chris Collins's quotes come from "The Last Curious Man." The Robert Ruiz quotes come from my interview with him.

Chapter 13

The quotes from and information about Ottavia Bourdain came from a confidential source. The quote from Eric Ripert that begins "Oh, my God" came from the documentary *Roadrunner: A Film About Anthony Bourdain.* Maria Bustillos's observations about Bourdain's life imitating his fiction appeared in the *Eater* Longform, "Fiction Confidential: Is the Real Anthony Bourdain Lurking in His Early Novels?" January 25, 2017. The Bourdain quote that begins "When you have too much painful history with a person" came from my interview with photographer Josh Cogan. The quotes about his experiences in Beirut came from "Anthony Bourdain Talks Travel, Food, and War," an interview with John Little, published in *Blogs of War*, July 20, 2014. The information about Ottavia's pregnancy and her asking Bourdain about a plan B come from a confidential source. The quote "We know you're tired but simmer down" came from Myleeta Aga. The story about Bourdain telling Scott Bryan how much money he was making came from my interview with Bryan.

Chapter 14

The information about Bourdain's email to Michael Ruhlman came from my interview with Ruhlman. Bourdain's description of Asia Argento as "a cancer that has taken over my whole body" came from a confidential source. Argento talked about her career difficulties on the *La Vanguardia* website ("Asia Argento: Lo realmente terrorifico es hacia donde va el mundo"), July 10, 2019, among other places. Argento appeared on the cover of the September 5, 2002, issue of *Rolling Stone* and referred to her "flying pussy" tattoo in the accompanying article. Ronan Farrow's initial article about Harvey Weinstein, "From Aggressive Overtures to Sexual Assault: Harvey Weinstein's Accusers Tell Their Stories," appeared in the October 10, 2017, issue of the *New Yorker.* The information about Bourdain's interactions with Laura Albert and about the intimate relationship between Argento and Savannah Knoop, the woman who posed as J. T. LeRoy, came from my interview with Albert, as well as the *Guardian* of November 1, 2008; "New Film 'JT LeRoy' Explores Bizarre Details of Early-2000s Literary Scam," by E. J. Dickson, rollingstone.com, April 26, 2019; and the 2016 documentary film *Author: The JT LeRoy Story.* Bourdain spoke at length about his television-making techniques in an interview with the Television Academy Foundation, recorded August 14, 2015. The quotes from Ottavia Bourdain about *The Layover* came from a confidential source. One place Bourdain told the story about the man who asks a woman if she'd sleep with him for a million dollars was his book *Medium Raw.* Chris Collins made his statement about CNN imparting confidence in "Tony's Compass: How Anthony Bourdain Became the Food TV Star of a Generation," by Alan Siegel, *The Ringer*, December 18, 2018. The Ralph Waldo Emerson quote is from his essay "Self-Reliance." Harley Flanagan told me during an in-person interview that Bourdain had called him during breaks in his conversation with Barack Obama. The quote that begins "It's very rarely a good career move" comes from *Medium Raw.*

Chapter 15

Ottavia Bourdain's quotes came from a confidential source, as did the information about Anthony Bourdain's marriage. The information about Asia Argento's emails, the emails themselves, and the information about her relationship with Bourdain also came from a confidential source. The Oscar Wilde quote comes from "The Critic as Artist," in *Intentions* (London: Methuen, 1891). The quotes from Zach Zamboni came from a confidential source. The information about Mario Batali and Laurie Woolever comes from communications provided by a confidential source, as did the information about Kim Witherspoon's sugestion that he come with her to Paris. The information about Annabella Sciorra and the email to David Remick were provided by a confidential source, as were Bourdain's texts with Ottavia. Ronan Farrow's follow-up article was "Weighing the Costs of Speaking Out About Harvey Weinstein," *New Yorker*, October 27, 2017.

Chapter 16

The information about Bourdain's experiences with Sandro Canovas came from my interview with Canovas. The *New York Times* article that supported Jimmy Bennett's claim, "Asia Argento, a #MeToo Leader, Made a Deal With Her Own Accuser," by Kim Severson, was published on August 19, 2018. The information about Tony hiring a private detective to dig up dirt on the actor Jimmy Bennett came from a confidential source. The quotes from Karen Reynolds appeared in "Anthony Bourdain Was 'Giddy' Just a Week Before His Death, Says Longtime CNN Coworker," by Ana Calderone and Karen Mizoguchi, *People*, June 8, 2018. The information about Eric Ripert listening at the wall came from a confidential source, as did the texts between Bourdain and Argento.

Epilogue

The Richard Holmes quote comes from *The Long Pursuit: Reflections of a Romantic Biographer* (New York: Pantheon, 2017). The details of Bourdain's death and his computer search history came from confidential sources, as did the information about the memorial service.

Bibliography

Alvarez, A. *The Savage God: A Study of Suicide.* 1971. Reprint, New York: Norton, 1990.

Anthony Bourdain: The Last Interview and Other Conversations. Introduction by Helen Rosner. Brooklyn, NY: Melville House, 2019.

Argento, Dario. *Fear: The Autobiography.* Goldaming, UK: Fab Press, 2019.

Batterberry, Michael, and Ariane Batterberry. *On the Town in New York: A History of Eating, Drinking and Entertainments from 1776 to the Present.* New York: Scribner's, 1973.

Blum, David. *Anthony Bourdain: The Kindle Singles Interview.* 2013, Kindle.

Bourdain, Anthony, with Joel Rose. *Anthony Bourdain's Hungry Ghosts.* Illustrated by Alberto Ponticelli, Irene Koh, and Paul Pope. Milwaukie, OR: Berger Books / Dark Horse Comics, 2018.

———, with José de Meirelles and Philippe Lajanunie. *Anthony Bourdain's Les Halles Cookbook: Strategies, Recipes, and Techniques of Classic Bistro Cooking.* New York: Bloomsbury, 2004.

———, with Laurie Woolever. *Appetites: A Cookbook.* New York: Ecco. 2016.

———. *The Bobby Gold Stories.* New York: Bloomsbury. 2002.

———. *Bone in the Throat.* 1995. Reprint, New York: Bloomsbury, 2000.

———. *A Cook's Tour: In Search of the Perfect Meal.* 2001. Reprint, New York: Ecco, 2002.

———, and Joel Rose. *Get Jiro!.* Illustrated by Langdon Foss. New York: Vertigo / DC Comics, 2012.

———, and Joel Rose. *Get Jiro: Blood and Sushi.* Illustrated by Joel Rose and Alé Garza. New York: Vertigo / DC Comics, 2015.

———. *Gone Bamboo.* New York: Villard, 1997.

———. *Kitchen Confidential: Adventures in the Culinary Underbelly.* New York: Bloomsbury, 2000.

———. *Medium Raw: A Bloody Valentine to the World of Food and the People Who Cook.* New York: Ecco, 2010.

———. *The Nasty Bits: Collected Varietal Cuts, Usable Trim, Scraps, and Bones.* 2006. Reprint, New York: Bloomsbury, 2007.

———. *No Reservations: Around the World on an Empty Stomach.* New York: Bloomsbury, 2007.

———. *Typhoid Mary: An Urban Historical.* 2001. Reprint, London: Bloomsbury, 2005.

———, and Laurie Woolever. *World Travel: An Irreverent Guide.* New York: Ecco, 2021.

Burroughs, William S. *Junky: The Definitive Text of "Junk."* Edited and with an introduction by Oliver Harris. New York: Grove Press, 2003.

CNN. *Anthony Bourdain Remembered.* New York: Ecco, 2019.

Cramer, Richard Ben. *Joe DiMaggio: The Hero's Life.* New York: Simon & Schuster, 2000.

Dinerstein, Joel. *The Origins of Cool in Postwar America.* Chicago: University of Chicago Press, 2017.

Domenburg, Andrew, and Karen Page. *Chef's Night Out: From Four-Star Restaurants to Neighborhood Favorites: 100 Top Chefs Tell You Where (and How!) to Enjoy America's Best.* New York: Wiley, 2001.

Dufresne, Wylie, with Peter Meehan. *Wd~50: The Cookbook.* New York: Anthony Bourdain/Ecco, 2017.

Durkheim, Émile. *Suicide: A Study in Sociology.* Translated by John A. Spaulding and George Simpson. Edited and with an introduction by George Simpson. Glencoe, IL: Free Press, 1951.

Farrow, Ronan. *Catch and Kill: Lies, Spies, and a Conspiracy to Protect Predators.* New York: Little, Brown, 2019.

Flanagan, Harley. *Hard-Core: Life of My Own.* Edited by Laura Lee Flanagan. Port Townsend, WA: Feral House, 2016.

Freeling, Nicolas. *The Kitchen and The Cook.* London: Big Cat Press, 2002.

Friedman, Andrew. *Chefs, Drugs and Rock & Roll: How Food Lovers, Free Spirits, Misfits and Wanderers Created a New American Profession.* New York: Ecco, 2018.

Greene, Graham. *The Quiet American.* 1955. Reprint, New York: Bantam, 1957.

———. *Ways of Escape.* 1980. Reprint, Harmondsworth, UK: Penguin Books, 1981.

Hamilton, Gabrielle. *Blood, Bones & Butter: The Inadvertent Education of a Reluctant Chef.* New York: Random House, 2011.

Hell, Richard. *I Dreamed I Was a Very Clean Tramp: An Autobiography.* New York: Ecco, 2013.

Jamison, Kay Redfield. *Night Falls Fast: Understanding Suicide.* 1999. Reprint, New York: Vintage, 1999.

Joiner, Thomas. *Why People Die by Suicide.* Cambridge, MA: Harvard University Press, 2007.

Kaplan, James. *Frank: The Voice.* 2010. Reprint, New York: Anchor, 2011.

———. *Sinatra: The Chairman.* 2015. Reprint, London: Sphere, 2017.

Luongo, Pino, and Andrew Friedman. *Dirty Dishes: A Restaurateur's Story of Passion, Pain, and Pasta.* Foreword by Anthony Bourdain. New York: Bloomsbury, 2009.

Maté, Gabor. *In the Realm of Hungry Ghosts: Close Encounters with Addiction.* Foreword by Peter A. Levine. 2007. Reprint, Berkeley, CA: North Atlantic Books, 2010.

McFarlane, Bonnie. *You're Better Than Me: A Memoir.* Foreword by Anthony Bourdain. Anthony Bourdain/Ecco, 2016.

Mitcham, Howard. *The Provincetown Seafood Cookbook.* Introduction by Anthony Bourdain. 1975. Reprint, New York: Seven Stories Press/ Tim's Books, 2018.

Morin, Frédéric, David McMillan, and Meredith Erickson. *The Art of Living According to Joe Beef: A Cookbook of Sorts.* Berkeley, CA: Ten Speed Press, 2011.

———. *Joe Beef, Surviving the Apocalypse: Another Cookbook of Sorts.* New York: Alfred A. Knopf, 2019.

Orwell, George. *Down and Out in Paris and London.* 1933. Reprint, Boston: Mariner Books, 1972.

Petroff, Bryan, and Douglas Quint. *Big Gay Ice Cream: Saucy Stories & Frozen Treats: Going All the Way with Ice Cream.* Foreword by Anthony Bourdain. New York: Clarkson Potter, 2015.

Real, Terrence. *I Don't Want to Talk About It: Overcoming the Secret Legacy of Male Depression.* New York: Scribner, 1997.

Reichl, Ruth. *Save Me the Plums: My Gourmet Memoir.* New York: Random House, 2019.

Ripert, Eric, with Veronica Chambers. *32 Yolks: From My Mother's Table to Working the Line.* New York: Random House, 2017.

Solomon, Andrew. *The Noonday Demon: An Atlas of Depression.* New York: Scribner, 2001.

Styler, Chris, ed. *Behind Every Great Chef, There's a Mom! More Than 125 Treasured Recipes from the Mothers of Our Top Chefs.* New York: Hyperion, 2005.

Szalavitz, Maia. *Unbroken Brain: A Revolutionary New Way of Understanding Addiction.* New York: Picador St. Martin's Press, 2016.

Thompson, Hunter S. *Fear and Loathing in Las Vegas: A Savage Journey to the Heart of the American Dream.* 1971. Reprint, New York: Vintage, 1989.

Vitale, Tom. *In the Weeds: Around the World and Behind the Scenes with Anthony Bourdain.* New York: Hachette, 2021.

Woolever, Laurie. *Bourdain: The Definitive Oral Biography.* New York: Ecco, 2021.

Illustration Credits

Page 17: Andrea Blickman
Page 70: Dae Bennett
Page 101: Michael Schnatterly
Page 169: Andy Menschel
Page 181: Jason LaVeris, Getty Images
Page 219: Courtesy of Nancy Bourdain
Page 237: Dimitrios Kambouris, Getty Images
Page 243: Pete Souza
Page 267: Sandro Canovas
Page 272: Charles Leerhsen
Page 275: Charles Leerhsen

Index

Page numbers in *italics* refer to illustrations.

Adrià, Ferran, 209
Aga, Myleeta, 211–12, 223–26, 234, 240
Agg, Jen, 257
Albert, Laura, 232
amphetamines, 30, 98
Andrés, José, 19
Anna C. Scott Elementary School, 23
Anthony Bourdain Appreciation Society, 21
Apocalypse Now (film), 140
Aretsky, Beth, 199, 207–8, 214
Argento, Asia, 20–21, 59, 61–62, 164, *181,* 218, 228–32
  AB's obsession with, ix, 228, 232, 244–46, 249–53, 256–64, 266, 276
  arguments with AB, 247–48, 251, 270–74
  career of, 228–30
  first meeting with AB, 245–46
  LeRoy and, 232
  sexual assault allegations against, 268–69
  television work with AB, 254–56
  Weinstein and, 230–32
Argento, Dario, 229
Aronofsky, Darren, 242
asshole (personality type), 95–96

Baker, Chet, 142
Barnes, Julian, 13, 66
Batali, Mario, 256–57
Beard, James, 74
Beirut, Lebanon, 222–23
Bell Jar, The (Plath), 71
Bell, W. Kamau, 15–16
Bennett, Dae, 25, 30–32, 33–34, 69–70, *70,* 76, 81, 92
Bennett, D'Andrea, 69
Bennett, Jessica, 87, 171
Bennett, Jimmy, 268–69
Bennett, Tony, 25, 69, 70
Bernhardt, Sarah, 20–21
Between C & D, 151, 154
Bigfoot, *see* Menschel, Andy
Bigfoot System, 119–29, 140–41
Binamira, Joel, 236
Birnbaum, Jan, 133
Black Sheep (restaurant), 172
Blake, William, 17, 190
Blickman, Andrea, 30–31, 32, 37

Blind Faith (band), 135
Bloom, Harold, 152
Bloomsbury Publishing, 190, 193, 200
B. Monkey (film), 230
Bone in the Throat (Bourdain), 107–8, 173–74
Booklist, 174
Bourdain, Anthony, *17, 101, 169, 181, 219, 237, 243, 267*
  AA/NA and, 157–58
  agoraphobia of, 219
  alcohol use by, 37, 58, 60, 63, 64, 77–78, 91, 117, 136, 141, 157–59, 166, 167, 168, 171, 187, 190, 197, 216, 220, 221, 236–38, 240, 248, 260, 266, 268
  anger of, 25–28, 47, 49–50, 54, 158, 169–71, 201–2, 241
  authenticity of, 86–88, 142–43
  awkward and shy nature of, 119, 177, 197, 238
  Batali accusations and, 256–57
  Busia and, *see* Busia, Ottavia
  cigarette smoking by, 30, 48, 65, 91, 117, 170, 171, 197, 215, 220, 221, 226
  conspiracy theories about, 59
  culinary skills of, 109–11
  dark side of, 57, 213, 216–20
  dating life of, 31, 67–69, 148, 207, 221, 233
  on desire, 20
  dickish behavior by, 13, 61, 77, 95–96, 127, 212
  as disappointed romantic, 25–26
  drawings of, 31, 33, 70, 169, 242
  drug use by, 19, 22, 29, 31–32, 35, 47, 58, 63, 65, 77–78, 81, 91, 92–93, 104, 117, 131, 136, 141–43, 144–47, 152, 157–61, 171, 197, 247, 265–68
  estate of, 20–21, 55
  fame and, 14–15, 59–62, 88, 97, 109, 128, 197, 199
  fear and, 60, 98, 103, 125, 158–59, 180
  finances of, 51, 64, 103–6, 112, 185, 189, 191, 194, 195, 220–21, 226, 233, 241, 258
  graphomania of, 168
  height of, 37, 75–76
  imposter syndrome and, 210, 219
  insecurity of, 152–53, 156
  as Jersey boy, 95
  knife tattoo and, 215–16
  memorial service for, 277–78
  musical tastes of, 27, 36, 76, 135, 138, 140, 142, 148–49
  nihilism of, 26, 70–71
  nunchucks and, 26, 63, 69, 81
  "outsider's eye" and, 66
  oyster epiphany of, 48–49
  performative behavior of, 31–32, 55, 142–43, 144
  as perpetual teenager, 28, 195, 244, 246
  personalities tried on by, 31–32
  pigs slaughtered by, 226, 243
  political views of, 25
  practical jokes and, 94–95
  prostitutes and, 216, 221, 233, 270
  Putkoski and, *see* Putkoski, Nancy
  samurai sword and, 81
  secretive nature of, 34–35
  self-criticism of, 88
  self-destructive nature of, 26, 57
  self-esteem of, 149
  squid stew and, 78, 99, 137, 173–74
  steroid use by, 252, 270

suicidal impulses of, 3–4, 216–17, 266, 268
suicide of, 4–8, 20–22, 57–58, 148, 219, 223, 232, 240, 275–77
therapy and, 260
truthfulness of, 84–88
verbal humor of, 33
"Vic Chanko" nickname and, 205
work ethic of, 12–13
Bourdain, Anthony, television shows:
AB's original pitch for, 10–11
Cook's Tour, A, 11, 22, 39, 195–212, 226, 242
experimental nature of, 11
Explore Parts Unknown, 236
Kitchen Confidential, 209
Layover, The, 14, 143, 235–36, 278
No Reservations, 13, 91, 136, 144, 202, 210–12, 214, 215, 221, 222–27, 235, 238, 240–42
Parts Unknown, 12, 13, 15, 30, 36, 62, 74, 96, 142, 144, 146, 158, *181,* 197, 202, 238, 242, 245–46, 253, 255, 261, 265, 271
Taste, The, 249
Bourdain, Anthony, writings:
Bone in the Throat (novel), 107–8, 173–74
Cook's Tour, 200–206
"Don't Eat Before Reading This," 183–88
"FAO," 154
Gone Bamboo (novel), 108, 175, 185, 217
Kitchen Confidential, 5, 14, 47, 48–50, 63, 74, 75, 77–79, 81, 83–88, 90, 96–100, 109, 110, 111, 112, 116–18, 119, 121, 127, 130, 136–37, 139, 140, 147, 148, 162, 163, 165, 167, 176, 178–79, 186–87, 189, 199, 207, 242, 256, 277
Medium Raw, 47, 68, 92, 97–98, 105–7, 116, 147, 171, 176–77, 205, 208, 216, 240
Nasty Bits, The, 173, 174
novels, 93, 107–8, 134, 151, 167, 173–74, 175
Typhoid Mary, 167
unpublished, 26, 28, 33, 67–72, 76, 77, 137–38, 149–54, 159–61, 165–70
Bourdain, Ariane (daughter), 7, 21, 62, 99, 110, 213, 223, 227, 233, 244, 248–52, 260, 261, 268, 276–77, 278
Bourdain, Christopher (brother), 7, 36, 46–47, 49–50, 53–55, 75, 82, 85, 105, 277–78
Bourdain, Gabrielle Riousse (grandmother), 38
Bourdain, Gladys Sacksman (mother), 6, 22, 37, 40–55, 63, 74, 80, 82, 93, 103, 119, 132–33, 185–86, 253, 254
Bourdain, Nancy Putkoski, *see* Putkoski, Nancy (first wife)
Bourdain, Ottavia Busia, *see* Busia, Ottavia (second wife)
Bourdain, Pierre (father), 5, 22, 35–40, 41, 44–46, 48–55, 63, 74, 80, 82, 103, 132–33
Bourdain, Pierre Michel (grandfather), 38
Bourdain Day, 19–20
Bourdain Market, 249
boxing, 246–47
Boyd, Chris, 28, 76–77
Boy Scouts, 29
Brasserie Les Halles, 6–7, 104, 108, 183–84, 186, 188, 189, 191–92, 199, 201–2, 205, 207

Bryan, Scott, 112, 126, 226
Burroughs, William S., 131, 142, 145–46
Busia, Ottavia (second wife), 7, 16, 21, 52, 61–62, 91, 99, 111, 164, 213–17, 219–23, 233, 234–36, *237*, 257, 260–64, 278
  AB's health and, 220–22, 236
  Argento and, 228–29, 244–45, 247–53, 261, 270
  introduced to AB, 215
  knife tattoo and, 215–16
  prostitutes and, 221
  and Sardinia episode of *No Reservations,* 226–27
  separation from AB, 7, 228, 232–34, 245, 249
  wedding to AB, 213–14
Bustillos, Maria, 217
Byron, George Gordon, Lord, 143

Canovas, Sandro, 265–68
Carême, Marie-Antoine, 136
Carey, Mariah, 176
Carver, Raymond, 154–55
CBGB (club), 135
chefs, as rock stars, 132–43, 148–49, 177
Chefs, Drugs, and Rock & Roll (Friedman), 133
Child, Julia, 45, 74
Cho, Helen, 243
Chuck Howard's (restaurant), 148
Civetta, Michele, 250–51, 264, 270
Civetta, Nicola, 252
Clark, Patrick, 137
Clément, Hugo, 271
Cleveland *Plain Dealer,* 108
Clockwork Orange, A (film), 27, 31, 77
CNN, 15, 19–20, 241–42, 269
cocaine, 98, 100, 131, 141, 246, 247
Coco Pazzo (restaurant), 162
Coco Pazzo Teatro (restaurant), 164, 178–80
Cogan, Josh, 217
Coleridge (Holmes), 276
Collins, Chris, 196, 198, 201, 203–5, 209–10, 221, 224, 242
Colmar, France, 7, 8
Columbia Records, 37, 39–40
comic books, 28–29, 33, 48, 126, 151, 152
Condé Nast, 184
Conrad, Joseph, 242
Cook's Tour, A (Bourdain), 200–206
Cook's Tour, A (TV show), 11, 22, 39, 195–212, 226, 242
Costello, Elvis, 13
crack cocaine, 35, 168, 268
Creole Gumbo and All That Jazz (Mitcham), 98
Cro-Mags (band), 36, 243
Cruisers, *17,* 29–33, 37, 76, 91, 130
Culinary Institute of America, 58, 73–75, 84, 87, 89–96, 120, 132

Danceteria (club), 138
Daniels, Elizabeth A., 67
Davies, Dave, 26
Demons 2 (film), 229
Denard, Henry (char.), 217
Dickinson, Emily, 20
dick (personality type), 95–96
Didion, Joan, 104
Diesel, Vin, 229
Dillon, Matt, 92–93
DiMaggio, Joe, 81–82
Dimitri, *see* Getmanov, Alexej
Dirty Dishes (Luongo), 164–65

D Magazine, 176
"Don't Eat Before Reading This" (Bourdain), 183–88
Doud, Ron, 132
Down and Out in Paris and London (Orwell), 14, 116, 193
Doyle, Christopher, 242, 255–56
Dracula 3D (film), 229
Dreadnaught, *see* Flagship (restaurant)
Dr. Strangelove or: How I Learned to Stop Worrying and Love the Bomb (film), 36
Drugstore Cowboy (film), 92–93
Duke, Raoul (char.), 27
Dupleix, Jill, 25
Dwight-Englewood School, *17,* 25, 29, 32, 33, 55, 63, 64, 69, 76, 91
Dyer, Geoff, 222, 236–37

Eater Upsell (podcast), 133, 149
Ecco Press, 147
Ed Sullivan Theater, 189
El Bulli (restaurant), 209
Emerson, Ralph Waldo, 242
Englewood School for Boys, *see* Dwight-Englewood School
Escoffier, Auguste, 136
Explore Parts Unknown (TV show), 236

Falco, Edie, 120, 123, 125
Fantasia (film), 37
"FAO" (Bourdain), 154
Farrow, Ronan, 230–31, 256–60
Fear and Loathing in Las Vegas (Thompson), 27
Fein, Esther B., 186
Femme Fatales, 229
Fieri, Guy, 128
Flagship (restaurant), 79–80, 83, 85–86, 96–97
Flanagan, Harley, 36, 243
Flaubert, Gustave, 50, 181
foodies, 50, 133, 188
Food Network, 201–2, 208–9, 210, 240
Formerly Joe's (restaurant), 110, 118–20, 123, 167–72, *169,* 175, 177, 188, 207, 277
France, Bourdain family trips to, 48–50, 132–33
Franks, Lucinda, 67, 72
Fresh Air (radio show), 26
Friedman, Andrew, 133
Froelich, Paula, 28, 217–20, 221, 249

Gandhi, Mahatma, 19
Gardner, Ava, 3–4
Geisha (restaurant), 214–15
Geneen, Daniel, 133
Genet, Jean, 75
Getmanov, Alexej, 97–100, 129, 131, 134, 139, 147, 148
Gianopoulos, Panio, 193
Giffords, William W., 72
Golden Unicorn (restaurant), 278
Goldman, Phillip "Flip," "Sam," 32–33, 92, 120–21, 125, 129, 130–43, 145–47, 148, 157, 163–64, 210
Gone Bamboo (Bourdain), 108, 175, 185, 217
Gotta, Zamir, 195–99
Gould, Joe, 168
Gourmet, 166
Greene, Graham, 8–9, 101

Hackensack (Bergen) *Record,* 22, 24, 29, 45, 46, 47, 51, 52

Halpern, Daniel, 22, 193
Harris, Bob, 71
Harrison, Jim, 242
Hatful of Rain (film), 145
Heart Is Deceitful Above All Things, The (film), 268
Heart Is Deceitful Above All Things, The (LeRoy), 232
Heart of Darkness (Conrad), 242
Hecker, Don, 40–41, 42–43
Hemingway, Ernest, 64
heroin, 92–93, 104, 131, 142–43, 144–46, 157, 159–61
Hiram's Roadstand (restaurant), 28, 35
Hitchens, Christopher, 166
Hoffman, Abbie, 27
Holmes, Richard, 276
Homeland Elegies (Akhtar), 91
Hotel de Russie, 271, 273
Howard, Gordon, 78, 172–73
human growth hormone, 270

Instagram, 248, 250, 253, 258, 261, 273, 276
In the Weeds (Vitale), 218–19, 242

Jamin (restaurant), 113
Japan, 189–90, 203–5, 237, 238
Jemail, Jimmy, 44
Jesus, 19
Joe Beef (restaurant), 112
Judd, Donald, 265
Junky (Burroughs), 146
JY's (restaurant), 271

Kaysersberg, France, 7, 8, 20, 219, 269, 271
Keefe, Patrick Radden, 15, 93, 208, 239
Kennedy, John F., assassination of, 28–29, 126
Kinch, David, 112–13
Kirkus Reviews, 107–8
Kitchen Confidential (catering company), 137–40, 148–49
Kitchen Confidential (Bourdain), 5, 14, 47, 48–50, 63, 74, 75, 77–79, 81, 83–88, 90, 96–100, 109, 110, 111, 112, 116–18, 119, 121, 127, 130, 136–37, 139, 140, 147, 148, 162, 163, 165, 167, 176, 178–79, 186–87, 189, 199, 207, 242, 256, 277
Kitchen Confidential (proposed TV show), 209
Kludt, Amanda, 133
Kubrick, Stanley, 27, 36, 253–54

Lagasse, Emeril, 128, 201, 226, 240
Lajaunie, Philippe, 183–84, 189–90, 205
Lakshmi, Padma, 233
Lamb, Caroline, 143
Lansky, Meyer, 94
La Pyramide (restaurant), 49–50
Larousse Gastronomique, 96
Larry King (TV show), 32
La Teste sur Mer, France, 48–49, 64–65
Lawson, Nigella, 233
Layover, The (TV show), 14, 143, 235–36, 278
Le Chambard (hotel), 6–7, 272, 276
Le Cirque (restaurant), 133
Lee, Andrea, 230
Le Madri (restaurant), 164, 178
Leonia, New Jersey, 22–33, 39, 46, 51, 71, 76
LeRoy, J. T., 232

Les Halles (restaurant), *see* Brasserie Les Halles
Lewis, Jerry, 28
Liebling, A.J., 113, 152
Lish, Gordon, 154–56, 165–66
Lohr, Pascal, 8
Lolita (Nabokov), 167
Lowry, Malcolm, 13
LSD, 30, 71
Ludlum, Robert, 23
Lunch, Lydia, 146
Luongo, Pino, 162–65, 177–80, 189, 225, 246, 254
Lush Life (Price), 145
Lynch, Kelly, 92–93

Manresa (restaurant), 112
Mansfield, David, 27, 29, 30, 37, 45, 47, 69
marijuana, 19, 30, 47, 58, 63, 65, 71, 91, 106, 117, 176
Mastering the Art of French Cooking (Child), 45
McFarlane, Bonnie, 13
McMillan, David, 14–15, 112, 127, 158, 194, 237, 239, 253
Medium Raw (Bourdain), 47, 68, 92, 97–98, 105–7, 116, 147, 171, 176–77, 205, 208, 216, 240
Meirelles, José de, 183–84, 188, 189
Menschel, Andy, 119–28, 130, 141, 163–64, 168, 171–72, 189, 225, 254
methadone, 8, 107, 157, 159–61
#MeToo movement, 59, 66, 232, 252, 257–58
Miami Ink (TV show), 215–16
Mike Douglas Show, The (TV show), 69
Miramax, 230
Mitcham, Howard, 98–99, 140
Mitchell, Joseph, 168
Monroe, Marilyn, 81–82
Montaigne, Michel de, 124, 126, 193, 227
Montana Eve (restaurant), 120–21, 128, 130
Moonlight Menus (catering company), 99–100
Morin, Fred, 144, 239, 278
Mudd Club, 135, 138
Mullally, Dennis, 110, 277

Nabokov, Vladimir, 167
Nasty Bits, The (Bourdain), 173, 174
Neville, Morgan, 253
New York, 136, 194
New York *Daily News,* 43, 44
New Yorker, 15, 21, 86–87, 93, 168, 183–88, 208, 230–31, 239, 256–58
New York Post, 218, 249
New York Press, 185
New York Times, 24, 40–42, 52–53, 67, 99, 140, 146, 157, 174, 186, 194, 201, 230, 232, 269
Nicolodi, Daria, 246
nitrous oxide, 81
No Reservations (TV show), 13, 91, 136, 144, 202, 210–12, 214, 215, 221, 222–27, 235, 238, 240–42
Nottle, Diane, 42
NPR, 26

Obama, Barack, 6, 12, 242–43, *243*
Odeon (restaurant), 137
Ohayon, Claudine, 125, 170–71
Oral History of Our Time, The (Gould), 168
organized crime, 107, 173

Oriental Garden (restaurant), 278
Orwell, George, 14, 19, 75, 85, 187, 193
Out of Sheer Rage (Dyer), 222

Parts Unknown (TV show), 12, 13, 15, 30, 36, 62, 74, 96, 142, 144, 146, 158, *181*, 197, 202, 238, 242, 245–46, 253, 255, 261, 265, 271
Pépin, Jacques, 74
peyote, 265–68, *267*
Phillips, Christopher, 42–43
Plath, Sylvia, 71
Poe, Amos, 252–53
Poole, Nancy, 79
Pop, Iggy, 142
Praver, Debbie, 167–71
Price, Richard, 145
Professional Chef, The, 96
"Proverbs of Hell" (Blake), 190
Provincetown, R.I., 78–80, 82–84, 96–97, 129
Provincetown Seafood Cookbook, The (Mitcham), 98, 99
Puccini (dog), 46
Putkoski, Nancy (first wife), 81, 156–61, 170, 171, 189, 193, 203–4, 206–9, 214, 248
  aversion to the spotlight, 93
  breakup with AB, 207–8, 216–17, 221, 260
  at Dwight-Englewood School, 32–33
  heroin use by, 146, 158
  in Saint Petersburg, 195–97
  shy and unambitious nature of, 103–7, 165, 194, 195–97, 206
  at Vassar, 63, 68–69, 72, 77–78, 82, 84, 92–93
  wedding to AB, 156–57, *219*

quaaludes, 30, 72, 173
Quacky Duck and His Barnyard Friends (band), 69–70, *70*
Queen Mary, RMS, 48
Quiet American, The (Greene), 101

Rainbow Room (restaurant), 115–19, 128–29, 175
Rai, Tatsuru, 237
Rakuichi (restaurant), 237
Raleigh Hotel, 144–45, 215–16
Ramones (band), 135, 140, 142
Ramsey, Gordon, 112, 113
Random House, 172–75
Ray, Rachel, 128, 201, 226
Ready . . . Set . . . Cook (TV show), 176
Reed, Lou, 142
Reichl, Ruth, 166
Remnick, David, 86–87, 186–87, 190–91, 258–60
Reynolds, Karen, 269–70
Rinaldi, Karen, 9, 190–91, 193
Ringer, The (website), 205
Ripert, Eric, 7, 19–20, 21, 99, 110, 112, 113, 214–16, *238*, 271–74
Ripert, Sandra, 214–16
Ritz (club), 138
Roadrunner (documentary film), 20–21
Roberts, Gene, 41
Robuchon, Joel, 112, 113
Rolling Stone, 27, 54, 139, 230
Rose, Joel, 13–14, 111, 150–56, 166, 167, 190–91, 193
Rosenthal, David, 173–74
Rosner, Helen, 21
Roth, Philip, 116
Ruby, Jack, 28–29

Ruhlman, Michael, 228–30, 257
Ruiz, Robert, 60–61, 110, 124, 126–27, 177–78, 180, 207
Ruth's Chris Steakhouse, 218
Ryan, Tim, 87, 92

Sacksman, Martha (grandmother), 43–44
Sacksman, Milton (grandfather), 43–44
Sailhac, Alain, 133
Saint Petersburg, Russia, 195–99
San Francisco Chronicle, 232
Sapore di Mare (restaurant), 164
Sardinia, Italy, 214, 226–27
Scappin, Gianni, 178
Schillinger, Jean-Yves, 271–73
Schnatterly, Michael, *101,* 108–9, 131, 135–36, 139, 140, 141–42, 148
Schutz, Diane, 205
Sciorra, Annabella, 258
Seinfeld, Jerry, 26–27
Shelley (Holmes), 276
Shoemaker, Willie, 148
Siberia (bar), 218
Simon, David, 12, 76
Simpsons, The (TV show), 93, 165, 204
Sinatra, Frank, 3–4
Sinatra, Nancy Barbato, 4
Something to Declare (Barnes), 13
Sears, Jimmy, *see* Tesar, John
speed, 71
Steadman, Ralph, 27
Steal This Book (Hoffman), 27
Steed, Michael, 255
Sullivan's (restaurant), 189
Supper Club (nightclub/restaurant), 172, 175–76, 177
sushi, 53, 90, 190, 203, 206, 238
Sydney Writers' Festival, 25

Taste, The (TV show), 249
tattoos, 215–16
Tempel, Steven, 109, 177–78, 202–3, 207
Tenaglia, Lydia, 76, 200–205, 209–10, 221, 224
Tesar, John, 165, 171–72, 175–77
Texier, Catherine, 151
32 Yolks (Ripert), 113
Thompson, Hunter S., 26–27, 142, 253–54
Three Stooges, 27
TMZ, 269
Tom H's, *see* Chuck Howard's (restaurant), 148
Toscorp, 177
Tower, Jeremiah, 133
Trauma (film), 229
Trauma: Life in the E.R. (TV show), 201
Travel Channel, 209–12, 217, 220, 221, 223–24, 226, 235, 240–42
Trilling, Lionel, 14
Trump, Donald, 6, 88, 96
Twitter, 245, 246, 271
200 Motels (film), 27
Typhoid Mary (Bourdain), 167

Under the Volcano (Lowry), 13
USA Today, 194

Valhouli, Nick, 90, 95
Van Sant, Gus, 92–93
Vassar College, 33, 55, 63, 66–72, 73, 75–78, 80–82
vegetarians, 187, 188
Ventures (band), 140

Verga, John, 139
Vidal, Gore, 96
Vietnam, 205, 225, 236, *243*
Vitale, Tom, 13, 218–19, 242, 243, 250, 254
Vladimir, *see* Getmanov, Alexej

Waters, Alice, 128
Wealthsimple, 50–51
Weinstein, Harvey, 59
  Argento and, 23–232, 247, 256
  sexual assault allegations against, 230–32, 256–57, 258, 260, 268
Wepner, Chuck, 26
Wharton, Edith, 66
Wheeler, Lisa, 169
Whitaker, Mark, 241–42
White, Marco Pierre, 133
White Album, The (Didion), 104
"Why Anthony Bourdain Matters" (Rinaldi), 9
Wilde, Oscar, 246
Wilson, Chris, 218
Witherspoon, Kim, 21, 191, 201–2, 241–42, 251, 277
Woolever, Laurie, 257
Works Progress (restaurant), *see* W.P.A.
Works Progress Administration, 132
World Poker Tour (TV show), 210, 223
W.P.A. (restaurant), 108, 130–37, 146–49, 175, 185

xXx (film), 229

Yasuda, Naomichi, 238, 240
Younge, Patrick, 210–11, 223–24, 240

Zamboni, Zach, 256
Zap (comic book), 29
Zappa, Frank, 27, 253–54
Zero Point Zero Production, 15, 61, 76, 127, 221, 234–35, 238, 254–55, 271, 278